BREAKING THROUGH!

BREAKING THROUGH!

Helping Girls Succeed in Science, Technology, Engineering, and Math

Harriet S. Mosatche, Ph.D.,
Elizabeth K. Lawner, and
Susan Matloff-Nieves

PRUFROCK PRESS INC.
WACO, TEXAS

Library of Congress Cataloging-in-Publication Data

Names: Mosatche, Harriet S., 1949- author. | Lawner, Elizabeth K., author. |
  Matloff-Nieves, Susan, author.
Title: Breaking through! : helping girls succeed in science, technology,
  engineering, and math / by Harriet S. Mosatche, PhD, Elizabeth K. Lawner,
  and Susan Matloff-Nieves.
Description: Waco, Texas : Prufrock Press Inc., 2016. | Includes
  bibliographical references.
Identifiers: LCCN 2015044131 (print) | LCCN 2016004984 (ebook) | ISBN
  9781618215215 (pbk.) | ISBN 9781618215222 (pdf) | ISBN 9781618215239 (ePub)
Subjects: LCSH: Science--Study and teaching--United States. |
  Mathematics--Study and teaching--United States. | Girls--Education--United
  States. | Sex differences in education--United States.
Classification: LCC Q183.3.A1 M68 2016 (print) | LCC Q183.3.A1 (ebook) | DDC
  507.1/073--dc23
LC record available at http://lccn.loc.gov/2015044131

Copyright © 2016, Prufrock Press Inc.

Edited by Lacy Compton

Cover and layout design by Raquel Trevino

ISBN-13: 978-1-61821-521-5

Printed in the United States of America.

At the time of this book's publication, all facts and figures cited are the most current available. All telephone numbers, addresses, and website URLs are accurate and active. All publications, organizations, websites, and other resources exist as described in the book, and all have been verified. The author and Prufrock Press Inc. make no warranty or guarantee concerning the information and materials given out by organizations or content found at websites, and we are not responsible for any changes that occur after this book's publication. If you find an error, please contact Prufrock Press Inc.

Prufrock Press Inc.
P.O. Box 8813
Waco, TX 76714-8813
Phone: (800) 998-2208
Fax: (800) 240-0333
http://www.prufrock.com

Table of Contents

Acknowledgments

The girls and women who are involved in STEM whom we interviewed for this book shared their experiences and insights frankly and enthusiastically with us. We are grateful to them for inspiring us and hopefully, you, the readers of *Breaking Through!* They captured the reality of what it's like to study and work in science, technology, engineering, and math—both the struggles and the rewards. Although we quoted only a couple of men, they represent thousands of fathers, teachers, and others who recognize the importance of encouraging girls to get involved in the exciting world of STEM.

We also thank Lacy Compton, our wonderfully supportive editor, who understood our vision for this book. She was a joy to work with—always responsive, encouraging, and open to our ideas.

We also appreciate the many people who helped us connect with STEM professionals—their introductions allowed us to reach individuals we might not otherwise have learned about. Finally, we acknowledge our debt to the researchers who understand the importance of collecting data about the barriers to female involvement in STEM and developing strategies for breaking through those obstacles.

Introduction

Just a few years ago, if the acronym STEM had appeared in the title of a newspaper article, some might have speculated that a new government agency had just been established. And if the term STEM had been used in conversation, many people would have been puzzled, wondering why the discussion suddenly included a reference to the stalk of a plant. Today, however, STEM is widely used and understood, a reflection of the growing recognition of the critical importance of science, technology, engineering, and math for dealing with the complex issues that face us.

We hear about STEM breakthroughs almost every day. Yet women face obstacles in breaking through in certain STEM fields and in reaching leadership positions. This book describes the obstacles that have prevented females' full participation in STEM, but also focuses on the actions we can all take to make sure that girls have opportunities to be successful. Not only do an increasing number of jobs require knowledge of and experience with STEM fields and methods, but most aspects of everyday life rely on some degree of competence in those same areas. STEM provides us with a framework for understanding and interpreting the world and offers the opportunity for lifelong enrichment and engagement with learning, cultivating an attitude of curiosity and a sense of wonder.

> *STEM is important for every person, not just girls, because so much of our society is based on STEM principles and ideas. There's so much technology in our world. There are issues that we vote on, even hearing the news, that require an understanding of science and engineering.*
> —Stacy Klein-Gardner, Ph.D., director of the Center for STEM Education for Girls at the Harpeth Hall School and faculty member in biomedical engineering and radiology at Vanderbilt University

CHAPTER 1

STEM—Critical to the World, Crucial to Your Daughter's Future

> 　*I love that I can take a property that was completely derelict and return it to function. I do the construction draws for all of our projects. I love seeing new homeowners walk into their house for the first time after it has been completed.*
> —Nancy Hohmann, construction engineer, Director of Development for Lemay Housing Partnership, Missouri

On a typical day, you may use your smartphone to set an alarm, calculate a tip at a restaurant, and send a text to your best friend. Using your laptop computer or tablet, you might keep a budget on a spreadsheet, pay your bills online, and check out the latest photos posted by your cousin. You may not understand all aspects of the technology you're using, but they have become an integral part of your everyday life.

When the news covers climate change, an oil spill, the dangerous condition of a local bridge, or the beginning of clinical trials for a new drug, your knowledge of STEM allows you to understand the information and to make educated decisions about your actions. You use math skills to decide which size breakfast cereal is the best buy at the grocery store, and your engineering know-how empowers you to fix a leaking toilet. When you integrate STEM experiences into your child's life, you will find your own life enriched by being exposed to discoveries that have pushed the frontiers of knowledge.

The Broad Reach of STEM

More and more people are working for companies that are directly related to science, technology, engineering, and math. In 2015, General Electric employed 307,000 people in 170 countries around the world, while 55,000 people were working at Google and 98,000 at Apple. Pharmaceutical companies employ more than 800,000 people; in 2015, Johnson & Johnson and Novartis each employed more than 120,000 individuals. Companies such as Estee Lauder, Avon, and L'Oreal, which focus on the development of beauty products and cosmetics, employ thousands of chemists to create and test their products.

> *I was ambitious and created drawings for the construction of chemical plants. Because I was involved in manufacturing, I had the opportunity to visit other countries. At one point, I was the chief negotiator and spent a lot of time as a project manager. What I really enjoyed about my work was the opportunity to keep learning new things, to be challenged, to keep thinking. That made life more colorful.*
> —Zihui Feng, retired chemical engineer from Shanghai

Numerous federal government agencies focus on STEM-related endeavors. One of the largest is the National Institutes of Health (NIH), which is made up of 27 institutes and centers, each focusing on particular diseases or body systems. NIH employs 6,000 scientists at its main campus in Bethesda, MD, and also funds the research of an additional 300,000 people at more than 2,500 universities. For example, scientist Nina Papavasiliou of Rockefeller University received an NIH grant in 2014 to create vaccines that act by stimulating a strong antibody response against specific targets, such as protein aggregates in Alzheimer's disease.

The National Science Foundation (NSF) is made up of seven research directorates and four research offices. While about 1,700 people work directly for NSF, about 2,000 universities, nonprofit organizations, schools, and businesses receive research grants from NSF annually. NSF uses the term STEM to include the fields of biology, computer and information science, mathematics, chemistry, physics, environmental science, psychology, social science (economics, sociology, anthropology, and political science), and engineering (NSF, 2015). That is the definition we use in this book.

With funding from NSF starting in 2009, industrial and systems engineers Julie Ivy, Irem Sengul, and Reha Uzsoy from North Carolina State University and Lauren Davis from North Carolina A&T State University teamed up with two major food banks to develop more effective processes for serving more than a half million people (meaning less waste and greater ability to reach those in more secluded areas). Researcher Lara Estroff, who received an NSF Faculty Early Career Development award, studies the role of crystals in gel formation in her lab at Cornell University. Applications for her work include the manufacturing of improved drugs and the production of biomaterials for bone and tooth repair.

Start-up tech companies and new technologies emerge almost every day. Facebook didn't make its appearance until 2004, Twitter in 2006, the global app-based taxi company Uber in 2009, and transportation network company Lyft in 2012. But these companies and others like them are already having a profound impact on the way we work, communicate, travel, and play. People who work in STEM-related jobs make all of the following possible: new drugs to fight debilitating illnesses; innovative processes to aid those with disabilities; ingenious discoveries to make driving, flying, and even playing sports safer; apps that make businesses run more efficiently; and medical devices and procedures to more effectively prevent, screen, and treat diseases.

> *Throughout my career, I have been involved in executive education programs helping executives understand technology trends and how the effective use of technology can help improve the bottom line. What I loved most was exposing students and clients to prototypic technology that was just being developed.*
> —Michele W., executive consultant, New York

The Importance of Diversity

As far back as 1999, William Wulf, then president of the National Academy of Engineering, noted that increasing diversity in that field was not just a matter of increasing fairness (although that is always an important consideration), but also a matter of increasing the understanding of problems and the development of creative solutions (Lazowska, 2014). Fields in STEM, such as engineering and computer science, in which females are underrepresented, would benefit by bringing more diversity of thinking into the workplace. An analysis by Dezso and Ross (2012), using 15 years of data of management teams from top companies, revealed that gender diversity increased managerial performance when the companies focused on innovation. In reviewing decades of research, Phillips (2014) noted that diversity of all kinds (including gender and ethnic background) is an important ingredient in the quality of decision making and problem solving because people from different groups contribute varying perspectives.

> *Not many women want to take a job where they are the only female employed. Not balancing sadly means a company will miss out on hiring some incredible women, and the world will miss out on some awesome scientific developments as great women's minds turn to other fields.*
> —Patty Laughlin, retired medical technologist and
> Microsoft-certified engineer, Missouri

Tragic examples abound of mistakes made when females were not part of teams in science and engineering. For decades, women were underrepresented as subjects in important medical studies, such as those done on heart disease, because male scientists didn't consider that diseases might manifest themselves differently in women and that treatments developed for male patients might not work the same way for women. Generations of doctors were trained to look for symptoms that applied more to men than to women, and treatments were typically designed for men but used by women, too. The outcome of this inequity was that, for many years, women's heart disease was likely to be inadequately diagnosed and treated. Another example was described by the American Association of University Women (Hill, Corbett, & Rose, 2010): A largely male engineering team designed the first car air bags but did not take into account the smaller stature of children and females, resulting in unnecessary injuries and even deaths.

> *If we have different viewpoints, not just men and women, but also different races and sexual orientations, you're ultimately going to make a better product. That is especially true if you're going to market that product to a wide range of people—sales will definitely increase.*
> —Christine Doherty, physiology and neurobiology major at the University of Connecticut.

When women are not fully represented and engaged in STEM workplaces, progress cannot possibly happen as quickly or as well. Questions that women might ask are not raised. Analyses that women might suggest are not conducted. It is not just women who lose out. Everyone does.

Where the Opportunities Are

In certain areas of STEM, such as computer science, job growth is occurring at such a high rate that the United States is unable to keep up with the demand, and filling those jobs often means outsourcing to skilled individuals from other countries. In fact, according to a 2012 report by the President's Council of Advisors on Science and Technology, economic projections indicate that over a 10-year period, the United States will fall short of meeting its need for STEM professionals by one million, and in order to meet that need, the number of undergraduates earning degrees in STEM would need to increase by 34%. That means that if your daughter decides to major in a STEM field, she will have many job opportunities to choose from. Moreover, because STEM professions often provide higher salaries than other jobs requiring the same degree of experience and education, when women enter those jobs they and their families are able to enjoy greater financial well-being. In addition, one study found that women in STEM fields actually had more flexible work hours and worked less over the typical 40 hours per week than women in non-STEM professional and managerial jobs (Glass, Sassler, Levitte, & Michelmore, 2013).

But the higher compensation for women pursuing STEM careers and the improved strategic benefits for companies that are more gender balanced do not tell the full story. Ensuring full participation in STEM is urgent for all girls, not just those who will pursue higher education and careers focused primarily in a STEM field. STEM provides us with essential tools to understand our world. Consider how important it is for girls to develop the following skills: thinking critically, revising processes when results are not achieved, interpreting and analyzing data, and using scientific inquiry to systematically weigh options when making decisions. These are all aspects of STEM learning that will allow girls to more effectively navigate through the decisions and actions that are part of growing up.

Beyond the practical applications, engaging in STEM activities can enrich our daughters' lives by providing them with creative outlets (ranging from making an animated movie to creating a garden with the kinds of flowers and plants that attract certain birds or butterflies), giving them access to a community of interesting people (whether they're attending a summer camp or participating in a virtual event), and discovering the answers to questions about the world (encompassing activities from researching the weather to using statistics to predict which team will win a basketball championship).

> *There are few careers today that don't require the basics of STEM. We need to encourage our daughters to stay in these classes at least through high school by helping them deal with any adverse social repercussions of doing so to make sure their world is not limited. My career has focused on the intersection of customers, marketing, and technology. STEM taught me critical, logical thinking, which is the core transferable skill. The scientific method is a great foundation for any analytically driven pursuit. In the war for talent, we need to embrace diversity of thinking of all kinds to get the best possible answers.*
> —Katrina Lane, Ph.D. in experimental physics, vice-president of Global Delivery Experience, Amazon

This book invites you, as a parent (or a girl's primary caregiver or another adult important in a child's life) to play a role in not just influencing your daughter's school and career path, but in transforming the broader world of education, business, healthcare, and the media in a way that will improve the lives of all of our daughters—and sons. Use the quotations, profiles, and activities in *Breaking Through!* to strengthen your advocacy for girls as well as your daughter's excitement about STEM. Share the information about programs, services, and other resources with your friends and your daughter's teachers. Transforming girls' participation in STEM is not a short-term endeavor; it requires a strong and lengthy commitment, which we hope you are ready to make. It is also a joyous journey that will expand your own horizons.

CHAPTER 2

Gender Diversity in STEM
The Changing Landscape

> *I knew that engineering was a male dominated and very demanding field. It wasn't until I started college that I realized how true this is. There have been times when I have been working with males on projects and have been questioned about whether I was sure I was right. It's tough when they're basically questioning you just because you're a female.*
>
> —Amanda McKnight, student majoring in chemical engineering and chemistry at College of New Haven

Historically, women have made significant contributions and discoveries in STEM fields. Women have persisted in spite of obstacles, sustained by their love of the work and the excitement of discovery. Although her name may not ring a bell for most people, British mathematician Ada Lovelace created the first computer algorithm way back in 1842. In the 1950s, Rosalind Franklin made the significant hypothesis that the spine for DNA was external; word of it prior to publication enabled Crick and Watson to "discover" DNA and subsequently win the Nobel prize (an award that many believed she should have shared in). Dorothy Hodgkin, who did win the 1964 Nobel prize for chemistry, was instrumental in discovering the chemical structure of penicillin using x-rays. Among many other accomplishments, Radia Perlman, an engineer and computer scientist, programmed an educational robot that could be used by children as young as 3—in the 1970s. Since that time, women have continued to play critical roles in STEM although often they have not received the recognition they deserve. Throughout this book, you will hear directly from girls and women who made a commitment to STEM and who shared their backgrounds and ideas with us. Initiate conversations using these quotes, and find out how the experiences and insights of a diverse group of females in STEM resonate with your daughter.

The Educational and Career Picture

Women have made great strides in educational attainment over the last few decades, now making up about 57% of students enrolled in undergraduate institutions. However, a 2015 report from the National Science Foundation found that women were still less likely than men to enter college with the intention of majoring in science and engineering. The report indicated that while women earned more than 60% of bachelor degrees in non-STEM fields in 2012, they earned only about 50% of bachelor degrees in STEM fields. Breaking it down by race and ethnicity presents a similar picture, but it does vary somewhat by group. African American and Latino students are underrepresented in STEM, regardless of their gender. Asians are more likely than other groups to earn bachelor degrees in STEM fields, but there is still a gender gap. This gender gap exists for all racial and ethnic groups, but it is largest for Whites and smallest for Blacks.

> *One of my undergraduates was doing an internship working on a team with graduate students. And she came back saying she needed to go into marketing because this guy told her she wasn't cut out to be an engineer. So I said 'How long did he know you? How does he know your skill level?' So I said 'I'm not helping you find an internship in marketing. I'm going to help you find an engineering internship, and I'm not going to sign off on your changing your major.' And now she's got her engineering master's degree.*
> —Karen Panetta, Ph.D., founder of Nerd Girls and associate dean of graduate engineering education at Tufts University

Women's representation in STEM fields varies widely. Specifically, women are now overrepresented in psychology, and earn degrees at similar levels as men in biological science, agricultural science, and social science. However, women are somewhat underrepresented in degree attainment in Earth, atmospheric, and ocean science; physical sciences; mathematics and statistics; and economics; and earn only a small proportion of degrees in engineering and computer sciences (NSF, 2015). Interestingly, those two fields have the most jobs of all STEM fields and the highest return on investment in terms of income compared to educational expenses (Corbett & Hill, 2015).

The picture is similar in terms of employment in STEM fields. Considering tech companies specifically, women made up only about 30% of the workforce, regardless of the type of job, at major tech companies such as Google, Facebook, and Apple, according to Securities and Exchange Commission data (Manjoo, 2014). The only company with a somewhat higher proportion of female employees was Yahoo, with women comprising 38% of the workforce, including its CEO Marissa Mayer, who attained the company's top position in 2012.

> *Information technology is an amazing career choice for women because it offers a wealth of opportunities. Not only does it provide a flexible work-life balance given the mobile nature of technology, but it is a rewarding industry as it allies people, business, and innovation and relies on talent to drive its evolution. People may think you have to be innately technically minded, but the reality is very different. Success in the IT field is rooted in skills of strategic and critical thinking; with some focus and persistence, the technical side can be learned.*
>
> —Sheila Flavell, Chief Operating Officer of the FDM Group, London

The current overrepresentation of women in the social and life sciences and underrepresentation in other areas of STEM was not always the case. Data from the U.S. Census Bureau on trends in women's employment from 1970 to 2011 show that women were once underrepresented in *all* areas of STEM (Landivar, 2013). Even in the social sciences, women were underrepresented, making up just 17% of the workforce in 1970. At that time, the gender gap in all areas of science was quite similar (although there was a much greater gap in engineering where women made up only 3% of the workforce). But some areas have made greater strides than others in achieving gender parity.

A curious fact is that women's employment in computer occupations grew significantly between 1970 and 1990 but then actually decreased, with women making up a similar proportion of computer workers in 2011 as they did in 1980 (Landivar, 2013). A 2014 story on NPR by Steve Henn attributed the drop in women in computer science to the rise in personal computers in the home. Early PCs were not particularly advanced and couldn't be used for much more than playing games (and some basic word processing). As such, they were marketed primarily as toys, and particularly promoted to boys. The result was that boys were more likely to grow up playing with computers, leaving girls with less initial experience with computers when they got to computer science classes in college. The American Association of University Women (Corbett & Hill, 2015) agreed about the role the personal computer played in decreasing the number of women in computing, but also noted that women were originally a major part of the computing workforce and actually were the majority of programmers in World War II. During the first half of the 20th century, these positions were considered to be clerical, but as the field became professionalized and more closely associated with engineering in the 1960s and 1970s, hiring and education practices changed to favor men and male attributes, even before the drop in women's representation in computing in the 1980s.

> *There are definitely challenges in being a woman of color in a STEM field. During my first internship in the consulting field, there were two interns in the department. There was a young man pursuing a degree in history, while I was pursuing a concentration in management information systems. The senior manager would always assign me tasks, such as writing the internal newsletter, while he would assign very technical tasks to my counterpart. We would swap tasks when the manager left the room. Also, since there were limited numbers of women and minorities in the field, it took more effort to get mentors and advocates. It didn't happen organically as it did for others.*
> —Racquel L. Santana, vice-president of ebusiness strategy and execution at Travelers Insurance, Connecticut

In addition to variation in the proportion of women in various areas of STEM, women's representation in STEM also differs by level, with women being even more underrepresented at the highest career levels. Data from the National Science Foundation (2015) showed that of the science, engineering, and health doctorate holders employed by universities and 4-year colleges, women are less likely to hold positions as presidents, provosts, chancellors, deans, department heads, or even research and teaching faculty, and are more likely to hold lower level positions as adjunct faculty or lab research and teaching assistants. Similarly, for scientists and engineers who work in business or industry, women are less likely to be managers.

The challenges to women in these fields can be stiff. According to Snyder (2014), women are more likely than men to be cited in annual evaluations for their personality traits. Although women are described as "abrasive" and told to "pipe down," men are given constructive suggestions. Similarly, women report feeling that they have to prove themselves, but are then liked less when they emphasize their ability to effectively do their job (Corbett & Hill, 2015). More disturbing are the findings from a study (Clancy, Nelson, Rutherford, & Hinde, 2014) in which 70% of women reported being sexually harassed and 26% said they were sexually assaulted during their STEM field research. Overwhelmingly, the harassment and assaults occurred while the women were trainees, which probably increased their sense of vulnerability. Clancy and her colleagues noted that men, too, were sometimes victims, but in considerably lower numbers. Corbett and Hill (2015) explained that sexual harassment is about dominance and control and may be viewed by men in male-dominated fields as a way for them to protect their "territory" when they feel that women are encroaching on it. For this reason, women in positions of power and women of color are more likely to experience sexual harassment. These instances of sexual harassment have negative consequences for women's mental and physical well-being, as well as their job satisfaction and intentions to stay in their jobs. However, these negative effects are lessened when women feel they have a strong voice in the organization (Corbett & Hill, 2015).

Within the video game industry, a campaign against women who spoke out against sexism in the industry escalated to threats of violence in 2014. Several professional women were forced into hiding for their safety in a scandal that came to be known as "Gamergate."

> *Before going to college I needed to take a prerequisite class for calculus, so I attended a local college for trigonometry over the summer. Even though I was getting straight A's the professor actually asked me, 'How did you manage to get into Vassar?' It was the first time that I encountered such a negative educator. The next month I entered Vassar and took on a rigorous course load with biology, chemistry, English, calculus, and French. My father was very ill, I was homesick, and while I passed every course, I didn't do well in biology. I began to think that maybe the trig teacher over the summer was right—How did I get into Vassar? At the end of my first semester I went home with no plans of returning to college. After 3 weeks at home and not having the freedom that I was accustomed to, when it was time to return, I eagerly went back to college.*
> —Michele W., executive consultant, New York

As public attention turned to the loss to society of potential contributions by women, companies began to react. In January 2015, Intel announced a $300 million initiative to increase the pipeline of qualified women and other underrepresented populations into STEM through scholarships and incentives, as well as a commitment to increasing the diversity of its own workforce. One of the country's leading STEM universities, Worcester Polytechnic Institute, selected Laurie Leshin as its 16th president in 2014—the first female in that position in the school's century and a half history. That same year, physicist France A. Córdova was appointed director of the National Science Foundation.

Across the Lifespan

We can also think of the changing STEM landscape in terms of the changes over time for an individual girl. In other words, how do girls' interests in STEM change throughout childhood, adolescence, and adulthood? The issue of females dropping out of STEM, whether in school or during their career, is often referred to as the "leaky pipeline." The pipeline that takes girls and women from science and math classes to become leaders in STEM fields has multiple leaks or points at which females tend to drop out of STEM, with some leaks even occurring years after beginning a STEM career. That means that we need to focus not only on making sure that STEM courses and careers seem engaging to girls to attract them to the field, but that once women are in a STEM career, they get treated well enough so they will want to stay.

Starting with the earliest major leak, girls' interest in math and science starts to decrease around early adolescence, which is also when they begin to lose confidence in their abilities in math and science, according to a 2010 AAUW report (Hill et al.). Importantly, this lack of confidence does not reflect actual performance, but rather is based on girls underestimating their abilities. At the same level of performance, girls tend to have less confidence in their abilities in math and science than boys do. This decrease in interest and confidence only gets larger as girls enter high school and can undermine their performance and participation in STEM.

The AAUW report shows that fewer girls than boys take Advanced Placement (AP) exams in math and science, but this varies by the particular test, with patterns similar to those discussed previously in degrees and employment. More girls than boys take the AP exam in biology and environmental science, but boys outnumber girls for all other STEM AP exams.

However, the picture is not all bleak. The AAUW report indicated that for many years some girls have defied the stereotypes, showing great interest and proficiency in STEM (both in school and in out-of-school settings) and pursuing challenging STEM-related careers, and not all girls lose interest and confidence in math and science during adolescence. In recent years, girls-only STEM programs have sprung up throughout the country. In addition, girls overall earn similar numbers of credits in math and science in high school compared to boys, and girls actually have a higher GPA in math and science than boys do in high school. And the gender gap for students scoring above 700 on the math section of the SAT has dropped dramatically over the past 30 years, showing that things can change for the better.

> *Both of my parents encouraged me to be independent and pursue a career in math and science where I can earn a decent income and be self-sufficient. One thing I recall my father saying many times was: 'Why settle for a B grade, when you can get an A?'*
> —Fehmida Mesania, Ph.D., consultant on water resources and environmental engineering, Pennsylvania

Breaking Through! sheds light on the obstacles that girls and women continue to face in pursuing interests in STEM, and what you can do to support your daughter's interest, aspirations, and success in the exciting world of science, technology, engineering, and math.

What the Research Tells Us About Obstacles and Opportunities

The solutions and recommendations for actions to encourage and sustain your daughter's involvement in STEM are informed by what current study findings tell us about obstacles and opportunities. Research can uncover issues and solutions that might be difficult to see otherwise and at times might even conflict with common sense notions. Keep in mind that the world is changing every day, and what are seen as barriers today might be transformed into real possibilities tomorrow.

CHAPTER 3

Double Trouble—
Stereotypes About
STEM and Gender

> Be prepared to struggle and be treated differently because, in my personal experience, women are not treated fairly or great in STEM fields. My advice is to let girls know that it's great to love science and math. It's not nerdy, or boyish, or weird, or uncool or any of those other adjectives that imply that a girl's interest in STEM is negative.
>
> —Ana, graduate student in biochemistry

Stereotypes about STEM fields as well as about gender roles influence whether girls decide to pursue education and careers in STEM. And if girls do decide to act on those interests, stereotypes may also create significant obstacles to their continuing in STEM. This chapter examines the major findings from the relevant research on these issues.

What Do the Statistics Say About Women's Quantitative Abilities?

A common myth of why women are underrepresented in STEM fields is that their natural quantitative abilities are not as strong as those of men. However, a review of the reasons for women's under-representation in science found that the evidence for a biological basis was contradictory and weak (Ceci, Williams, & Barnett, 2009). That doesn't mean that gender differences in math ability don't exist at all, just that any differences are more likely to be caused by sociocultural factors rather than biological ones.

Although earlier research had found gender differences in math performance, with boys outperforming girls on average, that is no longer the case, at least in the United States (Hyde & Mertz, 2009). Not surprisingly, the size of gender differences in math performance in various countries is related to measures of gender equality. In other words, when women and men have equal status, they perform equally in math. In addition, Riegle-Crumb and Humphries (2012), using data from the Education Longitudinal Survey of 2002 (a survey of a nationally representative sample of 15,000 10th-grade students) found that while White males outperformed all other groups in math test scores, White females had higher GPAs in math than White males. Furthermore, the advantage girls had over boys in their grades was greater among students in more advanced math classes. Unfortunately, this study only used White males as the comparison group, so it is not possible to examine gender differences among other races or ethnicities in this study.

Some of the research that has looked at gender differences in math ability has focused not on whether boys do better than girls on average, but whether more boys than girls get the top scores; presumably only those who have high scores in math have the potential to succeed in fields that rely heavily on math, which is true of many STEM fields. Once again, gender differences vary by culture and over time, indicating that societal factors are likely at play. However, unlike average scores, gender differences still exist if you look just at the top scores of standardized assessments. According to Ceci et al. (2009), the greater percentage of males receiving the highest scores on the quantitative sections of tests such as the SAT and GRE that determine acceptance into top-tier college and graduate programs may partially explain women's underrepresentation in STEM because it restricts their access to the best programs. In addition, not achieving the highest scores on these tests can reduce women's motivation and interest in STEM by making them feel that they don't have the level of ability that's needed to truly excel. Importantly, Ceci et al. (2009) reported that those women who score at the highest end of quantitative tests are more likely than men who score at the same level to also have similarly high verbal scores, which gives them more education and career options outside of STEM. Unfortunately the high course loads in STEM majors make it difficult for students to take courses in other areas, which may discourage women who have strong quantitative and verbal skills from choosing STEM majors (Corbett & Hill, 2015).

> *Tell stories—about how someone built a wheelbarrow or took apart a watch to see how it ran (me!). It's okay that the watch never got put back together; the object of that lesson was in seeing how things are put together. Most importantly, let the girl tell her parents what she wants to explore. If it's being a ballerina, fine. Learn how toe shoes are made to support the human structure without breaking it! Find ways to bring stories to life around STEM that relate to their passion.*
>
> —Karen W. Solorow, President of Coaching for Success and former banker, New York

Despite the fact that gender differences in math ability only show up at the highest end of the score distributions, vary by culture, have decreased over time, and are likely due to sociocultural factors rather than innate biological differences, the stereotype that boys are better than girls at math remains strong. In addition, female students of color may face further stereotypes about their academic abilities based on their race.

The Assumption That Math Ability Is Innate

Even when girls and women do not believe the stereotype that females are "bad" at math, they might still believe that some people are *innately* good at math and related fields, and others are not. Although these beliefs may intuitively seem to be beneficial for girls who are gifted, a practice guide by the Institute for Education Sciences (Halpern et al., 2007) and a report by the AAUW (Hill et al., 2010) both stated that these types of beliefs about the fixed nature of ability, particularly in relation to math, can be detrimental for girls. An enlightening 2015 study by Leslie, Cimpian, Meyer, and Freeland found that the more university researchers (graduate students, postdocs, and faculty) in a particular field believed that innate ability was required for success in their field, the fewer women received doctorates in that field. When researchers strongly believed in the importance of innate ability to do successful work in a subject, women were more likely to be viewed as not cut out for that area's high-level work. These findings suggest that beliefs about the importance of inborn abilities combined with stereo-types about women's lack of competence create an environment that is not welcoming to women.

For many years, Carol Dweck of Stanford University has researched the effect of beliefs about intelligence, particularly looking at what happens when people believe it is a fixed quality versus one that is more flexible (Dweck & Sorich, 1999). She found that students who believe that intelligence and academic abilities are fixed or inborn tend to focus on performance to *demonstrate* their skills, while students who think that cognitive abilities are malleable tend to set goals related to learning to *improve* their skills. As a result, students with a fixed mindset choose tasks that are easier rather than taking on tasks that might be challenging initially.

In elementary school, children often don't have a choice about learning something new or tackling difficult material. By the time students get to high school, they have some choice in their courses, but regardless of those choices, they are very likely to be faced with new and challenging material. When students with a fixed mindset encounter such difficulties, they tend to lose confidence and not persist because they interpret having trouble with a task as meaning they just aren't skilled enough and there's nothing they can do about it. As a result, their grades often suffer when they encounter challenges. In contrast, those with a growth mindset persist longer in the face of challenges, gain confidence because they feel that they're learning, and often end up improving their grades. The research conducted by Dweck and Sorich (1999) found that this pattern is particularly prominent during the transition to junior high or middle school because of the many changes and challenges typical of that age.

Holding the belief that abilities are fixed can be particularly problematic for girls in their relationship with math because of the stereotype that girls are bad at math—they see having difficulties with math as an indication that they just don't have the ability to succeed and that the stereotype is true of themselves. Research by Good, Aronson, and Inzlicht (2003) found that teaching seventh-grade students that intelligence was malleable was particularly helpful in areas where students face negative stereotypes about their abilities and led girls to do better on standardized tests in math.

> I had 90 students in my first engineering class, and no women. At the time there was a renewable energy program here, and so I said to a bunch of young women, 'I think this is the way of the future.' I took this group of talented girls who had unbelievable test scores but very low self-esteem and said, 'Let's take a project where I have no experience,' so they could see that it's really not about what you know now, but what you can do as a team and what you can do with the skills that you're learning in the classroom, which is essentially how to do the research and how to solve problems. So together we built a solar car. We got the parts in July and had it running in October. I got everything funded by corporate support and told the past dean I want to do this project and call it Nerd Girls. So we built the solar car, and when we were done these girls would go to companies and talk about what they had done and what they learned, and you could just see the exponential difference in their communication skills, their confidence, between them and all their peers. They were getting five, six job offers.
> —Karen Panetta, Ph.D., founder of Nerd Girls and associate dean for graduate engineering education at Tufts University

A 2012 study by Good, Rattan, and Dweck found that it is not just females' beliefs about math ability that can have a negative effect, but also their perceptions of the beliefs of those around them. Among college women taking a calculus course, just perceiving that the other students in the class believed that math ability was fixed and that women were not as good as men at math predicted a lower sense of belonging in math, which in turn predicted lower grades in the course and decreased their intention to take future math courses. In contrast, believing that other students recognize that math ability can be developed protected women's sense of belonging. That seemed to be the case even when they perceived that the other students endorsed negative stereotypes about women and math, probably because beliefs about women's math skills are less critical when those skills can be improved. This line of research indicates that developing a growth mindset can protect females against the effects of stereotyping.

Connecting and Helping People

The stereotype that STEM careers do not fulfill and can even get in the way of *communal* goals (which include helping, working with, and connecting with others) may lead girls to opt out of STEM careers. These goals can be fulfilled either through the style or set-up of the workplace, such as collaborative work that encourages people to make connections with others, or through the nature of the work itself or the end product, such as performing a service or creating a project that improves the lives of others. Research has found that men and women believe that STEM careers are less likely to fulfill communal goals compared to non-STEM careers (Diekman, Brown, Johnston, & Clark, 2010; Diekman, Clark, Johnston, Brown, & Steinberg, 2011). These studies also found that, in accordance with typical gender role stereotypes, women tend to feel that communal goals are more important than men do. Combining the stereotype of STEM as not particularly communal with the importance of communal goals to females results in women expressing less interest in STEM (Diekman et al., 2010;

Diekman et al., 2011) or choosing biological and medical fields over careers in the physical sciences and engineering (Corbett & Hill, 2015).

> *There are many misconceptions about what it means to "work in tech"; many believe it is all about coding and incredibly technical work, but the reality is that not everyone in tech does this. There are many career paths in IT, some of which more heavily rely on skills in problem-solving, communication, and team-working abilities.*
> —Sheila Flavell, Chief Operating Officer of the FDM Group, London

Diekman and her colleagues (2011) followed up on their initial findings by conducting two experimental studies: one showed that reminding people of their communal goals decreased their interest in STEM careers (regardless of gender) and another showed that emphasizing the collaborative nature of science increased the perception of science as fulfilling communal goals, which in turn resulted in more positive attitudes toward science careers by both females and males.

Nerd Stereotype of STEM

STEM fields are also often stereotyped as being "nerdy," and those who are interested in STEM are classified as nerds. In addition, this stereotype of STEM as nerdy tends to be specifically masculine and excludes girls and women. As a result, girls may learn the nerd stereotype of STEM and feel that they don't fit it or don't want it to fit them. This contributes to girls choosing to pursue non-STEM interests over STEM when they are talented at both.

> *I find that I'm not interested in the same kinds of things as the guys. For example, I don't want to attend events that are part work and part social and involve going to a bar after work. Also I sometimes feel like there's an 'old boy network' mentality that I don't fit into at all.*
> —Caroline Hecht, computer programmer and web developer at Cornell University

Stereotyping was investigated by Cheryan, Plaut, Davies, and Steele (2009) with a study that involved finding out about the objects that people associate with the stereotypical computer scientist, computer science major, or computer science geek. After compiling a list that included Star Trek posters, comics, video game boxes, and energy drinks, the researchers tested the effect of those objects on men's and women's interest in and identification with computer science. They set up computer science classrooms with objects that were or were not associated with the computer science stereotype. Water bottles, nature posters, and art were used as more neutral objects. The results indicated that college women were less interested in and identified less with computer science than men only when they were exposed to the stereotypical computer science classroom; when men and women were exposed to the nonstereotypical computer science classroom, no gender difference in interest or identification emerged.

In a similar line of research, Cheryan and her colleagues studied the effect of stereotypical computer science role models on women's interest in computer science (Cheryan, Drury, & Vichayapai, 2013; Cheryan, Siy, Vichayapai, Drury, & Kim, 2011). First, they tested what clothing, hobbies, magazines, movies, and TV shows were associated with computer science majors. They then conducted studies in which college students interacted with real or virtual role models who either wore clothing considered stereotypical of computer science majors (unfashionable clothing and eyeglasses and a T-shirt that referenced coding) and had stereotypical hobbies (anime, programming, and video games) and favorite movies, TV shows, and magazines (*Star Wars*, *Mystery Science Theater 3000*, *Electronic Gaming Monthly*), or wore nonstereotypical clothing and had nonstereotypical hobbies and favorite movies, TV shows, and magazines. Women were less likely to believe they could succeed and had less interest in computer science when they interacted with the stereotypical role model, regardless of the role model's gender. The decrease in believing they could succeed in computer science in response to the stereotypical role model was mediated by their perceived dissimilarity to the role model. In other words, women felt they were less similar to the stereotypical role model than the nonstereotypical role model, which caused them to believe they would be less likely to succeed in computer science.

Although Cheryan's work focused solely on stereotypes regarding computer science, similar stereotypes exist for other areas of STEM. In reality, scientists and engineers are complex people with a wide range of interests. But if girls are largely exposed to stereotypical portrayals of scientists and engineers, they will likely think that the stereotype of STEM as a nerdy field is true, feel that they don't belong in STEM, and be less interested in those fields, especially those most strongly associated with nerd stereotypes. You play a critical role in debunking the stereotypes for your daughter by exposing her to a broader view of STEM professions.

> *I definitely loved the aspect of biomedical engineering that involves helping others. I think that's why the field appeals to a lot of women. Within biomedical engineering, my specialty was in cardiac MRIs. I really love computer coding and getting more information out of a noninvasive way of looking inside your body.*
>
> —Stacy Klein-Gardner, Ph.D., director of the Center for STEM Education for Girls at the Harpeth Hall School and faculty member in biomedical engineering and radiology at Vanderbilt University

CHAPTER 4

Bias and Discrimination— Looking at Attitudes and Behaviors

> *Getting through engineering school as a girl has really opened my eyes to some of the ways women are still treated differently in STEM fields. It's almost as if acting girly and being considered a serious engineering student are mutually exclusive. If I want respect, I have to demand it, I have to firm up my handshake, speak loudly, stand tall, learn to compete. I have to be okay with shouting over the guys in my group project who start talking over each other in order to get a point across, defending my work in front of a classroom of 30 guys. Engineering school is like boot camp, but for your brain, and I've had to toughen up a lot in the process. Sometimes I feel like engineering is a field that's decided there isn't a lot of room for stereotypically 'feminine' behaviors, which is unfortunate because it's going to keep turning women away.*
> —Michelle DePinho, civil engineering major at Manhattan College

Although there is no doubt that active discrimination against women and girls in STEM has occurred in the past, there is some debate over how much and how often acts of discrimination occur these days now that explicit demonstrations of bias are generally viewed as unacceptable. However, biased attitudes still seem to be widespread, and this chapter looks at how much they affect women's representation in STEM.

Bias Against Women in the Workforce

An investigation into bias against females in hiring by science faculty at research universities was conducted by Moss-Racusin, Dovidio, Brescoll, Graham, and Handelsman in 2012. About half of the faculty in the study were randomly assigned to receive an application with a female applicant name, while the others received the same application, but with a male applicant name. Female applicants were rated as less competent and less hirable and were offered lower starting salaries and less mentoring than the identical male applicants, by both male and female faculty. Statistical analyses showed that faculty were less likely to hire the female applicant *because* she was viewed as less competent. Not surprisingly, faculty who scored higher on a measure of "modern sexism" (which assesses unintentional negativity toward women) rated female applicants more negatively in terms of competence and hiring and offered female applicants less mentoring compared to faculty who were less sexist. However, faculty members' modern sexism scores did not affect their ratings of the male applicant. Interestingly, men and women faculty did not differ in their bias against female applicants.

> *Although a lot of faculty members who work with students at the college or graduate level consciously strive to support their progress, there are these internal biases that undermine the ways in which female students are assessed, rewarded, advanced and mentored in these STEM fields, which are traditionally and stereotypically male-dominated and thought of as masculine.*
> —Corinne A. Moss-Racusin, Ph.D., assistant professor of psychology at Skidmore College

Another study (Reuben, Sapienza, & Zingales, 2014) found that men were twice as likely as women to be hired for an arithmetic task (one that actually showed no gender differences). In addition, men tended to exaggerate their performance on the task, while women underreported their performance, which led the bias to continue when those making hiring decisions were given candidates' self-reported past performance. Bias was only reduced, but still not eliminated, if objective measures of candidates' past performance were included.

On the other hand, in their reviews of research on the reasons for women's underrepresentation in STEM, Ceci and his colleagues (Ceci, Ginther, Kahn, & Williams, 2014; Ceci & Williams, 2011; Ceci et al., 2009) concluded that although discrimination and bias played a role in the below-average representation of women in STEM in the past, it is not a primary contributor to the low proportion of women in STEM now. This is not to say that bias against women and girls does not exist, but that other factors may be more important in creating a gender gap in STEM. However, their 2009 review article did indicate that one of the barriers to women's success in certain areas of STEM is the penalty they face in promotions when they have children or temporarily reduce their hours or interrupt their careers for childbearing and care.

> Gender discrimination has been prevalent since the day I was interviewing for jobs. I had gone to a school that had previously been all men, and I was part of the first class of women. So when I signed up for the interview as Chris, I'm sure the interviewer expected Christopher to show up, and he was totally taken aback. And he told me that women make terrible sales representatives because they don't know how to change tires, they're not as good drivers as men in general, they don't want to get their hair wet if it rains. I had a comeback for each one of those. I stopped caring about my promotions when I had a child. I continued to work, but when somebody was promoted over me, I said to my husband that if I had not had a baby, I would've gone ballistic because he was an idiot, but I wanted the flexibility and the reduced level of responsibility so I could be with my child. I never really had the support, and I lacked the self-confidence to really go in and be the leader that I knew I was intellectually capable of being.
> —Christine H. Kaufman, Principal at CHK Consulting LLC (pharmaceutical industry), New Jersey

Although many researchers have focused on bias and discrimination in the workforce, Halpern (2014) noted that discrimination is more likely to exist before women even enter the workforce and in the earliest stages of their career paths. Thus it is important to focus on how bias affects the development of girls' academic and career interests.

Effects of Bias During Girlhood

Focusing on bias that occurs during childhood, Gunderson, Ramirez, Levine, and Beilock (2012) described how bias by teachers and parents can influence girls' attitudes toward math. Their literature review concluded that both teachers and parents tend to view children's successes and failures in math differently depending on the child's gender. When girls do well in math, adults are more likely to believe it was because they tried hard, whereas when boys do well, adults tend to view it as being due to natural abilities. These patterns are reversed for poor performance, with adults thinking that when girls don't do well in math, it's because they don't have the natural ability for it, but when boys do poorly in math, it's because they did not try hard enough. This gender dependent reasoning leads parents and teachers to think that boys have higher math abilities than girls, even when they have the same level of objective performance. Basically, the tendency to attribute success to effort in girls and to ability in boys, and the converse for failure, effectively causes adults to underestimate girls' abilities and overestimate boys' abilities.

In addition, parents' and teachers' views of children's math abilities and their expectations for children's success in math influences children's own perceptions of their skills in math. In fact, parents' beliefs about their children's math abilities were a stronger predictor of children's perceptions of their own math abilities than their past achievement in math. In turn, children's perceptions of their math abilities predicted their achievement in math later on. Importantly, Gunderson and her colleagues (2012) noted that the evidence of gender bias in parents' and teachers' perceptions of children's math performance and abilities is strongest for middle and high school students (with similar patterns for elementary school students, but the findings are not as clear-cut for the younger age level).

Almost all of the studies referenced by Gunderson and her colleagues (2012) on the effect of parents' and teachers' beliefs about children's math abilities were conducted before 2000 (mostly in the 1980s and 1990s), and the few studies from 2000 or later were conducted outside of the United States. This does not necessarily mean that their findings or conclusions should be ignored. Parents and teachers are key influencers of children, so the impact of bias from parents and teachers on children's attitudes toward math is presumably just as strong now as it was when these studies were originally conducted. However, it is important to establish whether bias from teachers and parents is as strong as it was previously.

> *I had negative experiences with many of my teachers as far as science and math go. I was told that girls don't need math. I tried to create a math club at my middle school, and the only teacher who was able or willing to do a math club wasn't willing to do it because I was a girl.*
> —Nicole Flaig, Ph.D. student in neuroscience
> at the University of Connecticut

Although a 2001 study by Helwig, Anderson, and Tindal found that third- and fifth-grade teachers' ratings of their students' math achievement were not influenced by gender, Lavy and Sand (2015) reported very different findings. Lavy and Sand began, in 2002, to track students in Israel when they were in the sixth grade and continued until they had completed high school. One of the most significant findings was the demonstration of teacher bias favoring boys. Although girls received higher math test scores than boys when they were graded anonymously, boys scored higher when teachers knew the students' names, an effect that did not occur with non-STEM subjects. Most disheartening was the finding that girls who had been discouraged in math and science while in elementary school were less likely than boys to sign up for advanced STEM courses in high school. Although the study was conducted in Israel, Lavy and Sand believed that these findings would be replicated in the United States and elsewhere.

A 2012 study by Riegle-Crumb and Humphries mentioned in the previous chapter examined whether 10th-grade math teachers perceived their female and African American and Hispanic students as having lower abilities than their White male students. Their analysis found that although female and African American and Hispanic students were less likely to be rated by their teachers as being in a math class that was too easy for them (which the researchers took as an indicator of having high math abilities) compared to White male students, when their grades and test scores were taken into account, this bias only existed for White females. In other words, White female students were less likely than White male students with similar grades and test scores to be viewed as having abilities greater than those required for the course they were in. Interestingly, although there generally wasn't evidence of bias in terms of ratings that a student's math class was too difficult for them, which would be an indicator of lower math abilities, Black female students in advanced math classes were less likely to be viewed as being in a class that was too difficult for them compared to White male students with similar grades and test scores in advanced math classes. Unfortunately, direct assessments of students' abilities were not included in the survey, and the researchers only made comparisons between White males and other groups, so we cannot see whether there is bias against female students within a particular racial/ethnic minority group.

Reducing middle school and high school teachers' bias in their attributions for boys' and girls' successes and failures in math was the focus of an intervention reported by Espinoza, Areas da Luz Fontes, and Arms-Chavez in 2014. Before the intervention began, teachers showed the same attribution bias discussed by Gunderson and colleagues (2012) in their review: teachers were more likely to say that girls' successes were due to effort rather than ability compared to boys' successes, and that girls' failures were due to a lack of ability rather than a lack of effort, compared to boys' failures. The intervention was designed to encourage teachers to adopt a view of intelligence as malleable, and immediately following the intervention, teachers actually reversed their bias—becoming more likely to attribute girls' successes to ability and their failures to lack of effort compared to boys. However, the change didn't last, and within a year teachers returned to their previous patterns of attribution based on gender.

> *Though some stereotypes remain to an extent, the great news is that perceptions are changing. We know that girls are interested in technology; in a 2013 CompTIA Survey of 1,000 teens and young adults in North America, 95% of girls said that 'they like technology' but 53% said they would 'definitely not' want a career in IT. This disconnect alludes to the problem that girls view technology as a product rather than a career choice, and this must be challenged. Through coding groups and interactive learning that enable girls to try out simple programming tasks, schools and clubs can encourage girls and invest in cultivating their interest in technology from an early age.*
> —Sheila Flavell, Chief Operating Officer of FDM Group, London

Perceptions of Reverse Bias

Now that we are living in an age when it is not generally acceptable to discriminate against specific groups, students and employees are often trained to be aware of and avoid acting on those biases. In addition, affirmative action programs have sometimes been used to increase representation by females and people of color in fields where they are underrepresented. These efforts are well-intentioned and often quite beneficial, but they can sometimes create the perception of a reverse bias against the dominant group, typically White males.

Focusing on affirmative action, a 1992 study by Heilman, Block, and Lucas found that when female employees were labeled as having been an affirmative action hire, they were rated as less competent than women who did not receive the affirmative action label, despite both groups having the same qualifications. A 2011 report from the Massachusetts Institute of Technology on the status of women faculty in the schools of science and engineering indicated that procedures in place to make people aware of possible bias against women in hiring and promotion can inadvertently create a false perception that the standards for hiring and promoting women are lower than those for men. This means that, in some instances, procedures designed to reduce bias against women have had the incidental effect of actually recreating that bias in the form of lower perceptions of women's competence. The result might be that even when women are hired and promoted, they are not treated fairly by their male coworkers who might view them as not having the same abilities as men at the same level. However, perception should not be a reason for avoiding practices that correct inequities in the workplace.

The Effect of Stereotype Threat

Negative stereotypes about girls and women can also have harmful effects even when they are not believed to be true, as long as there is an awareness of those stereotypes. The phenomenon of stereotype threat occurs when a person's behavior can be judged in terms of a negative stereotype about a group, and in which the behavior could potentially confirm that negative stereotype (Steele, Spencer, & Aronson, 2002). Stereotype threat regarding females and math was first shown in a set of studies by Spencer, Steele, and Quinn in 1999. Their findings demonstrated that stereotype threat decreased college women's performance on difficult math tests, but when stereotype threat was removed by telling women that the test had not shown gender differences in the past (making the negative stereotype irrelevant to the task at hand), their performance was equivalent to that of men. These results also indicated that under normal test conditions when a test was difficult, stereotype threat was present.

Since 1999, the effect of stereotype threat on girls' and women's math performance has been widely studied and found to occur with children as young as 5 (Ambady, Shih, Kim, & Pittinsky, 2001) and with college women enrolled in rigorous math courses as requirements for degrees in STEM (Good, Aronson, & Harder, 2008). However, a meta-analysis (a statistical analysis of the results from many studies) by Picho, Rodriguez, and Finnie (2013) concluded that the effects of stereotype threat for girls and math are stronger for middle school and high school students, compared to college students. Unfortunately, there were not enough studies with elementary school students to make comparisons for that age level.

Importantly, many of the studies on stereotype threat for females and math have demonstrated that girls do not have to believe in the stereotype that they are bad at math for stereotype threat to negatively impact their performance; they just have to be aware of the stereotype. A 2008 review by Schmader, Johns, and Forbes concluded that stereotype threat negatively impacts performance through physiological stress responses and attempts to actively monitor performance and suppress negative thoughts and emotions, all of which use up executive resources that would otherwise be focused on the task at hand.

> *Parents should not stereotype science as a 'boy subject' or 'nerdy' or discourage daughters from taking certain classes because they will be 'too hard.'*
> —Teresa, Ph.D., analytic chemist for drug company, New Jersey

A review of research findings on stereotype threat by Steele, Spencer, and Aronson (2002) elucidated the conditions under which the effects of stereotype threat tend to be stronger. Stereotype threat generally occurs only when the task is difficult and when the purpose of the task is to assess one's abilities. The effects increase with one's identification with the relevant domain. For example, the more important girls think it is for them to be good at math and the more important math is to their sense of identity, the greater the impact of stereotype threat. Similarly, girls who feel that being female is an important part of their identity and girls who tend to look for bias against females are more likely to be impacted by stereotype threat.

These findings should certainly not be used to discourage girls from seeing math as important, being strongly identified with their gender, or being cognizant of bias in the world. Numerous interventions have been studied as ways to reduce or eliminate the effects of stereotype threat on performance. Those with the greatest research support include: learning about the malleability of intelligence and adopting a growth mindset; being exposed to female role models; mentoring with both high standards and positive feedback about ability or potential; and reflecting positively on one's important values, also called self-affirmation. You will find more information about applying these strategies in Sections IV and V of this book.

Understanding Bias From Within

Girls often internalize the biased messages they receive from society so that they end up having biased views of themselves, their performance, and their abilities. A review of the gender and motivation literature by Meece, Glienke, and Burg (2006) reported that girls were more likely than boys to cite effort, as opposed to ability, for their success in math and science, whereas they showed the reverse pattern for failures, with girls more likely than boys to blame failure on a lack of ability. This can cause girls to underestimate their own abilities and lower their expectations for success, particularly as they face more advanced work. These kinds of explanations are similar to those given by parents and teachers for children's performance.

> *In my experience I am my own worst enemy, and it was usually me thinking I couldn't do it. You have to remind yourself that you are capable of so much more. You'll still fail sometimes, but as long as you can learn from it there's nothing you can't achieve.*
> —Jessica Kay, B.S. in genomics and molecular genetics and M.P.H., marketing rep at Detroit Medical Center

The review by Meece and her colleagues (2006) also found that girls rated their own ability to succeed in math lower than boys did, even when they objectively had equivalent skills. However, this gender gap in competency beliefs narrows, but doesn't disappear, as children get older because although both boys and girls tend to view their skills as worse as they get older and encounter more difficult material, this decrease is larger for boys. Interestingly, the reverse gender gap occurs for children's beliefs about their ability to succeed in verbal domains during the middle school years, with girls rating their ability to succeed higher than boys do, in line with gender stereotypes regarding verbal skills.

Self-efficacy, the confidence in one's ability to learn and achieve specific performance goals, such as solving a certain number of math problems correctly or getting an A in a course, is a concept worth examining for its role in the underrepresentation of females in STEM. Similar to the findings on competency beliefs, the review by Meece and her colleagues (2006) found that girls tend to have lower self-efficacy in math, science, and computers compared to boys. However, unlike competency beliefs, the gender gap for self-efficacy in STEM domains tends to be highest during adolescence and smaller before and after, possibly due to increased pressure to conform to gender roles during adolescence. It is important to note that despite gender differences in attributions for success and failure, competency beliefs, and self-efficacy in math and other STEM areas, girls do not value math less than boys. We need to leverage that value to create greater STEM equity.

> *In the end, the reason I chose electrical engineering over other areas of engineering was that people said it was the hardest, and I was always trying to challenge myself. Also, there are so many cool things you can do in electrical engineering, such as in the medical field and in robotics.*
> —Bettina Chen, electrical engineer and cofounder of Roominate Toys, California

CHAPTER 5

Opening Your Daughter's World to STEM Experiences

> *I had exposure to programming in high school, and I found [it] so engaging and interesting to me, I wanted to know more.*
> —Karen Panetta, Ph.D., Founder of Nerd Girls and associate dean of graduate engineering education at Tufts University

Although many people think of STEM as subjects taught in school, exposing your daughter to the field through visits to museums and participation in afterschool programs can be a powerful way to support your daughter's engagement in science, technology, engineering, and math. Science, natural history, and children's museums; colleges and universities; and youth programs offer both coeducational and girls-only programs from the preschool through the high school level. Activities that your daughter can participate in at home and online can also foster both engagement and competence in STEM.

What makes a quality, relevant STEM experience for girls? This chapter describes the types of programs that have been found to be effective in promoting girls' competence and confidence in STEM.

What Does the Research Tell Us?

In the early 1980s, Eccles (2005) developed a psychological and social framework to explain the choices young people make, such as those about course selections, college majors, and career aspirations. Many people in the youth development field apply this framework to develop and assess their programs. Using this model, girls evaluate the decision to engage in STEM from the following perspectives:

- ¤ Do they enjoy it?
- ¤ Do they value it?
- ¤ Can they expect to succeed at it?
- ¤ Does it fit their long- and short-term goals?
- ¤ What do they have to give up to engage in these activities?

As a parent, you are influential in helping your daughter answer these questions and weigh her choices.

> *Parents should introduce their daughters to classes or activities that encourage them to explore STEM fields, which can vary from STEM-related toys to afterschool programs. FEMMES, the organization I work with at Duke, provides an amazing opportunity for elementary school girls to learn about STEM subjects in fun, interactive ways.*
>
> —Sammi Siegel, student at Duke University

In recent years, practitioners and researchers have worked together to define and articulate the most effective strategies for promoting girls' interest and success in STEM. Studies of exemplary programs such as The Girl Game Company, The Lang Science Program of the American Museum of Natural History, Queens Community House's Access for Young Women Program, Techbridge, and Sisters4Science provide insights that present a remarkably consistent picture of what works. Fancsali provided a comprehensive survey of the field in 2002, and McCreedy and Dierking (2013) conducted a study in which they interviewed women who had participated in girls' STEM programs 5 to 25 years earlier to determine their long-term influences. A consistent picture of the characteristics of effective experiences emerges from these diverse studies.

Forming Relationships and Building a Community

Research has consistently indicated that girls prefer cooperative and collaborative learning over competitive and individualistic settings. One organization that has intentionally included cooperative learning in its implementation is The Girl Game Company, which was created to teach computer programming to Latina middle school girls who have had limited technology experience (Denner, Bean, & Martinez, 2009). Girls valued the social relationships that were formed as they worked in groups and were paired up to do programming. The program facilitators are trained to be mindful of the cultural values and background of participants. An important caution has been sounded by researchers (Fancsali, 2002; McCreedy & Dierking, 2013) who have reported that when cooperative learning occurs in coed groups, girls' involvement drops as boys tend to dominate the discussions and control the equipment.

> Science and tech have solved some of the world's hugest problems, and there are some really huge ones left. Problem solving is more than just science and theory; it also involves cooperating and figuring out how to work together. I think you need a large degree of women's talent in there to take problem solving away from competition and into collaboration.
> —Kathy Callahan, retired chemical and business executive, Pennsylvania

Building a sense of community and other positive effects are more likely to happen when programs last for an extended period of time. The Lang Science Program was developed to provide STEM experience for youth, largely from underrepresented groups, from sixth grade through high school at the American Museum of Natural History in New York City and allows girls free range of the museum so that they can meet women working across disciplines in the museum setting. Adams, Gupta, and Cotumaccio (2014) described four major effects of long-term participation in the Lang program on female participants: a sense of belonging to a particular place (in this case, a museum); varied exposure to STEM topics and careers; the development of a collective identity in which girls bonded with peers who also liked and were competent in STEM; and a pathway to college. The formation of an identity as part of the STEM field shapes future aspirations and increases confidence, and the opportunity to develop friendships with like-minded girls adds to girls' enjoyment of STEM programs.

Programs that offer multiyear engagement with increasing levels of responsibility provide long-term reinforcement of girls' STEM expertise and identity. A longitudinal analysis of the impact of the Access for Young Women program, conducted by Mosatche and Lawner (2010), showed a stronger effect after 2 years than after one in girls' belief that women can succeed in careers in STEM. Similarly, participants' knowledge of gender equity issues increased the longer they were in the program.

Engagement Starts With Girls' Interests

To foster engagement in STEM, programs should maintain the "fun factor" in activities. Mosatche, Matloff-Nieves, Kekelis, and Lawner (2013) described several different STEM programs that had in common the creation of activities that girls would choose because they enjoyed them. Mosatche and her colleagues noted that staff must be knowledgeable about child and adolescent development as well as STEM content. Staff who are uncomfortable with STEM will unconsciously communicate this negative attitude to the girls. Those who do not understand or relate well to girls will also fail to engage them in STEM.

> *This year I'm taking a research class before school, and even though I have to wake up an hour before normal, I jump out of bed—I love waking up to science!*
>
> —Marina Tosi, high school student, New York

Emphasizing the joy of discovery is an essential and appealing aspect of STEM. In a 2012 editorial in *Science*, editor-in-chief Bruce Alberts criticized the trend in science education that emphasizes strict attention to memorizing complicated concepts and facts, which deprives students of the joy of discovery and an appreciation of the aesthetics of the natural world. This wonder can be experienced through out of school activities. In looking for STEM experiences, keep in mind that working scientists, engineers, and mathematicians use words like "joy," "elegance," "play," and "beauty" to describe their work.

> *It may seem odd that art and music and poetry would be at all helpful in science, but I think it helps you think more creatively and see a broader picture. If you think about it, science and art are pretty much the same thing in the sense that you're looking for beauty and truth.*
> —Mona Xiaomeng Xu, Ph.D., assistant professor of experimental psychology at Idaho State University

STEM draws on creativity, and engaging in and appreciating the arts can enhance STEM skills and enjoyment. For instance, music uses intervals and sequencing that are also used in math, and engineers use creativity to solve physical problems. Field trips and exposure to physical environments where STEM takes place are fun and memorable experiences that bring girls closer to the professional world of STEM—whether that means visiting a veterinarian's office or talking to an engineer at a construction site.

Making It Real

STEM programs that connect concepts to real-life applications are more powerful than those that don't seem relevant to girls' lives. Consider how girls might react to the opportunity to explore the science behind making ice cream, or to gather and present statistics on teen dating violence, or to make a film on climate change with cutting-edge special effects. Knowledge and skills that girls can apply to their own lives increase the value that they place on STEM.

> *I analyze a lot of process data, trying to determine the cause and effect of certain variables. I also run a lot of cost reduction trials, substituting cheaper chemicals and determining if they have any negative effects on the process. I basically try to figure out what is wrong with the process and how to make it run right.*
>
> —Melissa Glifort, process engineer, Maine

Theme-based programs with a choice of topics allow girls to explore areas of high interest and to personalize their experience. Giving girls the opportunity to participate in creative workshops rather than structured design challenges, and holding exhibitions rather than competitions have broader appeal and make the idea of engineering more accessible. For example, the Crickets and Crafts program run by Boys and Girls Club of America for girls ages 9–12 transitions from familiar arts and crafts to engineering over the course of the program.

Setting High Standards

Allowing girls to use specialized equipment and to tackle complex issues challenges them and maintains their interest. According to Denner and her colleagues (2009), effective technology programs promote fluency in programming (ability to adapt and shape content and functions of programs) rather than literacy (ability to simply use technology). Program staff should encourage participants to make mistakes and learn by trial and error, particularly in groups with other girls. Becoming comfortable making mistakes is essential to the scientific method of experimentation and is contrary to the experiences girls may be having in school where correct answers on tests are often the measure of mastery. As noted by Alberts (2012), high standards in STEM are not defined by rigor in content knowledge but rather by the opportunity to learn the methodology of experimentation and discovery. Girls need hands-on experiences with the kinds of tools and equipment that are often not found at home or in school.

Your daughter needs the opportunity to work with soldering irons, Bunsen burners, and similar tools that are often off-limits because they are seen as too risky or too complicated. Learning to use powerful machines safely empowers girls. It is important to not only set the bar high for performance in areas in which individuals are negatively stereotyped, but to also reinforce the message that they can achieve those high standards (Steele et al., 2002). Programs in which girls teach others (as happens in the Lang program) recognize their expertise while reinforcing their fluency in STEM concepts.

> *I enjoy the flexibility of being able to work with numbers and people. Having knowledge about those two areas means I can develop best-in-class solutions. Some people are good with relationships and don't understand the financial impact of their actions. Some folks only look at the bottom line and don't regard the people involved. I can interpret both, and use financial language (which most organizations care about) to convey my thoughts.*
> —Angie Pace Kirk, human capital strategist and professional development coach

The cultural competence of staff is essential for delivering high-quality STEM programs to girls from every background. For girls who are recent immigrants, staff can create opportunities that allow girls to build their language skills by conversing in English and their native language. For instance, Denner and her colleagues (2009) described how staff of The Girls Game Company employed Spanish-speaking staff and paired girls who were bilingual in English and Spanish with those who were not yet fluent in English so that their language skills would not hold them back from engaging in the program's challenging STEM content.

Developing Leadership Skills

Quality STEM programs support leadership development and prepare girls to recognize barriers related to gender, ethnic group, and class and to develop strategies to confront and overcome bias. For example, Mosatche and her colleagues (2013) noted how the Queens Community House Access for Young Women program integrates STEM content within a leadership framework. Girls learn about gender as a protected legal status, develop an understanding of gender bias, and strengthen their assertive communication styles and skills in public presentation.

Coming into contact with female scientists and successful peers is an important mechanism for promoting leadership. That is exactly what happens in the Lang program at the American Museum of Natural History (Adams et al., 2014). Working as an integral part of a science museum, girls develop a sense of belonging in this important STEM institution and become experts in transmitting knowledge to others.

For teen girls, experiences in museums and laboratories provide authenticity: a connection to real-world work by scientists. Program activities at an automotive factory where engineers work, internships in clinical labs, and tours of museums all provide girls with opportunities to meet women with careers in STEM, to experience the settings where they work, to ask questions about work/life balance, and to visualize their potential future.

> My decision to become a med tech came after volunteering at a local hospital from 14 to 18 years old. I had thought I would become a nurse, but I worried too much about the patients and their suffering. I loved science classes in high school, especially biology and chemistry, so it was natural to stay in the medical environment by working in the laboratory.
> —Patty Laughlin, retired medical technologist and Microsoft-certified IT engineer, Missouri

Although many programs attract girls who are already doing well in STEM, some welcome girls who are not excelling academically at math or science. One such program is Project Exploration's Sisters4Science (S4S) program in Chicago, which offers a safe space for low-income African American and Latino girls from schools that do not offer strong science and math experiences (Lyon & Jafri, 2010). The S4S program intentionally integrates specific elements to foster girls' confidence by: (a) designing female-led programs around girls' experiences and strengths; (b) instilling a sense of pride in being female and having respect for female peers; (c) helping girls recognize and overcome inequities; and (d) addressing the mistaken belief that combining family responsibilities with the demands of a STEM career is not possible.

S4S, Access for Young Women, and other community-based programs also recognize that some girls are expected as teens to assume adult responsibilities within their families, which can hinder the engagement in academic and personal development outside of school.

Creating STEM-Friendly Home Environments

If organized programs are not available or accessible in your area, or you would like to create a STEM-friendly environment at home, you will find lots of ideas in the next section of this book. But here are some general ideas to keep in mind as you expose your daughter to STEM experiences.

Trips and outings are a wonderful way to experience STEM as a family. If a science museum or aquarium is located nearby, consider a family membership, which permits unlimited free entry, invitations to special events, and a sense of belonging to a STEM institution. In the absence of a nearby museum, trips to factories or processing plants and nature walks provide opportunities to engage with STEM as a family. Look for those everyday opportunities when you can encourage your daughter to formulate questions, use data, write down her observations, and draw conclusions based on the information she has collected.

> *When I was little, my mom got me a weather kit that you put outside and it could measure the temperature. It came with a little cup that measured precipitation and the direction the wind was blowing, and I thought it was the coolest thing. I would go out every day and record the weather stuff in my little book. My recordings of the weather for the month became my second-grade science project.*
>
> —Christine Doherty, physiology and neurobiology major at the University of Connecticut

Keep in mind that younger children are concrete thinkers who prefer projects that can be completed in one or, at most, a few sittings.

Teenagers can work on longer projects that stretch out over a period of months and are capable of abstract thinking.

Even if STEM experiences don't result in your daughter choosing a future in STEM, remember that there is still inherent value in engaging your daughter in science, technology, engineering, and math activities. McCreedy and Dierking (2013) found that women who had extensive STEM experience earlier in their lives were likely to continue their involvement in STEM-related careers and hobbies, gained feelings of empowerment and self-confidence, and developed leadership skills and a strong self-image in areas of gender and culture. Some participants in the study even felt that the programs impacted their skills as parents and that the role models they met provided excellent examples of women balancing careers and family responsibilities. This finding supports the notion that even when females do not ultimately choose a career in STEM, the experience they have had in STEM allows them to use that competence in navigating the complexities of the world today.

CHAPTER 6

How Role Models and Mentors Make a Difference

> *In my computer science class, my professor often highlights a well-known female computer scientist, which I have found to be interesting and motivating. It's important for girls to be able to see someone they can identify with in these positions or fields, and that exposure provides a source of necessary inspiration.*
>
> —Sammi Siegel, student at Duke University

Why Role Models Matter

Although a great deal of research has investigated how STEM role models influence girls in terms of their interests and aspirations, the data have not yielded a clear picture of what works and what doesn't. Research suggests that STEM role models are probably most helpful for girls who are good students and see a career in STEM as a possibility, but less motivating to girls who are not already interested in STEM.

Do Role Models Have to Be Similar to Have an Impact?

Some studies have demonstrated that women are more powerful role models than men, resulting in female college students making more of an effort on a math exam, having stronger feelings of competence in STEM, and identifying implicitly more with STEM fields, and that these changes were driven by identification and feelings of connection with the role models (Stout, Dasgupta, Hunsinger, & McManus, 2011). However, exposure to female (as compared to male) role models did not reduce the stereotypes about STEM fields being "masculine domains." Stout and her colleagues suggested that women may be leaving the STEM school-to-work pipeline because they are not seeing sufficient numbers of same-sex role models in books, on television, in movies, and in classrooms.

Many research investigations have specifically examined the effect of female role models on girls' and women's performance on math exams. A meta-analysis (statistical analysis of results from multiple studies) by Weisz, Lawner, Quinn, and Johnson (2015) found that while there is a small positive effect of female role models on female students' math performance, this effect is only significant for studies that were done in the lab. In other words, female role models only seem to help students' performance when they are tested under very controlled conditions, rather than in a natural setting, such as a classroom. However, some of this may have to do with differences in the characteristics of role models in lab and field settings that may make them more or less effective. For example, the meta-analysis found that in lab studies, role models who were portrayed in a purely positive way were more effective than those who had some sort of undermining flaw, such as being doubtful of their abilities or not deserving their success. However, it should be noted that this particular analysis combined studies that looked at females' performance on a math test with those that examined the performance of African American students on any sort of academic exam. In addition, the vast majority of these studies were done with middle school and college students, so it is unclear whether role models have the same effect on girls of other ages as well as on women. Among all field studies (those focusing on females and math as well as those focusing on African American students), only those done with middle school students showed a significant effect.

To complicate the picture even further, Betz and Sekaquaptewa (2012) noted that while exposing middle school-age girls to feminine role models engaged in STEM is "well-intentioned," the effect may actually cause girls to feel threatened and less motivated. Combining feminine qualities, such as wearing makeup and enjoying fashion magazines, with high ability in a field such as math, may make girls see that kind of success for themselves as unattainable. In general, research has found that role models are more effective when girls can easily identify with them. But if women's characteristics make girls feel that they could never reach their level, it's less likely that girls will be influenced by them, and their interest in STEM might even decrease.

STEM programs that bring in role models for girls typically try to include women who share characteristics such as race or ethnic background with participants. For example, the Girl Game Company, an afterschool and summer program designed to increase participation of Latina females in IT fields, connects girls with Latina women already working in those jobs. According to the founders of the Girl Game Company (Denner et al., 2009), girls become more interested in using and learning about computers in school as a result of their participation.

In a similar vein, research by Price (2010) found that when African American students had a STEM college instructor who was the same race as they were, they were more likely to stick with the STEM major they had chosen. In that same study, Price also found that fewer than a third of Black students who had declared themselves as STEM majors were still studying in a STEM field after 3 years of college as compared to their White counterparts, in which almost half persisted as STEM majors. In analyzing the database from all of the public universities in Ohio, Price noted that more research needs to be conducted to determine the underlying mechanism for the commitment to a STEM field. Do the African American faculty members serve simply as role models or are they actually acting as mentors to students of the same race?

> *The instructors for Charles Drew Science Scholars courses were incredibly helpful in providing support and networking opportunities that allowed me to succeed in STEM. For me, the most effective instructors I had were ones who were passionate about the subject they taught. It made learning from them much easier and showed me that there are many pathways you can take with a STEM degree.*
> —Jessica Kay, B.S. in genomics and molecular genetics and M.P.H., marketing rep at Detroit Medical Center, Michigan

Role Models Close in Age

Although many programs and much of the research has focused on role models who are fully established in their careers, a series of studies was conducted by Cheryan and her colleagues (2013) with role models who were third- and fourth-year computer science majors. The outcome depended on whether those role models were portrayed as stereotypical or nonstereotypical. A stereotypical role model might be described as playing video games as a hobby with *Electronic Game Monthly* as a favorite magazine, while a nonstereotypical role model would be presented as enjoying hanging out with friends and reading *Rolling Stone* magazine. The results of these studies showed that the gender of the role model didn't matter (surprisingly, males and females could be equally influential), but that female college students increased their interest in computer science when the role model had nonstereotypical interests. On the other hand, when the role model was portrayed in a stereotypical way, female students actually became less interested in the computer science field than when no role model was presented. That piece of information is critical because it runs counter to the assumption that all you have to do is expose girls to people in a STEM field and you'll increase their interest in it. This research tells us that only the "right" kind of role model is effective. One further finding of Cheryan's work was that role models are more effective when they evoke a sense of belonging, basically the feeling that "I can fit in here." Similarly, the meta-analysis by Weisz and colleagues (2015) found that among lab studies, only those that used role models who were close in age, such as an older student, were effective at increasing performance in the stereotyped domain.

Taken together, the research indicates that role models may be helpful in increasing girls' interest and possibly even their performance in STEM fields, but only under certain conditions, and male role models in many instances can be as effective as female role models. Role models seem to be more effective when girls can identify with the role models and feel some sort of connection with them, when they increase girls' sense of belonging in STEM, when girls feel they could potentially attain the same level of success as the role model, and when role models show that they are not stereotypical "geeks."

Role Models in the Media

For many years, at least some television shows have depicted females as physicians, but more recently, programs have begun to expose girls to other STEM careers such as forensic and computer scientists. However, television characters in STEM-related roles are still overwhelmingly male, fitting into the stereotype of a male-dominated STEM world. And when television shows that focus on physicists and engineers, such as *The Big Bang Theory*, include female characters involved in science, those characters fit the stereotype of nerdy, socially awkward individuals, not exactly a way to win over ambivalent girls.

A 2014 film has given girls a new role model. Keira Knightley played pioneering computer scientist Joan Clarke in *The Imitation Game*, which told the story of how Alan Turing, with Clarke's brilliant assistance, decoded the German Enigma machine, helping to defeat the Nazis and end World War II. In an early scene in the movie, the men were shocked when Clarke completed a complicated puzzle before anyone else and was asked to join the all-male team. How effective Keira Knightley is as a role model remains to be seen, since her skills and appearance might well make girls view them as unattainable. But, the movie might become a motivator in the same way as a television show such as CSI inspired girls to explore a career in forensic science. And its commercial success may encourage the film industry to create more movies that highlight previously unknown contributions by women to STEM.

> *Shonda Rhimes, the head writer and creator of Grey's Anatomy does a fantastic job of including a diverse cast, but you never think of them as the 'woman doctor' or 'Black doctor,' just the neurosurgeon or the orthopedic surgeon. I wish more shows were like this.*
> —Elise Sarvas, D.D.S., M.S.D., M.P.H., clinical assistant professor of pediatric dentistry at the University of Minnesota

Parents as Role Models

Parents have long known that their actions have a significant impact on their children. Numerous research studies have looked at parental influence in a wide variety of areas from school performance to ski helmet usage. For example, Hurd, Zimmerman, and Xue (2009) reported that when parents were actively involved in their children's schooling, educational outcomes were more positive. Some of the favorable results may come directly from actions parents take to encourage their children in their academic pursuits, the way they ask their children questions that foster critical thinking, and the variety of educational opportunities to which they expose their children. And part of the explanation may be based not on what parents do with and for their children, but how they live their lives and solve challenges. Whether they are asking probing questions, using creative solutions to everyday problems, or exploring their world by reading or traveling, they are serving as role models.

> *My dad always explained to us how things in the world happened. Actually, I loved it as a kid when he would stop on the highway, get us out of the car, and show us corn or wheat. Or when we toured rubber tree and tea farms when we traveled internationally. And my mom always had us help hold a flashlight, screw in a light bulb, fix something under the sink. I enjoyed seeing and physically interacting with how things worked—my parents really fostered that in day-to-day life and in travel.*
> —Karen Laughlin, Ph.D. in ecology and evolutionary biology, cofounder of Compassionate Use REform (CURE), California

Many of the STEM professionals we interviewed for this book described their parents as role models—not only by what career they had, but also how they pursued knowledge, resolved problems independently and collaboratively, and took reasonable risks to explore the world. How you live your life may have even more influence on your daughter than what you tell her to do.

> My dad is a computer scientist. When I was growing up he would always be talking to me and asking me questions: 'What do you think about this and what do you think about that?' If we passed something, he would say, 'Let's go see what this is.' My dad especially felt that you should be doing something that you love, that matters in a very broad sense and that matters to you. Maybe you can help other people or do something worthwhile.
> —Mona Xiaomeng Xu, Ph.D., assistant professor of experimental psychology at Idaho State University

The Role of Mentors

Although many school and afterschool programs designed to encourage girls to participate in STEM include the use of role models, very few set up girls with individual mentors. In general, mentors are difficult to recruit since the process involves a long-term, one-on-one relationship between a girl and a mentor, background screening, and ongoing supervision. That kind of commitment of time and effort is very different from what is typically required of a role model who may only be asked to allow someone to shadow her at work or to make a brief appearance at a school assembly or afterschool workshop.

Those girls who do have an opportunity to spend time with a mentor are able to have a powerful experience of guidance—whether that person is studying mutations in earthworms, the long-term effects of watching televised violence, or the efficiency of various designs of energy-saving solar panels. Programs that provide mentors for girls high school age and younger are expensive and labor-intensive and typically reserved for those who have won contests or gone through a grueling and competitive application process.

Online mentoring programs have both the advantage and disadvantage of not requiring face-to-face interactions, which means that regardless of where a girl lives, she could be potentially matched with a STEM mentor. However, when all the exchanges are in the virtual world, girls get a limited view of what a STEM workplace looks like and what day-to-day life is like for people in those fields.

> *In the places where I've been trained, there's a very strong tradition of mentorship—good, fair, and nurturing mentorship. The horror stories I hear about mentorship in the basic science realm would never happen in my field of epidemiology. I've had incredible mentors, one after another, in this field, and that's what has helped me excel.*
> —Hilary Robbins, doctoral student in epidemiology at Johns Hopkins University

Dasgupta (2011) suggested that programs pair advanced students with those who are somewhat below that level. This peer mentoring model could be an effective approach at all levels from elementary school through professional positions in business and academia. More experienced students and workers would benefit by having their knowledge reinforced each time they share their expertise while at the same time feeling good about their contribution to another person's growth. For those who are mentored, the advantages are obvious—the opportunity to learn from someone who has recently experienced what the mentee is now going through and a chance to be inspired by what's ahead in their school or work life. One thing to keep in mind with programs that use mentors and mentees who are close in age is that a mentor's superior achievement might make a mentee feel that she could never reach that level, which can be demotivating. To overcome this potential issue, mentors can be trained to emphasize the potential for their mentees to reach their level of expertise and to discuss how much they improved from where they started—thus inculcating a growth mindset.

For college women, mentors are more readily available, but that doesn't mean it's easy for students to find someone in the specific STEM field who interests them and who is willing to spend the time and energy exposing them to critical aspects of work and helping them make connections. Many scientists and engineers talked to us about specific professors who served as role models and mentors to them, not only encouraging them to stay in the field when the work was tough but also helping them see that this was a field that could be personally and professionally rewarding.

> *I went to school at a time when my peers would say, 'You should be home having babies,' and my professors didn't think girls should be in the classroom. After fighting all that, I felt that if I could do this I'm going to give back by being a good mentor to women and showing all students how to work together.*
> —Karen Panetta, Ph.D., founder of Nerd Girls and associate dean of graduate engineering education at Tufts University.

Although more research needs to be done to determine the specific attributes and actions of ideal role models and mentors, it is evident that having access to those who are already successful to some degree in STEM can play a role in guiding girls toward a future in which STEM plays a significant part. And when STEM mentors or role models provide a welcoming community to girls who have yet to make decisions about their educational and professional pathway, they show that STEM can give them an opportunity to grow in knowledge, self-confidence, and a sense of belonging.

> *My most significant mentors thus far have been my research advisers in undergraduate and graduate school. Their values and dedication to helping their students are and were very inspirational to me and kept me motivated in chemistry research.*
> —Teresa, Ph.D., analytical chemist for drug company, New Jersey

How Can We Transform the Picture of Girls and Women in STEM?

The findings described in the previous section have drawn a picture of the obstacles that have prevented females from full representation in STEM. But the research has also pointed to opportunities that we can take advantage of to transform the landscape to a more equitable one. Change needs to happen on many different fronts, from implementing policy initiatives at the national level to increasing access to role models. This section describes how we can turn obstacles into opportunities.

CHAPTER 7

Advocacy

A Key Way to Transform Obstacles Into Opportunities

> *The biggest obstacle I faced when I was in school was there was no one to tell me I could be a scientist, an engineer, a mathematician, or a computer whiz. There was no one who understood the possibilities. Today, the potential and need for girls in STEM is higher than ever and the opportunities are exciting.*
> —Sylvia Barsion, Ph.D. in educational research, measurement, and evaluation; writer and consultant, New York

Parents can play an active role in transforming obstacles to opportunities for girls in STEM through their participation as citizens in influencing public policy. Elected public officials have a keen interest in hearing from voters about their concerns, and it can be surprisingly easy to be heard; they (or their staff) do read their mail and e-mail and note telephone calls from constituents.

All levels of government make decisions that influence the opportunities for girls in STEM. The federal rules are universal for all states, while state laws apply to all areas of the state. The local level legislates only for your city, county, or town, but this can be the easiest level of government to influence because of its accessibility.

In general, there are two major types of governmental functions that impact girls and STEM: funding and regulations. Both are key. Many of the programs that promote girls' involvement in STEM rely on funding from the federal, state, or local government. Regulations protect women's rights in education and at work, including the right to equal access to STEM education. Governments may also provide incentives to educational institutions to promote gender equity as well as leverage penalties for failure to provide equal access and to protect girls and women from harassment. Government institutions may also provide nonbinding guidelines for effective practices among government-funded institutions.

An additional role of government can be to convene stakeholders to analyze evidence-based practices. The President's Council of Advisors on Science and Technology (PCAST) delivered an extensive report in February 2012 that included recommendations on engaging and retaining girls in STEM called, "Engage to Excel: Producing One Million Additional College Graduates in Science, Technology, Engineering and Mathematics."

Private companies are concerned with their image among consumers and the general public. Advocacy campaigns that encourage fairness and general awareness of issues influence private companies to reflect on and change their practices. For instance, in January 2015, Intel announced funding for a more effective school-to-work pipeline in STEM. That same year, Google appointed two women to its highest levels: Ruth Porat as its Chief Financial Officer and Susan Wojnicki to run YouTube. Both had already established themselves as powerful forces in the finance and tech worlds. The growing public concern about the lack of women at high levels of STEM companies and online harassment of women in the computer and gaming industries has been expressed formally and informally. During the 2014 Grace Hopper Celebration of Women in Computing in Phoenix, a storm of Twitter protests arose in response to a "Male Allies Plenary Panel" at which male leaders of tech companies placed responsibility for changing toxic environments on women rather than discussing their own roles and efforts to make necessary changes for a female-friendly environment. In a much-publicized case, Ellen Pao sued venture capital firm Kleiner

Perkins Caufield and Byers for gender discrimination. Although she lost the case, the publicity generated was widely hailed for highlighting the issue. When she was CEO of the social media company Reddit, Pao banned salary negotiations because she believed it was an area in which women experienced discrimination in comparison to male colleagues.

> *There are tons of studies that show the benefits of having many viewpoints on teams, and the benefits of having women on boards and women in leadership positions. The challenge I see at my job is that the pool of applicants for junior positions are overwhelmingly male. So the lower levels don't start off with an even gender mix.*
>
> —Jennifer Tosi, BA in engineering, vice president at Morgan Stanley, New York

What Can Local Governments Do?

Local governments, particularly in urban areas, are a major funder of STEM activities for girls. After school and during summers and weekends, girls can explore STEM on their own terms, free of the mandates of state curricula. In addition, many decisions about school curricula and school-sponsored extracurricular activities are made at a local level. School officials can decide, for instance, to sponsor an all-girls robotics team. Local authorities can also be educated on the best practices for inclusion of girls and underrepresented groups, such as sponsoring exhibitions rather than competitions. By attending local meetings of school boards and civic organizations, you can become informed and have the opportunity to influence local decisions.

As a parent, you have the right to expect that the local education authority will be accountable for providing an equal education for your daughter. Among the data they should provide is the gender balance in Advanced Placement courses. Requests for this information sometimes promote discussion resulting in changes; if not, the information can be incorporated into a campaign to increase educational equity.

According to Title IX of the Education Amendment of 1972, every school is required to have a written public policy prohibiting gender discrimination, including addressing sexual harassment. Title IX applies to all public schools and any other entity accepting federal funding. Many districts have antibullying protocols. Both of these can protect girls from negative peer interactions in the spaces that should be safe for learning. Teacher training is also a local or state issue, and professional development in bias awareness is a policy in the local domain. Title IX provisions are beginning to be used by advocates to press for changes in educational institutions to provide girls with equal access to STEM opportunities.

Local governments also grant funds to museums. As a condition of receiving government money, museums are generally required to provide free access during certain hours (such as an admission-free evening or day) or to particular groups such as children, or to institute a "pay what you wish" policy for admissions. School districts and individuals at all government levels also give awards to students and could be encouraged to think about STEM and girls in this context.

What Can the State Government Do?

It is at the state level that many educational decisions are made, including funding formulas and decisions about priorities for education and youth work. States can be encouraged to pay for expanded learning time, adequate school budgets to support quality STEM experiences for all children, and funding for afterschool and summer youth programs. In addition, many states sponsor scholarships focused on STEM. For example, as of 2015, the New York State STEM Incentive Program was providing a full tuition scholarship to any state or New York City public college for the top 10% of students in each New York State high school if they pursued a STEM degree in an associate's or bachelor's degree program and agreed to work in a STEM field in New York for 5 years after graduation. New Jersey has a STEM Scholars program through which promising students receive exposure to STEM and mentoring by professionals. As of 2015, the National Governors' Association has supported six states—Colorado, Hawaii, Minnesota, Ohio, Pennsylvania, and Virginia—in advancing STEM education policy agendas.

State governments may also establish their own guidelines around school climate and reporting and addressing instances of harassment. When there is a conflict between state and local regulations, state law takes precedence. For instance, if a state mandates certain educational standards, the locality must comply. Science education standards have been particularly contentious in some areas due to controversy over how to teach evolution and sexual education.

Oversight of the Federal Government

The federal government has the broadest oversight and the most authority in many matters, and states cannot overrule or ignore federal laws. The federal government also allocates national level funding to states to distribute. For instance, 21st Century Community Learning Centers are federally funded afterschool programs with money distributed to states to grant to schools and community organizations. This has been an important source of funding for afterschool STEM experiences.

Higher education is also governed by federal guidelines, and public and most private colleges accept some federal funding, including financial aid that is distributed to students (support that is essential for many young women). These institutions must abide by federal law as a condition of receiving funds. The laws that colleges and universities must observe cover issues of student privacy and educational equity. Enforcement of civil rights (including access to education) fall under the U.S. Department of Education and U.S. Department of Justice. The U.S. Department of Labor includes a Women's Bureau, which addresses working women's issues, including equitable policies and family leave initiatives.

One of the major protections for girls and women in education is Title IX. Initially applied mainly to the right of girls to have equal access to sports, in recent years, women have used it to gain equal access to educational activities related to STEM. Educating girls about their rights under Title IX can promote better access to educational opportunities in STEM and fair treatment within educational institutions. The Women's Educational Equity Act (WEEA) program was enacted in 1974 to promote educational equity for girls and women, including those who suffer multiple forms of discrimination based on gender, race, ethnicity, national origin, disability, and age, and to provide funds to help education agencies and institutions meet the requirements of Title IX of the Education Amendments of 1972. For many years, WEEA provided funding for research on programs to promote gender equity, including for STEM education for girls. However in 2010, WEEA was defunded, and without resources WEEA could not complete its mission. The American Association of University Women and other organizations have been advocating for the resumption of WEEA funding.

Family leave policy is another area protected by federal regulations. One of the obstacles to women's pursuit of STEM careers has been the balancing of family and work responsibilities, which is most often a heavier burden for women than for men. Childcare and other domestic issues are also realms governed by federal law. Gender equity is protected under the Equal Employment Opportunity Act, another set of federal regulations. Women who experience gender discrimination at work can file a federal complaint seeking back wages or other redress.

The White House and Congress have the authority to establish Task Forces and Commissions to study social problems and propose solutions. US2020 is an initiative developed from a White House call to generate large-scale, innovative solutions to STEM education challenges. Announced by President Obama at the 2013 White House Science Fair, US2020's mission is to dramatically scale the number of STEM professionals mentoring and teaching students through hands-on projects with a focus on serving underrepresented communities—girls, students of color, and low-income children.

> *Our goal is to match one million STEM mentors with students from kindergarten through college via youth-serving nonprofits by the year 2020, creating millions of moments of discovery—life-changing events when students conduct experiments, build model rockets, and program robots.*
> —Michael Valentino, communications and foundations engagement specialist, US 2020

Established in 2008 by President Obama, The White House Council on Women and Girls had a mandate to ensure that federal agencies, departments, and offices were scrutinizing how they were addressing the needs of women and girls; the results are described in their April 2012 report: *Keeping America's Women Moving Forward: The Key to an Economy Built to Last.* Congress mandates a Committee on Equal Opportunities in Science, and the National Institutes of Health has convened several relevant working groups, including The Working Group on Women in Biomedical Careers and the Women of Color Research Network. These initiatives had as their impetus the advocacy of citizens working collectively to bring issues to the attention of their elected officials.

A Role for Community Organizations and Companies

Civic and business associations can encourage greater participation of girls and women in STEM by offering prizes and awards. Local organizations that honor "women of the year" could choose to select a woman in a STEM field or offer a specific award for women in STEM. Media can offer press coverage of girls in STEM as well as related issues and advocacy campaigns. Publicity campaigns make people aware of available opportunities and create a climate that promotes girls' involvement in STEM.

> *It is important to leverage social media to get people talking about STEM initiatives because the only way that policy will be made in the future is to get people talking about it now.*
> —Michael Valentino, communications and foundations engagement specialist, US 2020

Every private company is governed by a board of directors appointed or elected by shareholders to ensure legal compliance and good governance of the company. Because boards appoint the chief executives, they can be sensitized by employees and the public to the benefits of women's leadership and encouraged to work with executives to establish incentive programs that increase the percentage of women in high-level positions.

Some companies fund scholarships and charitable donations to groups that work with girls in STEM. Many corporations in the STEM arena have separate foundations that support nonprofit organizations, which support youth involvement in STEM. Many national and local organizations take advantage of those kinds of funding opportunities, proposing programs in which girls gain experience doing hands-on science or engineering projects, learning how to code, or using the latest technology. In addition, some corporations in STEM fields encourage their employees to get involved in activating the pipeline to STEM careers through mentoring. As an example, SanDisk, through its engagement with Citizen Schools, has 20% of its workforce signed up as mentors for youth through the US 2020 initiative.

> *The first building that I had my lab in was built at a time when the only role women had at DuPont was as secretaries. So the building I was in didn't have any restrooms on the second or third floors for women because women only worked on the first floor in the office. So my first 3 years working at DuPont I had to go down two flights of stairs to get to a restroom.*
> —Carol L. Ensinger, Ph.D., retired pharmaceuticals industry chemist and project manager, South Carolina

Honorable Sylvia Sanchez, Member of Congress
2302 Rayburn House Office Building
Washington, DC 20515

Dear Representative Sanchez:

As a concerned parent who is a constituent of your district, I am writing to urge you to support funding for the 21st Century Community Learning Centers in the reauthorization of the Elementary and Secondary Education Act. My children attend Public School XYZ where they have benefited greatly from the afterschool program. In particular, my daughter has discovered a keen interest in science through the exciting STEM component of this program. This was not a topic that interested her prior to attending the afterschool program.

Afterschool programs are also very important to me as a working parent, so that I know that my children are safely supervised, providing peace of mind at work. In addition, they are making friends and learning to communicate with peers and adults. I appreciate your past support for our afterschool program and urge you to continue this support.

Sincerely,

Jane Smith

Figure 1. Sample letter to Congress member.

How to Advocate Effectively

If you don't know who represents you in Congress or in your local legislature, you can obtain this information online or though the local election board or League of Women Voters. Figure 1 includes a sample advocacy letter that could be used for requesting more funds for an afterschool program that can be adapted to any relevant issue.

Get your friends, neighbors, and local PTA or other organization of parents involved. Elected officials depend on votes and are sensitive to their reputation. If they see a widespread community concern, they are generally eager to take action. Be very clear when you write or speak about the solution that you propose. See this as an opportunity to educate officials about your area of expertise, which is your child's development. As with any interpersonal interaction, the more personalized a communication is the better; a typed letter with an original signature "counts" more than a signature on a petition. Specific stories and data are particularly important. The details of how the proposed change will impact an individual is powerfully persuasive to the uncommitted and provides ammunition for those who are already convinced in helping to persuade their colleagues. Increasingly, officials are following Twitter and other forms of social media, which may be an engaging way to involve your children. Make sure to send thank-you acknowledgements to those who do take a positive stand to encourage their future support and to build a relationship with the official. Because many people forget to take this step, officials are likely to remember who thanked them.

Organizations That Support Women and Girls at the Policy Level

Many organizations are working to promote girls' participation in STEM. It is easy and free to sign up for alerts and informational newsletters that can help shape your advocacy efforts. Here is a sample of national organizations that engage in advocacy for STEM-related education:

- The American Association of University Women (http://www. aauw.org) has been advocating for women in education for decades. The "Budget 101" section of its website includes a concise synopsis of current federal policy issues.
- Association for Women in Science (http://www.awis.org) advocates for policies to sustain women in science careers, including family-friendly policies and applying Title IX to STEM fields.
- National Coalition of Women and Girls in Education (http:// www.ncwge.org) educates the public about issues concerning equal rights for women and girls in education; monitors the enforcement of relevant current legislation; and conducts research and analyses of issues concerning equal rights for women and girls in education.

¤ The Afterschool Alliance (http://www.afterschoolalliance. org) is the largest organization that advocates for funding for afterschool programs, including those that foster STEM engagement.

As your daughter is growing up, an important role you play is preparing her for independence. Teaching her from an early age to assertively speak up for herself, to work with peers to bring injustice and inequities to the attention of authorities, and to recognize and act on her convictions all prepare her to make the most of the world of STEM. By engaging in advocacy actions with your daughter, you model assertiveness and help her develop her self-confidence and foster a sense of belonging to a broader community.

CHAPTER 8

Preparing Girls to Recognize and Respond to Gender Bias

> *As a young and small female, I often find there is a completely different experience over the phone, where my technical skills are apparent without physical appearance creating a stereotyped impression. In person, it often takes longer for men to trust my technical judgment until I find a mistake or point something out that they haven't thought about.*
> —Ashley Odom, B.S. in computer science and public policy, M.B.A.;
> senior consultant at the Public Consulting Group, Massachusetts

In the previous chapter, we described ways to impact girls' opportunities in STEM through advocacy. Critically important is educating them to recognize gender discrimination as it occurs and to respond to it in an assertive manner. When girls are better prepared to respond effectively to discrimination, they are more likely to find success in STEM. As girls develop a repertoire of actions they can take when faced with bias about their skills and backgrounds, they become more confident and are better able to take effective action (Muno, 2014).

What Does Gender Bias Look Like?

Girls and women often note that they are more likely than males to be ignored or not called on in class or in meetings. Even in casual conversations, females say their opinions are often not sought or their ideas are quickly dismissed. Rather than feeling inferior when these situations occur (as if they don't deserve to be recognized), girls can use critical analysis to recognize a social pattern that is not about them personally, but rather is about the way bias manifests itself. As a parent, you can encourage your daughter and her friends to talk to each other about their classroom experiences, for example, to collectively identify patterns of behavior that reflect unconscious bias. It is never too early for children to begin to learn about fairness. Even toddlers and pre-schoolers can exhibit empathy (Saliquist, Eisenberg, Spinrad, Eggum, & Gaertner, 2009)

> *Bias can be everywhere—even in the questions posed in textbooks.*
> —Ruthe Farmer, chief strategy and growth officer at the National Center for Women and Information Technology, Colorado

Girls can use data to find out the truth for themselves and use this information as a reality check and also for advocacy purposes. For instance, if a student learns that only 20% of girls at her high school are taking AP Calculus but 75% were eligible, that would suggest a systemic issue. If girls are given the opportunity to develop their analytic skills, they will recognize that often it is the setting, rather than their talent, that is limiting their options.

The research described in previous chapters indicates the continuing existence of systemic barriers to girls' participation in STEM. Particularly as girls move through higher levels of education and the world of work, they are likely to encounter instances of discrimination. If they learn to build the resilience that allows them to solve problems as they run into tough situations, they are more likely to achieve success at a high level. Parents, teachers, and program facilitators can find those teachable moments to ask questions and provide relevant examples, which will foster the critical thinking that allows girls to make sense of situations, including the presence of stereotypes and bias.

> *I am a strategy consultant and leadership educator. STEM thinking, at its base level, is the application of logic and reasoning. I deconstruct issues and identify solutions, and I work with teams of people to implement the answers. Engineers function similarly.*
> —Daria Torres, M.B.A./M.S.E., managing partner and founder of the Walls Torres Group, New Jersey

Many youth programs that focus on girls and science incorporate strategies for responding to gender discrimination as part of their programming. For example, Queens Community House's Access for Young Women's program integrates curricular sessions that include STEM topics while building skills in assertive communication, leadership, and advocacy (Mosatche et al., 2013).

Skills and Behaviors to Cultivate

Key to responding effectively to discrimination is the development of skills and behaviors that promote success. Earlier, we reviewed the research relating to growth mindset. If you praise your daughter for effort more than for outcomes, she experiences the value you place on hard work and learns that improvement is possible. You can reinforce her efforts to be persistent and work through challenges, which is a part of how scientists and engineers work. Enhance her confidence with well-deserved praise and also by allowing and encouraging her to take reasonable risks and to challenge herself. Foster her awareness of social injustice, which will also help her recognize and avoid being derailed by discriminatory comments and practices.

> *In high school, when I participated in Math League, one of the math teachers would 'jokingly' tell my female friend and me that we better not make him 'regret putting two girls on the calculus team.' Even though the comments were meant as jokes, it reinforced the idea in the back of my mind that women aren't as represented in fields like math, and the stereotype that women aren't as good at math as men.*
>
> —Sammi Siegel, student at Duke University

An ability to navigate systems will help girls make the most of potential opportunities. For instance, locating contests and competitions relating to STEM requires research. Likewise, finding scholarships and STEM programs requires initiative if school guidance counselors and teachers are unable or unwilling to help. Creating a network and using mentors well requires initiative and assertiveness. Many girls are uncomfortable requesting that someone spend time guiding them—giving them academic and career advice—without compensation. However, when girls do take these kinds of actions, their feelings of insecurity and frustration lessen while their sense of pride builds.

Fighting the Imposter Syndrome

Self-awareness helps girls put external feedback on their performance in perspective. Coupled with self-confidence and a reality-based assessment of their strengths, young women can push back against discriminatory practices by "owning" their strengths. Some women are prone to the "imposter syndrome": believing that their successes are accidental and fearing that their inadequacy will be uncovered (Clance & Imes, 1978). Those who live with that perception have trouble taking credit for their achievements. Experiences with discrimination in the classroom reinforce the imposter syndrome. Help your daughter cushion herself against feeling like a fraud by keeping track of her accomplishments in a way that she can refer to when she encounters situations that might provoke feelings of insecurity. Encourage her to think about peers and adults who can serve as her professional "panel of advisors" for support.

> *During my Ph.D. work, I almost always felt that I wasn't as good as all of my peers. I'm not sure if this was due to being a woman, being me as an individual, or simply the lot of every Ph.D. student. I found the attack culture of academic talks off-putting. There was more emphasis on asking hard questions than finding good answers.*
> —Karen Laughlin, Ph.D. in ecology and evolutionary biology, cofounder of Compassionate Use REform (CURE), California

The Beauty of Assertive Communication

Communicating effectively is a vital tool in dealing with gender discrimination. Your daughter will benefit from understanding the three basic communication styles: aggressive, passive, and assertive. Aggressive communication contains a hostile element and is ineffective because it makes the other person defensive or angry. The aggression can be shown in words or in tone. Passive communication is too indirect to achieve the desired end. Assertive communication, on the other hand, enables girls to express their needs without demeaning or antagonizing the other person.

Assertive communication employs "I" statements that enlighten the other person as to the impact of their actions. Provide opportunities for your daughter to practice ways to respond assertively in challenging situations that she may encounter in the future. Encourage her to use "I" statements when faced with hurtful comments from others. An example is: "When you state that girls can't do this, I feel resentful and less confident. If you give me a chance to try this activity then I can test my skills and find out for myself."

Using data combined with expressing honest feelings can also be helpful to bolster her arguments, as shown in this example: "I feel frustrated that you are not calling on me as often as I would like, and I noted that in the last class, 11 out of 12 students who spoke were boys."

> *Everyone in my life told me 'YOU CAN' from teachers to parents. Or perhaps I blocked out those who didn't. I have a unique ability to absorb what I need from people and leave the unhelpful information on the table.*
> —Yvette L. Campbell, B.A. in applied mathematics and dramatic art-dance, past president and CEO of the Harlem School of the Arts

When your daughter does encounter gender discrimination, encourage her to come up with her own solutions rather than rushing to solve problems for her. Giving her an opportunity to strategize about how to handle a difficult situation fosters self-reliance and confidence that she can solve her own problems.

In the 1960s at a time when STEM was a male-dominated field, Frances Oldham Kelsey, M.D., Ph.D., saved countless children in the United States from being born with major deformities, such as phocomelia or flipper-like limbs, by her assertive behavior. A drug called Kevadon (known by its generic name as thalidomide) had been used by pregnant women in Canada, Europe, and the Middle East to decrease the nausea of morning sickness, and an application for its approval came to the attention of Dr. Kelsey at the Food and Drug Administration in 1960. She became concerned after reviewing the safety data and asked the drug manufacturer for more information. The company responded, but Dr. Kelsey wasn't satisfied and requested more evidence. She continued to withhold approval as pressure on her grew. Supported by her colleagues, pharmacologist Oyam Jiro and chemist Lee Geismar, Dr. Kelsey stood her ground as the evidence of the toxic effects of thalidomide on the developing fetus emerged and the drug was never officially approved for use in the United States (until recently when it was shown to be effective against multiple myeloma). Dr. Kelsey was a true hero, combining science expertise, leadership, and courage—a great role model for girls today.

Bolster your daughter's awareness of women who have overcome barriers to help her recognize that experiences with discrimination may be part of the STEM experience but they do not have to derail her aspirations. You can practice role-playing assertive responses to hurtful experiences, thus giving her a lifelong skill that is transferable to many situations.

CHAPTER 9

Providing Girls With Engaging STEM Experiences

> *Children just going about their daily lives will have lots of opportunities to encounter messages that boys are good at science. Parents can counteract that idea by saying that girls are great at this, too, and it's wonderful if you're interested in these STEM fields. Or take the opportunity to point out women doing good work across the STEM universe. Parents can make the effort to explicitly encourage these interests and highlight role models who are in these fields already. It is powerful to give young girls and women the sense that this is an option for them.*
>
> —Corinne A. Moss-Racusin, Ph.D., assistant professor of psychology at Skidmore College

Creating Gender Neutral Environments

Creating environments for children that are not biased allows them to openly explore a variety of interests. However, many places are not gender neutral—sometimes intentionally, but often inadvertently. When girls experience messages that STEM in general or in specific subfields is mainly for boys, girls are less likely to become engaged even if the subject matter or activity itself would appeal to them.

In a gender-neutral environment, behaviors, policies, and language are not differentiated according to an individual's sex or gender. Unfortunately, toys, children's books, clubs, games, academic subjects, and roles are often created or taught in ways that distinguish between those for boys and for girls. Examples are everywhere. Teachers ask boys and girls to line up separately. Toy packages often depict girls and boys differently—for example, a boy playing with a chemistry set while a girl looks on or a girl making a craft with pink and purple fabric with no boy in sight. Many toy stores even separate toys and games into boy and girl aisles. Main characters in television shows and movies are more likely to be male than female.

> While I was growing up in Ho Chi Minh, Vietnam, my family did not have a lot of money. Most of the time, the games and toys I played with were improvised from what was available and made more interactive with other players. Tennis balls and chopsticks were used for games of speed and agility, while napkins were used to create origami shapes, which I believe trained my brain to think in terms of structure in 3D and solving problems. When I did get modern toys, I tended to take them apart due to my curiosity about how they worked. I took apart a doll to find out why her eyes closed when you lay her down. I often stayed in a safe area at my family's factory where I could see my parents operating the machines. I was also introduced to hammers and nails and bolts and screws pretty early on.
>
> —Young Le, transmission engineer working on helicopters at Lockheed Martin

As a parent, you can become a critical observer of environments and help your daughter do the same. Many of the gender-biased marketing messages are explicit, but perhaps even more insidious are the subtle ones. Consider these kinds of questions:

- ¤ How would you feel if a girl were featured on this (STEM-related) game? Would you be more likely to want to purchase it? How do you think your daughter would react to it?
- ¤ How could this product be marketed in a way that is more gender neutral?

   ⊠   What would make this book about science more appealing to your daughter?

Encourage your daughter to ask questions about her environment and to critically think about changes that would make STEM activities more relevant and exciting for her. The very act of asking questions and brainstorming possibilities is STEM in action.

> *One of the toys that I thoroughly enjoyed was 'Capsula.' It primarily was made up of different gears and motors that you connected to form motorized-based toys for land or water. You could build cars, boats, pulleys, or even a fan. I brought the fan to school in sixth grade and everyone was jealous and in awe.*
> —Meghan Rushing, Ph.D., research chemist at BASF

What Needs to Happen at Home?

Young children typically spend most of their time at home, and what parents do and say are powerful forms of influence. As they get older, other people and their outside environment become increasingly important, but parents remain significant sources of inspiration. That means that you have opportunities over a period of years to engage your daughter in STEM. If you show enthusiasm, curiosity, and openness about the world of STEM, your daughter is likely to develop those attitudes. An extensive research literature points to the way parents' views and actions affect their children's sense of competence in STEM. A review by Gunderson and colleagues (2012) noted that parents' perceptions of their children's math competence are often gender-based. Even when contradictory evidence exists, parents believe that their sons are better at math than their daughters. As a parent, you need to recognize your own biases and how you might be translating those beliefs into your behaviors and expectations.

> *My father is an engineer, and my mother is a science teacher. I couldn't wait until third grade so I could finally do a science fair project at school. They were little projects, but my father brought me through the entire process of understanding what I'm doing—let's make the experiment in our kitchen, let's see what this does. And there were these kits, like a chemistry kit and a microscope kit. We made slides of random things we found and just looked at them under the microscope. I had experience observing the world through a different kind of lens.*
>
> —Nicole Flaig, Ph.D. student in neuroscience
> at the University of Connecticut

Recognizing That STEM Is Everywhere

One of the easiest and most important ways parents can engage their children in STEM is by helping them see that STEM is everywhere and a part of their everyday experience. Whether you are preparing a meal in the kitchen or unclogging a stopped-up toilet, think about what STEM principles are involved and how your daughter can learn about them by seeing what happens when you mix ingredients or use a plunger. Instead of passively watching television (even commercials), engage her by asking the kinds of questions scientists and engineers ask:

- What do you think will happen? (You're asking her to make a hypothesis.)
- How could you improve that product? (You're asking her to be a product engineer.)
- What's another way to solve that problem? (You're asking her to be a civil engineer, a computer scientist, or a psychologist.)
- How much time do the commercials take up while you're watching a program scheduled for one hour? (You're asking her to be a mathematician.)

Jacobs, Davis-Kean, Bleeker, Eccles, and Malanchuk (2005) noted that parents influence their children both directly by what they say, but also through "opportunity structures" or the experiences to which they expose their children. For instance, a father might encourage his daughter to join a math club at school, and a mother might play math games on the computer with her daughter. An afternoon at the beach or the lake or a walk on a hiking trail in the woods or through a new neighborhood provides you and your daughter with ample opportunities to engage in STEM questions and activities. From experimenting with methods of purifying water to studying the ecosystems of various outdoor spaces, you are experiencing STEM. Simple machines, such as levers and inclined planes, are all around us. At the playground, you can point out that the seesaw your daughter and her friends are playing on is a lever, and when you see a ramp for wheelchair access, tell her that it's an inclined plane in action. Ask her to tell you how it works. The key point is that STEM experiences should be part of her daily life. Make it fun to question and observe, and your daughter will use you as a role model for how to interact with and understand the world.

> We didn't realize that we were learning when Dad asked us to 'hold the flashlight' as he worked. Most of us are pretty handy with tools and electricity now. The influence of career was certainly not direct, but oriented us to how things work and the world of engineering.
> —Patty Laughlin, retired medical technologist and Microsoft-certified IT engineer, Missouri

As part of observing the everyday world, listen to conversations and help your daughter really hear what's being said. When a woman states, "I've never been good at math," that's a teachable moment for you, an opportunity to ask your daughter about the effect of women making those kinds of self-denigrating comments about their math skills. Help her see that it's not okay to be unable to or uncomfortable doing basic math tasks.

Identifying Friends and Family With STEM Interests and Jobs

People often focus on networking in a business context, but consider the impact on your daughter of connecting with people who either work in STEM fields or have interests that are related to STEM. Make it a game the two of you play together identifying people one or both of you know who has either a job or a hobby that involves STEM and might be willing to share their knowledge and interest with your daughter. If you and your daughter use a spreadsheet to track people and areas of expertise and experience, make sure you mention how using this computer application makes this exercise manageable and organized. Questions you can ask to identify people in your STEM network include:

- ¤ What networks am I part of? Your list could be quite long, ranging from Facebook and LinkedIn to school alumni groups and community associations. Your coworkers can also be a possible network, even if you don't work in a STEM field. There are likely some people in your office who have STEM-related jobs, such as the IT person, or who have STEM-relevant interests outside of work.

- ¤ How can I find out who in these networks is working in a STEM-related field? You might use simple keywords, like "engineering" or "science" to do a search for those networks that are online.

- ¤ Which relatives have STEM-related hobbies or jobs? Get your daughter involved in getting answers.

- ¤ How can we use technology to find out about relatives we're not in touch with on a regular basis? People send out mass holiday e-mails—you and your daughter could send out a mass STEM search e-mail.

- ¤ Which neighbors have STEM-related hobbies or jobs? When your neighbors know about your STEM project, they will let you know about their connections. This activity is a great way to introduce your daughter to the important role networking plays in our lives.

Once you've created your list, what's next? The answer depends on your daughter's age, her level of interest in this project (it's supposed to be fun and educational for her), and available time (both yours and hers). Before either of you reaches out to the people in your network, think about the result you want since you and/or your daughter will need to make that clear through questions or requests. The outcomes might include: opportunities for your daughter to shadow employees in STEM workplaces, interview people about their jobs, learn about new technologies, discover a new hobby, and think about how STEM fits into her future. Especially if your daughter is younger, you can also talk to these individuals about their ideas for how you can integrate their particular area of STEM into everyday life for your daughter. The experience of reaching out to adults for information cultivates an important skill that will benefit her in college and beyond.

> *My parents opened doors for me to figure out what I wanted to do, and let me meet a lot of different people. I met lots of other faculty members, and it seemed normal at the time to have all these bright people around. They never pushed me toward anything, but they never stopped me from doing anything either.*
> —Stacy Klein-Gardner, Ph.D., director of the Center for STEM Education for Girls at the Harpeth Hall School and faculty member in biomedical engineering and radiology at Vanderbilt University

What Is the Role of Schools?

The school curriculum and those who teach it influence children's attitudes toward STEM in direct and indirect ways. Like parents, teachers bring their own experiences and bias into their interactions with children. Research by Beilock, Gunderson, Ramirez, and Levine (2010) indicated that teachers' anxiety about math rubs off on their elementary school students. They found that girls who were taught math by female teachers who had relatively high levels of anxiety about the subject showed lower math performance than did those girls who had female teachers with lower levels of anxiety about math. Moreover, girls who spent a year in school with highly math-anxious teachers showed greater agreement with the stereotype that boys are better at math while girls are better at reading. Results like these suggest that interventions need to be focused not just on students but also on their teachers. Training that helps teachers recognize and decrease their biases and increase their comfort and confidence with math is critical in turning around the adverse effects on their female students' math achievement and anxiety.

> What the research literature is telling us is that even very egalitarian, well-meaning people can often express subtle biases. In our work and in other research, we don't find these biases are held differentially by different groups of people. So female faculty were just as likely as male faculty to express these biases, young and old, physicists and chemists. We're all pretty exposed to these stereotypes and affected by them. As an educator, I just try to be as aware as possible of the ways in which these subtle biases may affect interactions with students. Try to be vigilant about moments when you may have encouraged a female student less than a male student or may have inadvertently downplayed the competence of a female student.
> —Corrine A. Moss-Racusin, Ph.D., assistant professor
> of psychology at Skidmore College

Learning About STEM Curricula

As a parent, you have a right to know what your children are learning in school and to raise questions about the curriculum. Learning facts is important but it is definitely not enough. Many states have adopted the Common Core State Standards, which specifies in great detail what higher order skills students at each grade level should be learning in English language arts and math. Find out more by visiting http://www.corestandards.org. If you live in a state that has not adopted the core standards, learn about them and see what aspects are missing from your school's curriculum and decide with other informed parents whether the absence of certain topics and learning strategies is depriving your daughter of an optimal educational experience. And, if you live in a place that has adopted the standards, that doesn't necessarily mean that you shouldn't investigate further. There's a big difference between what's contained in a document and how that material comes alive in a classroom.

As of 2015, the Common Core State Standards only had standards for the mathematics part of STEM. Some states have adopted standards for other subjects, including science, engineering, and technology. For instance, some states have adopted the Next Generation Science Standards (http://www.nextgenscience.org/next-generation-science-standards), which emphasize the scientific method more than memorization of facts and encourage teachers to delve into a few topics deeply rather than broadly.

STEM should be part of the curriculum starting in kindergarten (or preschool if that level is available in your community). Because research has shown that girls enjoy science when it is hands-on and relevant, the curriculum should reflect that approach. Technology can and should be introduced to girls at the beginning of their formal schooling—before they've had too much time to develop a fear of it. The engineering piece of STEM is the one that is most neglected in elementary and middle school education. Unless a child personally knows an engineer, she probably doesn't have any idea what engineers do and what the engineering design process is, although it is a key way to solve problems and create innovations. Most schools need to do a better job of inserting engineering into the curriculum, not as an add-on or an enrichment, but rather as a basic subject. When kindergartners play with blocks, for example, their teacher can help them understand why the ramps they constructed allow their cars to quickly slide down, an aspect of engineering. As for the math component of STEM, it can and should be integrated into the curriculum, not just saved for arithmetic lessons—whether it's dividing up a snack or saving for a class trip. Section V in this book will give you more ideas about how you can advocate to get your daughter the best STEM education possible.

> *Teachers should emphasize that STEM subjects help us deal with social and societal challenges, instead of focusing solely on technological challenges of the work.*
> —Fehmida Mesania, Ph.D. in civil/environmental engineering, consultant on water resources and environmental engineering, Pennsylvania

Are Teachers Prepared to Teach STEM?

As noted earlier, teachers need to feel confident in their own ability to teach STEM before they can pass on a positive attitude to their students. Because elementary school teachers are overwhelmingly female, their attitudes about STEM are particularly impactful on girls.

In looking at the middle school and high school levels, far too many teachers do not have the kind of background that allows them to competently teach STEM subjects. In a survey of almost 7,800 teachers, Banilower et al. (2013) found that only about one third of the middle school math teachers had a degree in that subject and that more than half of the elementary school teachers said that they didn't feel "very well-prepared" to teach science. Another disturbing finding from that study was that only 29% of high school science teachers emphasized the relevance of science to real life, something that is particularly important to maintaining girls' interest in STEM. Teacher education and training need to address this critical issue.

> *Teachers should have classroom activities that make science more fun for children. The lessons mean nothing without applying [science] to the real world through experiments and other projects.*
> —Amanda McKnight, chemical engineering and chemistry student at the University of New Haven

The Importance of Out-of-School Experiences

Although your daughter's formal school experience has a broad impact on her attitudes and achievement in STEM, informal education opportunities should not be ignored. Indeed, when your daughter's school experiences are not satisfying her needs and interests in STEM, afterschool STEM programs can make the difference between a girl becoming actively engaged or becoming STEM-avoidant for a lifetime. Rahm (2008) suggested that out-of-school time STEM programs are particularly critical for children from underrepresented groups (for example, low-income youth or students of color) who are more likely to attend schools with limited resources.

Instead of viewing the relationship between formal and informal education as a competitive one, schools and community organizations need to see how they can establish effective partnerships. Project Exploration, a Chicago-based education organization that focuses on science, creates written contracts with schools delineating each party's responsibilities, which might range from training scientists to providing appropriate space for the planned activities (Lyon & Jafri, 2010).

> *I get to spend my time and effort turning the current around for girls—helping them navigate the pathway to a career in tech that is meaningful for them and giving them that crucial social group of peers to support and encourage them.*
> —Ruthe Farmer, chief strategy and growth officer, National Center for Women & Information Technology, Colorado

Techbridge for Girls, an organization created to inspire middle school girls to learn about engineering, has partnered with schools in the San Francisco Bay area, providing girls, particularly those from underrepresented groups, with career exploration and hands-on activities, such as building solar night lights and creating green environments. These activities are not only engaging but teach collaborative, problem-solving strategies that are critical in STEM learning and work (Kekelis, Larkin, & Gomes, 2014; Mosatche et al. 2013). Science Club for Girls, based in Cambridge, MA, focuses on increasing girls' understanding of STEM topics, ranging from astronomy to oceanography. Like Project Exploration and Techbridge, Science Clubs for Girls reaches out to students who are likely to attend schools with inadequate STEM education. Another similarity among these programs is that their hands-on activities are interesting to girls and relevant to their lives. Schools might do well to replicate some of their methods and topics.

> *At Science Club for Girls, we provide opportunities for girls to explore STEM who are from underresourced areas and may never have had a meaningful STEM engagement. Many girls tell us that Science Club is where they first understood what STEM was, or where they first discovered their interest in the field. For many of these girls, that interest is piqued at a time later in their schooling when they don't have access to advanced STEM classes. For many, when they discover this interest, they are ineligible for local internship programs because they don't have the grades, or haven't had the classes or experiences they need. Additionally, many don't have any idea who to go for support—there may be no one in their immediate sphere of influence who has experience in a STEM field or can guide them as they progress through college.*
> —Kate Pickle, deputy director of Science Club for Girls, Massachusetts

Identifying Effective Afterschool Programs

Gil G. Noam (2010), the director of the Program in Education, Afterschool and Resiliency at Harvard, has described the components of a high-quality afterschool STEM program:

- Activities are planned with individual elements fitting together in a cohesive way.
- A program facilitator is clear about each activity's purpose.
- The materials used for an activity are age-appropriate and appealing to children.
- The program is structured in a way that is safe.
- Sessions provide sufficient time for participants to complete activities.
- The space has room for children to move around and doesn't feel like a classroom.
- The environment encourages children to explore STEM topics.
- Children are engaged in STEM work and not distracted by other things. Instead of simply trying to get a task completed, they are focused and attentive.
- Activities and facilitator questions provide opportunities for children to explore and to receive feedback, which they can use to extend their learning.

◻ The facilitator encourages children to use the scientific method in their work—observing, making hypotheses, and asking questions.

◻ Children are encouraged to think about how STEM learning relates to other subjects, including current events and careers.

◻ The activities are relevant to children's lives in terms of culture, language, and socioeconomic status. Children are able to recognize themselves as STEM "professionals."

Based on the evaluation of STEM programs with adolescent female participants, Mosatche and her colleagues (2013) described the following critical elements:

◻ Facilitators need to be trained so that they know the subject matter, understand the importance of making STEM learning fun, have high expectations for girls, and can interact effectively with participants in their programs. Girls want facilitators who have a sense of humor, are "cool," and show a comfort level with STEM methods and topics.

◻ Participants should be able to see how activities are related to real-life issues and challenges. Girls need to know that they can work in an exciting career related to the STEM topics they are exploring.

◻ Long-term participation is typically more effective than one-time learning. When the scientific method is used repeatedly in a variety of activities or when the engineering design process is demonstrated in numerous projects, girls are more apt to incorporate those strategies into their daily lives.

◻ Girls need to be exposed to role models, particularly when they make the work that they do exciting and show that they have "normal" lives and interests. Role models can speak as part of a panel discussion or facilitate activities.

◻ Having the opportunity to make mistakes and learn from them is a part of STEM, and girls need to know that making a mistake is an opportunity to learn, not a failure.

◻ Field trips to college campuses and STEM workplaces allow girls to see STEM in action but also give them an opportunity to meet women in these careers. These kinds of trips encourage girls to see that they can be part of a STEM community.

Keep the above information in mind when you are looking at a program and deciding whether you want your daughter to participate.

Exploring Weekend Community Activities

Although many out-of-school programs are conducted in school buildings right after school, your daughter can also explore STEM in the community on weekends. Museums, public parks, botanical gardens, zoos, aquariums, and nature centers often offer special events or longer term programs for children. Even when formal programs are not available, you can create your own activities, using these rich environments to investigate STEM.

Boys and Girls Clubs of America, Girl Scouts, Science Club for Girls, and other community organizations may run STEM programs on weekends. Although more weekend resources are typically found in urban and suburban areas, if you live in a rural area, farms, 4-H programs, and local colleges might be available for STEM activities. Even if structured activities are not easily accessible, you can create your own STEM weekend learning environment. Section IV provides more information about how you can do that with your daughter.

CHAPTER 10

Increasing Access to Effective Role Models

> *I love sharing with teachers what engineering is and what the engineering design process is about. I'm helping them see that it's the way people naturally solve problems. I still consider myself an engineer first and foremost—applying that way of seeing the world and solving problems.*
> —Stacy Klein-Gardner, Ph.D., director of the Center for STEM Education for Girls at the Harpeth Hall School and faculty member in biomedical engineering and radiology at Vanderbilt University

Although many questions still exist about the way role models affect girls' perceptions of and aspirations in STEM, research has demonstrated that role models can have an impact. This chapter looks at how the media, the educational system, out-of-school activities, and technology can facilitate the connection between girls and STEM role models.

Finding Role Models in the Media

Because children and adolescents spend a lot of time watching television, using the Internet, and reading books and other materials not required for school, these media sources offer an opportunity to inspire girls to get more involved in STEM activities and see themselves in STEM careers. However, currently, the media are not providing the kind and number of role models that can make a difference. That needs to change.

How Can Role Models in the Media Change Perceptions and Aspirations?

A report by FEMInc (Bhatt, Blakely, Mohanty, & Payne, 2012), an organization created to promote "diverse and empowering images of girls and women in popular entertainment," suggested that media can shape perceptions by constructing stereotypes or tearing them down. Bhatt and her colleagues have expressed concern about the media's relatively limited depiction of females in a wide variety of roles while most often presenting females in stereotypical roles.

One of the reasons for media's power is its ability to spread information to huge numbers of people very quickly. And if that information is embedded in an interesting storyline, the impact is greater. For example, when the television program *Numb3rs* aired an episode that focused on organ transplants, many viewers who were not already registered as organ donors were moved to do so (Morgan, Movius, & Cody, 2009). In the same way, when movies and TV shows depict women as uncomfortable with math or needing a man to save them, viewers become more stereotyped in their perceptions of women's abilities.

Another important factor in changing attitudes is the amount of time or number of exposures to a different way of viewing the world. Although there has been limited research in this area, Bhatt (2012) suggested that repeated exposure to nonstereotypical female role models might be able to reduce stereotyped views.

> " *In the 60s and 70s, it was TV that had a great impact on me in choosing STEM. Shows with women like That Girl (groundbreaking career girl), Agent 99 (Get Smart), Emma Peel (Avengers), and Gidget showed me that women could be smart, sassy, skilled, respected, and independent! I also loved the Star Trek series, mostly because it showed people of all races and backgrounds working together, where everyone was equal and judged on their merits and not their gender or race. Even though now that I think about it, Uhura was basically a high-tech receptionist at the control panel and Nurse Chappell was a nurse (who eventually become a doctor)—both stereotypical fields for women in the 60s—but the exciting part was that they worked alongside, and not behind, men using the latest technology.* "
>
> —Denise Scribner, high school teacher of ecology,
> biology and forensic crime science, Kansas

What Needs to Change on Our Screens—
Television, Movies, and Online

When 86 British women who worked in STEM were asked about the impact of the media on their career choices, they noted that females were not adequately represented in their fields (Kitzinger, Haran, Chimba, & Boyce, 2008). The same television dramas, such as *CSI* and *Silent Witness*, were cited repeatedly as examples of shows that portrayed positive role models. The fact that the same examples were mentioned over and over points to the need to increase the number and diversity of female STEM role models as main characters.

The participants in the Kitzinger et al. study (2008) generally suggested that the media need to show more women in STEM careers as competent and in control, but not necessarily extraordinary and exceptional. In other words, they should be presented in a realistic way to encourage female viewers to identify with them. However, some women in the study wanted the media to show that women in STEM could be glamorous and feminine. Some suggested that women in STEM be depicted as having a family life, that their lives not be shown as totally focusing on work and achievement. Other recommendations from the group included: women serving as presenters on documentaries focused on STEM topics; increased representation of women from diverse backgrounds; depiction of more women in STEM programming developed for children and adolescents; appearance of women in all fields of STEM; representation of female scientists and engineers as enthusiastic rather than overly emotional; and exploration of a wide variety of motivations and paths to a STEM career. The women we interviewed for this book made similar comments and are living in a variety of roles and life stages. Your daughter needs an opportunity to see the full breadth and depth of a life in STEM.

> Between reading books and watching TV shows as I was growing up, forensics became a huge interest. Michael Crichton was one of my favorite authors—he always touched on science concepts, even if they were fiction.
> —Meghan Rushing, Ph.D., research chemist at BASF

What About Fictional Characters and Nonfiction Profiles?

Girls generally spend more time reading than do boys. But, as is the case with television and films, many more of the characters are male, particularly in children's books in which animals are portrayed (McCabe, Fairchild, Grauerholz, Pescosolido, & Tope, 2011). McCabe et al. (2011) found that more than twice as many children's book titles included a male's name compared to a female's name. When girls don't see their gender portrayed equitably in books, they are deprived of models who depict a full range of experiences.

> I remember a giant book called Questions and Answers that had all these random types of questions about how the world works. I really enjoyed that and learned so much from it. Reading those kinds of books drew me toward engineering because I realized I could build something worthwhile and do something very cool.
> —Bettina Chen, electrical engineer and cofounder of Roominate Toys, California

Although women have accomplished a great deal that is STEM-related, many more biographies are devoted to male scientists and engineers. Particularly for girls who do not have access to real-life STEM role models, the opportunity to read about actual women would help them see that women have a place in science, technology, engineering, and math. When people are asked to name famous women in STEM, Marie Curie is the name that jumps to mind. But there are many others. Below are some examples:

- ☐ Linda Brown Buck, who earned a Ph.D. in immunology, was awarded the 2004 Nobel Prize in Physiology or Medicine, along with Richard Axel, for their work on olfactory receptors. Their research significantly advanced the understanding of the mechanisms of smell.

- ☐ Lillian Gilbreth was a psychologist and industrial engineer who made significant contributions to industrial engineering fields such as time and motion studies. Together with her husband Frank Gilbreth, Sr., she wrote the book *Cheaper by the Dozen*, which tells the story of how they applied principles of efficiency to their family life, which included 12 children.

- ☐ Hedy Lamarr, best known as an actress during the 1930s through the 1950s, was also an inventor whose work on communication technology was used to control torpedoes during World War II. Her inventions continue to be important, playing a role in wi-fi and bluetooth technology. In 2014, 14 years after her death, she was finally recognized for her work and inducted into the National Inventors Hall of Fame.

- ☐ Evelyn Boyd Granville earned a Ph.D. in mathematics from Yale in 1949, one of the first African American women to do so. As a university professor, she inspired other African American female students to pursue doctorates in math. She also worked as a computer programmer for IBM and later worked on space-related projects, such as the Apollo program. Her influence as an educator includes her development of enrichment programs in math for the elementary school level.

- ☐ Carolyn Widney Greider is a molecular biologist and professor at Johns Hopkins University. She discovered the enzyme telomerase in 1984 as a graduate student and pioneered research on the structure of telomeres, the ends of the chromosomes. She was awarded the 2009 Nobel Prize for Physiology or Medicine for her contribution to the discovery that telomerase protects telomeres from shortening, research that continues to play a significant role in our understanding of aging.

Research has demonstrated that providing girls with real and fictional STEM role models can reduce the effect of stereotype threat (Dasgupta & Asgari, 2004). Even something as basic as changing textbook pictures so that girls can see women doing STEM activities would help to expand girls' choices (Good, Woodzicka, & Wingfield, 2010). Publishers need to know that parents and teachers are looking for more gender-balanced images and characters in the books they purchase or recommend.

> *As a child, I read a lot of sci-fi fantasy books, like A Wrinkle in Time. Books are a big influence on girls, and if the stories are all about romance and fairy tales, we are missing a huge opportunity. One of the best STEM movies ever is Chitty Chitty Bang Bang. There is so much engineering in that film. Today's equivalents might be Chicken Run or Spy Kids.*
> —Ruthe Farmer, chief strategy and growth officer at the National Center for Women & Information Technology, Colorado

Commercials and Advertisements Count, Too

Commercials on television and advertisements in magazines and newspapers are designed to market particular products. When females are portrayed in biased ways or underrepresented, girls receive direct as well as subliminal negative messages. A set of studies by Davies, Spencer, Quinn, and Gerhardstein (2002) found that when women were exposed to commercials depicting females in stereotyped roles, they subsequently avoided math questions on an aptitude test, did worse on the math questions they did complete, and became less interested in educational and career opportunities related to math. Think about how much your daughter is influenced by the countless commercials she watches on television, the advertisements that appear in her favorite magazine, and those that show up online—whether she's using Facebook or e-mailing a friend. Become more attentive to the messages she's receiving from the various media she interacts with and suggest that she critically analyze the words and images she views. Ask her questions and encourage her to do the same. Help her focus on the more subtle messages. For example, you could discuss the following:

- Is the expert who's touting a product male or female?
- What message is conveyed by the clothing a woman is wearing?
- Who has the power in that scene?
- How would the message change if women and men changed roles in the ad or commercial?

As a parent and consumer, consider the potential power you and your daughter can exert to convince companies to change their messaging so that there is less gender bias in selling their products and services to the public. Previous campaigns by consumers, such as one in 1992 that pressured Mattel to remove a Teen Talk Barbie that was programmed to say, "Math class is tough," have been successful and forced corporations to take products off store shelves and remove commercials from the air.

Change the Way Teachers Are Trained

Teachers are important models of behavior and attitudes for children. For them to be effective as role models, educators need opportunities to: (1) develop their confidence in covering a wide range of STEM topics and show their enthusiasm, (2) demonstrate the importance of using STEM problem-solving strategies, (3) share the relevance of STEM to real-life issues and situations, and (4) learn to recognize and respond to gender bias in their classrooms (particularly when STEM subjects are taught).

In college I had a terrific professor who had a lot of passion for engineering. He really helped me understand all of the possibilities that engineering could offer me as far as a career.
—Jennifer Tosi, BA in engineering, vice-president
at Morgan Stanley, New York

Strengthening Their Skills and Building Their Enthusiasm

Teachers can model being comfortable with STEM subjects by strengthening their own skills and knowledge of these content areas through ongoing professional development. A practice guide called, "Encouraging Girls in Math and Science" published by the National Center for Education Research (Halpern et al., 2007) outlined recommendations for teachers, including checklists for implementing suggested practices. Among the recommended strategies is exposing girls to female role models who have succeeded in math and science. Classroom guest speakers, biographies, and field trips to workplaces all expose students, regardless of gender, to women who are accomplished in STEM. Teachers can also model a positive attitude toward STEM by sharing their joy in STEM investigations and discovery and encouraging their students to do the same. Another recommendation is for teachers to promote a growth mindset in their students, which teachers can model by working to extend the boundaries of their own knowledge and keeping abreast of developments in STEM fields, as well as praising students' effort and improvement rather than just their abilities.

Teachers need to be aware of the skills of all of their students. They need to be fair and make subjects such as math and science fun and challenging for everyone. Smart kids want challenge, and they also want engagement and fun. If math is boring, teachers need to change it up, to find ways to relate the very essence of math to everyday life.
—Elizabeth Dodson, cofounder of HomeZada, California

Using STEM Strategies

Analyzing situations from different perspectives, using critical thinking to solve problems, predicting outcomes, designing processes, and modifying products as a result of evaluations are all strategies that people in STEM use. When teachers incorporate these strategies in their classes, they serve as role models and help girls understand how useful and widespread these practices can be. Training and practice can help teachers feel comfortable using these methods in a variety of classroom situations. And they shouldn't be reserved just for science and math classes. For example, teachers might ask middle school students in a social studies class to collect and analyze data related to an upcoming election. Once teachers learn about the engineering design process (see Figure 2), they can figure out ways to use it with a variety of school subjects, ranging from having their elementary school students create a three-dimensional map (when learning geography) to asking high school students to design (and redesign, if necessary) a public service announcement to effectively encourage seat belt usage. By not just demonstrating these practices but also making sure their students recognize that they are actively using the engineering design process, teachers can expose students to the field of engineering, something that typically doesn't happen before college.

Demonstrating the Relevance of STEM to Real-Life Issues

Because research indicates that girls are more likely to be interested in STEM when they can see how these subjects are relevant to real-life issues and situations, teacher training in these subjects should include ways to make those connections. Teachers can provide examples of how to connect science and engineering concepts with alleviating global challenges, such as increasing sanitary water where there are shortages or preventing the spread of diseases such as Ebola. When teachers engage students by using real-life examples, their students learn to do

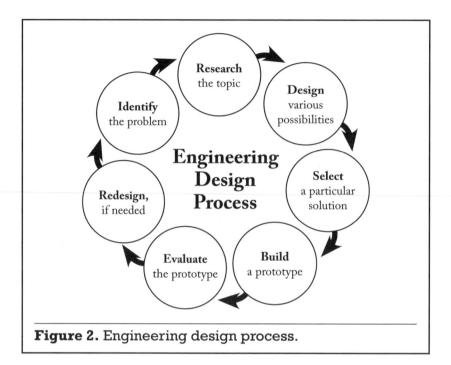

Figure 2. Engineering design process.

the same. The result is students eager to learn more about their world and solve its problems.

> *I knew that I wanted to do something that would help people and realized that engineering was the way to take the cool things I learned in physics and make something practical that actually helps.*
> —Bettina Chen, electrical engineer and cofounder of Roominate Toys, California

Recognizing and Dealing With Gender Bias

When teachers behave in gender-neutral ways, they serve as models of equity in the classroom. In a summary of research on gender bias shown by teachers, Scantlebury (2009) noted that small and subtle inequities add up over time. Research done three decades ago (Tobin & Gallagher, 1987) revealed that "target students," those who ask and answer most questions, are typically White boys. And when girls had trouble, particularly with a complex science question, instead of helping girls arrive at the answer, teachers often turned the question over to a boy to answer. The same thing didn't happen when boys had trouble coming up with an answer. In those instances, teachers often broke down the question into a sequence of simpler questions, which allowed boys to respond correctly. Among Scantlebury's (2009) recommendations is for teachers to videotape themselves teaching and then to review those tapes either independently or with a colleague, looking for which students are asked questions and called on, and whether there are differences in the kinds of questions asked of girls and boys.

As part of professional development in the area of behavior management, teachers can learn to set and maintain ground rules in which children are not permitted to interrupt or talk over classmates (which "target students" are likely to do) and to wait a few seconds before calling on a student to give time for more children to become engaged and ready to respond. Liu (2006) found that teachers often gave girls fewer critical and meaningful comments and focused on a project's appearance, which results in girls' work being undervalued. Girls and boys should be praised equally for insights as well as encouraged to expand upon their comments in class. The Delaware State Education Association provides a simple checklist for teachers to self-assess their classroom behaviors (see http://www.ccctc.k12.oh.us/Downloads/Gender%20Bias%20in%20the%20Classroom2.pdf). These include paying attention to the ratio of calling on girls and boys; distribution of classroom tasks, including leadership and technical tasks vs. note-taking and clean-up; and use of gender-free language in the classroom.

> *When I was at MIT, about 10% of the class were women, so there were women when I got there who always looked out for everybody. I had people who were very supportive and who kind of knocked down some of the roadblocks before me.*
>
> —Gail Ruby, MS in computer science, senior product manager at Motor Information Systems, Michigan

Awareness of Societal Trends

Teachers who have an understanding of how social institutions perpetuate gender bias can better prepare students to challenge inequity. Within schools, teachers can educate themselves to promote awareness of Title IX, laws about sexual harassment, and the rights of access to advanced coursework such as AP classes. They can also support equal participation of girls in STEM activities during and after the school day. When teachers encourage girls to take leadership roles, they are promoting equity beyond the classroom as well as in it. Textbooks may also reinforce gender and racial stereotypes, both in problems given and in pictures. Teachers can model awareness of gender bias by pointing out issues in the language and pictures in textbooks, such as when girls are depicted in passive roles with boys as active participants. They can also make sure to use or create handouts and tests that do not reinforce stereotypes.

For the above strategies to be successful, educational systems must be adequately funded to ensure that there are resources for a rich array of materials, well-equipped laboratories and supplies, and field trips. When teachers have the necessary tools, training, and experience, they can create engaging STEM experiences for all their students.

> Students get tracked in math early on and sometimes not accurately, and that really limits some of the things they can go into. So we need to be careful not to do that and to allow students to develop at different paces.
> —Stacy Klein-Gardner, director of the Center for STEM Education for Girls at the Harpeth Hall School and faculty member in biomedical engineering and radiology at Vanderbilt University

Providing Role Model Training for Youth Workers

Like parents and teachers, youth workers can be potent role models for girls. People who work in afterschool programs have the opportunity to model STEM skills, emphasize a growth mindset, encourage participants to make and learn from their mistakes, and be aware of their own unconscious biases as well as the stereotyped expectations young people bring with them to their programs.

Modeling STEM Skills

STEM activities may be implemented in a way that accounts for the interests of particular girls and relates STEM to other domains by integrating STEM with the arts, literacy, recreational activities, and community service, which heightens the engagement of girls.

The youth work approach is designed to foster intrinsic motivation rather than compliance and reactive behavior. Activities should stress the joy of discovery and the pleasure of investigation (which are key aspects of STEM learning), rather than relying on rote knowledge and worksheets. Although the ability to create engaging activities may be impacted by budget limitations, some curricula and activities, such as Junk Drawer Robotics developed by 4-H, are available at low or no cost.

> It's so important for women in youth work to show enthusiasm for science-related activities; and also to make sure that those activities are available for girls in the program. One day, we had girls dissecting owl pellets while boys were doing an arts and crafts activity, and everyone was happy.
> —Allison Leah Weingarten, program director, After School Enrichment Program, Queens Community House, New York

In reviewing resources, keep in mind the difference between curriculum, which is sequential and builds upon the knowledge and skills gained in previous lessons, and activities, which can be implemented without experiencing the earlier sessions. Depending on the goals and nature of the youth program, one or the other may be preferable. Staff should understand the difference, and their training should include an ability to state the aim or goal of an activity. For instance, rather than stating, "This is a lesson about water," they should be able to articulate that "we are going to understand how the properties of water change at different temperatures."

Some websites that offer lesson plans, activities and curricula are listed below:

- ¤ The After School Corporation (TASC) has developed *STEM After School: How to Design and Run Great Program Activities* (http://expandedschools.org/sites/default/files/STEM_Guidebook_Update2014.pdf)
- ¤ Exploratorium in San Francisco has an open access Learning Commons with a searchable database at http://www.exploratorium.edu/education/learning-commons
- ¤ Youth Development Institute offers a course called, "Integrating STEM Into Youth Programs." This course not only offers guidance on how to integrate STEM into out-of-school time, but also provides information about evaluating STEM activities (http://www.ydinstitute.org).
- ¤ 4-H offers a STEM curricula for a modest fee (http://www.4-h.org/resource-library/curriculum)
- ¤ Project 2061 of the American Association for the Advancement of Science lays out a blueprint for scientific literacy that may help guide program planning. (http://www.aaas.org/program/project2061)

Modeling a Growth Mindset

Due to the limited funding for youth work, STEM activities in youth programs are often taught by staff and volunteers who lack specific expertise in STEM content. Although this may be seen as a drawback, research by NASA indicates that youth workers without a STEM background may increase engagement by sharing the joy of discovery (National Institute on Out-of-School Time, 2007). The lack of content experience provides a wonderful opportunity for youth workers to model a growth mindset as they learn new content along with the participants. However, their training must include the opportunity to become comfortable with this role as learner and the ability to balance the learning role with their authority within the group.

As with parents and teachers, youth workers should be trained to speak to young people in ways that promote a growth mindset. Offering specific, descriptive feedback and asking children to explain their answers and results is more effective for their long-term growth than praising them simply for being smart.

Youth workers who are college or graduate students, particularly those who are studying some field of STEM, serve as role models for the pursuit of higher education for girls in their programs. And those studying for a college or more advanced degree should be encouraged to discuss with participants how they navigate college and university systems and how they prepared for that level of education.

> *Science Club for Girls seeks to create a network—a sisterhood—of support and experiences so that these young women are empowered to make the choices that are right for them in life and careers and are not held back by a lack of knowledge, exposure, or experience.*
> —Kate Pickle, deputy director of Science Club for Girls, Massachusetts

Modeling Making Mistakes

Girls Incorporated has offered *Operation SMART*, three girl-focused STEM curricula, for many years through its affiliates. They have identified four elements of their successful approach as: (1) assume girls are interested in STEM, (2) encourage them to see mistakes as an opportunity for learning rather than a sign of failure, (3) help them embrace messiness ("getting past the 'yuck' factor"), and (4) expect them to succeed. These attitudes can be taught to any youth worker who then models them in working with girls. Showing that mistakes are a way of learning helps young people become comfortable with trial and error as an important scientific investigative technique.

Above all, STEM activities in youth programs should be fun and engaging. Project-based work in which youth work in teams to solve problems may be particularly appealing to girls. STEM-related field trips can foster interest as well.

Training for youth workers is best when it takes place over time, with a cohort of staff who can form a learning community. This can be conducted among the staff of a single agency or a learning community can be formed with members of multiple programs and organizations learning together and bringing in multiple perspectives. Sources of training include colleges with youth work departments, professional associations such as New York City's Partnership for After School Education and The After School Corporation, 4-H clubs (which are supported by land-grant colleges), and science museums.

Modeling Equitable Behavior

Most systems of describing the core competencies needed by youth workers address the importance of skills related to promoting social justice. For example, one of the competencies described by the Youth Development Institute is understanding of power dynamics regarding race, culture, and gender (http://www.ydinstitute.org). Youth work is distinguished in part by putting youth at the center of program design. Fusco (2011) defined it as a practice that does not focus on individuals but rather places them in a community and historical context. As such, well-grounded youth workers will bring to their interactions with young people an understanding of gender, race, class, and other aspects of culture obtained and sustained through professional development that is ongoing. Youth workers model this awareness through the language they use when addressing youth and by ensuring equal participation in activities and discussions. Within programs that employ professionals in STEM, training in working sensitively with youth may be required for staff to succeed in engaging youth in STEM content. Youth workers should get to know young people individually and be able to identify their interests and passions, connect youth to each other in supportive and positive peer relationships, and foster an environment of equity and respect in which youth can speak up freely.

> *I started judging FIRST ROBOTICS this year and plan to continue volunteering. I judged two high school events last month and was thrilled to see so many young women working side by side with young men as equal partners.*
> —Marykate Noonan, podiatrist, New Jersey

Connecting Girls and Role Models in Person and Through Technology

In addition to the role models girls may already encounter through the media and the teachers and youth workers they interact with, direct efforts can also be made to connect girls with effective STEM role models, both in person and through technology.

How to Find Role Models

Some STEM-focused programs for girls incorporate role models into their activities, using real STEM professionals to work with girls on activities. STEM-related clubs or organizations at colleges and universities, such as college chapters of the Society of Women Engineers, also organize events for community youth to allow them to interact with STEM students and professionals. Museums, organizations, and even government agencies also host events to provide role model experiences. For example, the Department of Energy holds STEM Mentoring Café events (http://energy.gov/diversity/stem-mentoring-caf), a speed-mentoring program in which middle school students, particularly those from groups that are underrepresented in STEM, and their teachers talk to federal employees and private sector professionals in STEM about their careers.

If these sorts of events are not available in your area, you can also find online databases of female STEM role models. For example, Women@Energy (http://energy.gov/diversity/listings/women-energy) showcases the talented women who work in the Department of Energy through pictures and interviews, and Women@NASA (http://women. nasa.gov) includes essays and videos of the women of NASA. Outside of government, there is FabFems, an international role model database of women in STEM (http://www.fabfems.org). You can use this database to find a local role model for a variety of in-person or online role model experiences, or simply browse the profiles to read about many amazing women in STEM. You can even search by field or ethnicity to provide the best match to inspire your daughter.

> *During high school, I lived on a construction camp site in the Middle East where my father worked as a senior engineer for a construction company. I felt that it was cool to be an engineer on a project site and be able to execute and oversee technical tasks. That's when I decided that civil engineering would provide me with the ability to plan, design, construct, operate, and research with an ultimate goal of serving people and protecting the environment.*
> —Fehmida Mesania, Ph.D. in civil/environmental engineering, consultant on water resources and environmental engineering, Pennsylvania

Longer term role model experiences are also possible through mentoring. These relationships tend to be one-on-one and can involve an adult or older student. STEM mentoring programs can vary in whether mentoring occurs in person or online (or both), characteristics of the target population (e.g., girls, college students, students underrepresented in STEM), whether they focus on a particular area of STEM, the length and amount of mentoring time, and the degree of structure or guidance. For example, MentorNet (http://mentornet.org) involves 15–20 minute weekly online mentoring sessions with specific prompts over a 4-month period (with an option for mentees to do additional 4-month cycles with the same mentor or a new one) and is open to all college students in STEM, but with a focus on women and underrepresented minorities. In contrast, the Million Women Mentors initiative (https://www. millionwomenmentors.org) focuses specifically on girls and women and recommends 20 hours of mentoring over the course of one year, which can be in person, online, or through internships, workplace mentoring, or sponsorships. Finally, mentoring programs for specific fields include the Association for Women in Mathematics' Mentor Network (https://

sites.google.com/site/awmmath/programs/mentor-network), which provides mentoring for girls and women of any age (including recent Ph.D. grads and teachers), and the ACE Mentor Program (http://www.acementor.org), which focuses on mentoring high school students in architecture, construction, and engineering.

> *To increase engagement, we must properly showcase female talent in IT—give young girls role models in the industry to show what it means to work in technology. Illuminating what these women actually do in their roles dispels myths and inspires others to pursue these amazing opportunities.*
> —Sheila Flavell, Chief Operating Officer of FDM Group, London

Your daughter can also receive mentoring outside of a formal program. If you and your daughter did a network search, as described in Chapter 9, you may have found someone you already know who could be a potential mentor for your daughter. If this individual doesn't already have mentoring experience, there are resources to help guide her through the mentoring experience, such as the National Center for Women and Information Technology's "Mentoring-in-a-Box: Technical Women at Work" (https://www.ncwit.org/resources/mentoring-box-technical-women-work).

What Makes a Role Model Effective?

Research on role models in general has found that a prerequisite for a role model to inspire is that their success must be viewed as attainable (Lockwood & Kunda, 1997). As mentioned earlier, if a role model's success is perceived as not being attainable, she can instead make people feel worse about themselves or less interested in a field. Role models who are very successful and also very close in age to target individuals may be viewed as unattainable because girls may feel they are already too far behind to achieve the same level of success (Lockwood & Kunda, 1997). Research has also found that girls viewed a successful STEM role model who was very feminine as unattainable (Betz & Sekaquaptewa, 2012). Role models who have achieved success in multiple domains may be less effective because they are seen as too much of a "superstar." Also, the same role model might be viewed as unattainable by an individual who has a view of intelligence as a fixed quality, but considered attainable by another girl who has a more incremental view of intelligence (Lockwood & Kunda, 1997). In order to increase girls' feelings that a role model's success is attainable, role models should emphasize how they improved through persistence and effort and try not to come off as perfect and innately destined for success.

Girls' ability to identify with a role model also influences how effective they will be. This idea is generally the basis for using female role models to inspire girls. However, as discussed previously, some research indicates that male role models can be just as effective if they are viewed as being nonstereotypical (Cheryan et al., 2011). Importantly, both role model gender and role model stereotypicality make role models more influential through their effects on girls' perceived similarity to the role model, identification with the role model, and feeling a connection to the role model (Cheryan et al., 2011; Stout et al., 2011). These findings indicate that while matching on gender, race, and other characteristics can make role models more effective, strategies to increase girls' identification that do not rely on demographic similarity can be just as effective. For example, role models can talk about what they were like when they were younger or share interests with girls to increase perceptions of similarity, and they can share a personal story to enhance the connection that girls feel with the role model.

> *I tell women and girls to cultivate a good mentor or role model relationship—someone you can go to for concrete advice and who also helps you envision doing this work, someone who looks like you or who you can identify with personally, someone who makes you feel like this challenge is worth it. Having those role models can over time help turn the tide a bit.*
> —Corinne A. Moss-Racusin, Ph.D., assistant professor of psychology at Skidmore College

Techbridge's role model guide advises role models to share their passion and why their work matters, to use activities that are fun and interactive, and to include academic and career guidance (Countryman,

Kekelis, & Wei, 2010). Mentors should follow the same recommendations as role models, but there are additional factors that are needed to make a mentor more effective, due to the lengthier and more intense and personal relationship of a mentor as compared to a role model. A study that statistically analyzed the effectiveness of 73 youth mentoring programs (of a variety of types and not specific to STEM or girls), found that programs were more effective when the mentor's educational or occupational background was in line with the program goals, the mentor and mentee had similar interests, and the program helped mentors take on an advocacy or teaching role with the mentee (DuBois, Portillo, Rhodes, Silverthorn, & Valentine, 2011). The researchers suggested that screening and training of mentors, clear expectations, and ongoing professional support are also important.

For role models and mentors, the main goal should be to show girls the exciting possibilities of a career in STEM, including helping girls see that they, too, can be successful in such careers and guiding them on how to pursue that path.

> *I had math and science teachers starting in junior high and going through high school who very actively encouraged my interest in math and science. They kept encouraging me to continue, to not let my parents' lack of encouragement keep me from pursuing what I definitely enjoyed. I was fortunate that my teachers were very vocal to my parents about that, even in my presence. So that gave me a lot of encouragement from people my parents' age who were not my parents, and that helped immensely.*
> —Carol L. Ensinger, Ph.D., retired pharmaceutical industry chemist and project manager, South Carolina

Time for Action
Activities and Guidelines

The previous sections have outlined the major research findings and suggested actions that will allow the field of STEM to become truly and fully equitable. The chapters in this section offer specific ideas and activities that you can implement to change your daughter's involvement in STEM now and in the future. The suggestions include strategies to help her become a critical viewer of media messages and recognize the power of her language and communication style. You will learn about finding toys, games, and activities that encourage STEM exploration as well as ways to inculcate a mindset of creative problem solving and persistence in your daughter. The final chapter in this section provides information that will be helpful to your daughter as she looks beyond the high school years. Whether your daughter is a toddler or a sophisticated teen, you can find tips and activities to help you create greater opportunities for her to become a participant in the rich world of STEM.

CHAPTER 11

Helping Girls Become Critical Viewers of the Media

> *For older girls, encourage movies and TV that show girls in STEM fields. Back in my early career days, you couldn't interest many boys or girls in laboratory work, but now with the advent of CSI, the field of criminal pathology (lab testing) is overflowing.*
>
> —Patty Laughlin, retired medical technologist and Microsoft-certified IT engineer, Missouri

Every day, girls are bombarded by media messages, whether it's from a character in a favorite television show or ads on the Internet. They see movies, photos, video games, book covers, cartoons, and cereal boxes depicting females and science in a variety of ways. Many girls select particular posters to hang on the walls of their rooms. Even when girls do not realize they are being affected by the words and images that surround them, the impact is evident. As a parent, you can influence how your daughter interprets what she sees and hears and help her to critically analyze those messages, rather than merely being a passive recipient of those messages. Be prepared, because attaining that critical attitude may have her questioning some of what you say or do. But that's part of using STEM in everyday life, and it will serve her well now and in the future.

Which Media Figures Are Influencing Your Daughter?

As a parent, it's important for you to know what your daughter is watching on television or the computer. Learn who her favorite characters and actors are. Encourage her to understand the complexity of most characters. Help her differentiate between the role an actor is playing and what she is like in real life.

A study by Levine, Bowman, Kachinsky, Sola, and Waite (2015) found that in one sample of parents, more than 65% of children younger than 3 were watching movies and television on mobile devices, such as cell phones and tablets, on a daily basis. And half of the parents in that study reported that their children were introduced to these devices before they turned 18 months old. Before you even think about monitoring what your young child is watching, you might want to think about when she should be introduced to computers, cell phones, and tablets. Are there better ways for your child to learn when she's very young? In many instances the answer is "yes," because research (Kremar, 2014) suggests that infants and toddlers do not increase their vocabulary by exposure to DVDs. Interacting with responsive adults is better than passively watching a program (even a so-called educational one) on a screen.

As your daughter gets older, she will be increasingly exposed to media images—real, illustrated, and animated. Sometimes, her exposure is indirect, such as when she is playing in a room where the television is turned on to a program you've selected for yourself. Although you may think she's fully engaged in her own activity, your daughter is probably picking up some of the messages from your show. As a key role model in her life, you give her important messages about using and interpreting media. The more you notice and question, the more your daughter will learn to do the same. Consider the following:

- ¤ What are you watching?
- ¤ How much time do you spend watching television or using a computer for nonwork activities?
- ¤ Do you comment about the characters and the roles they play in the storyline or do you just passively stare at the screen?
- ¤ How many males and females are portrayed in starring roles?
- ¤ Are females shown as problem solvers or as passive players?

> *There are amazing TV channels these days, such as National Geographic and Animal Planet. So you can watch those programs with your kids, and if you learn something new, go ahead and tell them that's new information for you and that you're glad to know it now.*
> —Kathy Callahan, retired chemical and business executive, Pennsylvania

What Messages Are Conveyed About Being Female?

Although media representations of attractive females can inspire girls to take better care of themselves, many of the images show girls and women with bodies that would be impossible (or unhealthy) to attain for most. When they set a standard that few can ever achieve, girls sometimes feel inferior. Many television shows and commercials portray females in stereotypical roles, such as getting excited about using household cleaning products or showing their emotions in an exaggerated way. While video games tend to have more male characters, particularly in lead roles, and sexualize female characters or portray them as damsels in distress, some games do include female characters in lead roles and provide them with problem-solving experiences. For example, *Portal 1* and *2* both depict a strong female character with story lines that involve successfully dealing with challenges. *Tomb Raider* shows a female as competent, and more recent versions are less sexualized.

Some companies have figured out that it's appropriate to show males and females in all kinds of roles—mom going off to work and buying a car, dad doing the laundry and choosing breakfast cereals at the supermarket. Make sure your daughter pays attention to those messages that show girls and women (as well as boys and men) in a variety of roles as well as those that do not. With the latter, ask her questions to help her recognize direct and subtle messages. If your daughter is preteen or older, try this activity with her: Watch two or three television shows together. Use the chart in Figure 3 to track the various ways females are depicted and then spend some time talking about what you learned— from what surprised you to what could have been shown differently to convey a more positive image of females.

Depending on your daughter's age and level of interest, you can make the activity more like the kind of study a social scientist would do by comparing the results you get across different factors, such as the TV channel or type of show. If your daughter collects quantitative data, such as by using numeric scales to make ratings for the answers to each question, she can even calculate averages and other basic descriptive statistics to help her draw conclusions.

You can do similar exercises with magazines, commercials, movies, books, video games, recorded music, and online ads. Create a list of questions that will highlight the way females are portrayed. Encourage your daughter to make up additional questions and to draw conclusions and possible actions she can take based on what she has observed. In addition, you can adapt this exercise to examine portrayals of other groups, such as people of color, individuals with disabilities, or even scientists and engineers.

Your discussion with your daughter of media portrayals of women will likely focus on what messages they send to girls and women and their roles in society, but it's important to also consider the messages they send to men and boys about gender roles and how girls and women should be treated. For example, research has found that playing violent video games against sexualized female opponents increased young men's negative attitudes against women, in terms of higher hostile sexism and lower empathy toward rape victims, if they were psychologically immersed in the game (LaCroix, Burrows, & Blanton, 2015). On the

Question	Television Show 1	Television Show 2
How many females have speaking parts?		
How many males have speaking parts?		
Of the main characters, what percentage are female?		
How much of the dialogue was spoken by females? By males?		
Are females depicted as being assertive, aggressive, or passive?		
How much of the action is driven by the female characters?		
Are the females more likely to be more physically attractive and younger than the male characters? Are they more likely to be sexualized?		
Are females as likely as males to be shown in work roles?		

Figure 3. Tracking depictions of females on television.

Question	Television Show 1	Television Show 2
How much of the time do female characters go to male characters for help? How often does the opposite occur?		
Are there female characters who are fully developed and realistic, occupying the middle ground between damsels in distress and perfect women who have no flaws and never need help?		
Are women used merely as plot devices or are they characters who move the plot forward?		
Does it pass the Bechdel test, which means that (1) it includes two women, (2) who talk to each other, (3) about something other than a man (Bechdel, 1985)?		
When you viewed the credits at the end of the program, how many (or what percentage) of the jobs other than actors were held by women?		

Figure 3. Continued.

other hand, media in general, and games in particular, can be used to change attitudes in a positive way. In 2014, two high school students, Andrea Gonzales and Sophie Houser, created "Tampon Run," an app-based game in which players throw tampons at their enemies instead of using guns or other weapons. In talking to *TIME* magazine about coming up with their idea, they explained that they wanted to challenge the idea that menstruation is taboo, even though it's something all women experience, while violence is rampant in video games (Dockterman, 2014).

If your daughter is younger, you can still have interesting and informative discussions about media messages about being female. Some questions you can use after you've watched a few commercials with her include:

- Which commercials seem to show that some products are for girls (or women) and others are for boys (or men)?
- How do they show that?
- How do you feel about companies that sell their products that way?
- Which commercials encourage both girls (or women) and boys (or men) to try a product?
- How can you change a commercial so that it seems to show both girls (or women) and boys (or men) in a fair way?

When discussing these commercials, make sure your daughter distinguishes between products that are used exclusively by females (such as tampons) and those that potentially could appeal to either gender but are marketed to either females or males (such as pink pens or sophisticated computers).

> " *I encourage all my kids to do STEM. These are steady careers and my kids also enjoy math and science. My oldest daughter is thinking about engineering or computer science. She also has an interest in sound design and other more technical aspects of the movie and gaming industry.* "
> —Christina Sormani, Ph.D., math professor at City University of New York

Although conversations about females' representation in the media are important and educational, your daughter and her friends might want to do some hands-on activities that are not only informative but also fun. Here is one idea: Suggest that they create a magazine, newsletter, website, or video segment that depicts girls' lives and aspirations today (or how girls have changed through some historical period). Encourage them to use various forms of technology to produce their work and to share it with others—maybe to their class, online to friends and relatives, or at a club meeting. (And be sure to review everything before it goes public—there may be some teachable moments in the course of doing this activity.)

Messages About STEM's Importance and Women's Role in It

Messages in the media are often very obvious, but sometimes their meaning is more subtle. With your daughter, track the depiction of STEM and women's participation in STEM in television, web series, and movies, using the questions below:

- ¤ Does the media reflect the importance of STEM in the way we live, work, and play?
- ¤ Are women shown as STEM experts? On what topics and in what kinds of settings?
- ¤ What is the ratio between males and females in STEM-related contexts?
- ¤ Who (in terms of gender, ethnic group, and age) has the more powerful STEM positions?

Discuss the significance of these questions and the answers. Press your daughter to explain not just what she has observed, but also what changes can and should be made. Ask her whether she can see herself in any of the positions played by women (and men) in the media portrayals. If not, what would allow her to see herself in those roles in real life? After you have done this exercise with your daughter, encourage her to find instances in which females do something positive related to STEM. For instance, on a television show a girl is the first student to solve a math problem or the voiceover on a commercial for a computer is female. And you can share your findings with her as you go about your regular daily routines. If she is disappointed with how women in STEM are represented in the media, she can brainstorm (possibly with her friends) a TV show, movie, comic strip, or video game that she thinks would better represent women in STEM and might inspire other girls. She and her friends can even make a pilot episode, trailer, or mock-up of their idea, which can also give them experience using video editing or graphic design software.

> *I was so impacted by the underwater exploration done by the character James Bond in the movies that I later became a certified and avid scuba diver and began studying marine biology on my own.*
> —Michele W., executive consultant, New York

It's never too early for girls to start exploring careers, and the media provides lots of opportunities to see role models (fictional and real) in a variety of different STEM careers. Some television shows, such as *Nova* and *Nature*, are gender neutral. On *The Magic School Bus*, the lead character is a female science teacher, and *Myth Busters* has a female myth buster. Inspire your daughter to start paying attention to women in STEM by pointing out examples in television shows, magazines, and video games. Then encourage her to find her own models in the media. You can even make a game of it, with a point going to the family member who has identified a woman or girl in STEM. The family member with the greatest number of points over a designated period wins a STEM-related prize, such as a box of snap circuits that can be used to make lights blink and wheels turn.

Some in the entertainment industry have recognized the role they can play in changing the kinds of roles actresses portray. In December 2014, the Entertainment Industries Council (a media trade group) in partnership with Google and the National Center for Women & Information Technology announced the first annual SET (Science,

Engineering, and Technology) Award for Portrayal of a Female in Technology, someone who encourages girls and women to pursue careers in computer science and other areas of technology. In May 2015, the actress Renée Felice Smith, who plays Nell Jones, an intelligence analyst, on the CBS television program *NCIS: Los Angeles,* was given the award.

Some actresses themselves also have a STEM background and can serve as role models. Actress Danica McKellar, best known for her work on *The Wonder Years* and *The West Wing,* is a summa cum laude graduate in mathematics from UCLA who has written several math books for adolescents and is an advocate for math education for girls. Mayim Bialik is familiar to older television audiences as the title character on *Blossom* and more recently as the neurobiologist Dr. Amy Farrah Fowler on *The Big Bang Theory.* Bialik is able to fact check the neuroscience on that show because she earned her Ph.D. in neuroscience from UCLA. Your daughter might know Karlie Kloss as a model, but she has turned to other endeavors, such as Kode With Karlie Scholarships, which allow high school girls to take a software engineering course.

Taking Action as a Consumer

Producers need people to purchase movie tickets and video games and watch television shows. You and your daughter can leverage that to get them to highlight STEM's role in everyday life and show females having their rightful place in STEM classes and workplaces. Figure 4 includes an example of the kind of e-mail message, letter, or website response you might want to write when you have noticed something amiss in terms of the depiction of STEM and/or females' roles.

In addition to writing to a show's producer as shown in Figure 4, you might also want to write to companies that advertise on that show. That's another kind of pressure. Because people are much quicker to criticize than to compliment, when you or your daughter observe a positive example of how females play a role in STEM, make time to write a complimentary note about the show or product, and be sure to

Dear Producer of Television Show XYZ,

I am writing to express my dismay about the way you portray women in your *JKL* program. My daughter is 14 years old, and observing television characters is one way she learns about careers and women's strengths. We have both noticed that the female characters on *JKL* have had to be saved consistently by the "smarter" male characters. Moreover, the male characters work in exciting careers in technology, while the females barely know how to send an e-mail message and, if they have jobs, they are likely to be in low-level positions.

Although you may claim that "it's only a fictional show," I know how much young people are affected by what they see and the subtle messages that are conveyed by shows such as *JKL*. I am requesting that you and your writers do better and create or change the characters so that our daughters will want to emulate and learn from them. Confident female characters who are competent in science, technology, engineering, and math can be exciting additions to your programming and can attract a loyal audience of girls and parents.

Sincerely,
Concerned Father

Figure 4. Sample letter to television producers.

mention how that portrayal makes you more likely to watch that show in the future or be a more loyal customer. In addition to traditional letter writing, you may also want to consider using social media, such as Twitter. These sorts of public campaigns can get a lot of other people on board quickly, especially if you have a clever hashtag, and may attract attention from celebrities and the media, making it more likely to have an impact.

> There are many moments, particularly when we think about products marketed to kids and media targeting kids, when children may be getting the message that STEM is for boys. If I were advising parents I would tell them to look for moments to encourage any counter-stereotypic interest. That would be an incredible gift to give children—to articulate that as an option for them.
> —Corinne A. Moss-Racusin, Ph.D., assistant professor of psychology at Skidmore College

As new forms of media and technology emerge, it may be your daughter and not you, who discovers them. Regardless of who learns about the latest ways to interact with media, continue to encourage your daughter to maintain her critical viewing habits and to actively engage with media rather than be a passive observer.

CHAPTER 12

Recognizing and Using the Power of Language and Expression

> *I was a shy girl and quite small, a late-bloomer, and I was intimidated by boys in the early part of high school. I do believe that the separation from that set of insecurities at a crucial time in my education allowed me to find my voice, realize that I could lead, and be great in any subject at school.*
> —Karen Laughlin, Ph.D. in ecology and evolutionary biology, cofounder of Compassionate Use REform (CURE), California

Although the media relay messages, girls, too, convey their own messages through the language they use, the tone of their voice, and their body language (posture and gestures). This chapter explores how girls impact others with the way they deliver their own messages to their friends, family, teachers, and the public. Developing strong communication skills will be important to your daughter in many avenues of her life—whether she's disagreeing with a lab partner in her chemistry class or letting her guidance counselor know she'd like to look at colleges that have strong engineering programs. She will need to show confidence when she responds to her uncle who says that girls aren't as good in math as boys and to speak clearly and loudly when people interrupt and try to talk over her.

Because girls may find themselves in situations in which they are the only female or one of the few in certain settings, such as an advanced calculus class or a math club, they need to learn to speak confidently in those situations and be comfortable with standing out. To start helping your daughter feel more comfortable in those sorts of situations, tell her about a time when you were "the only one." Maybe it was when you took a stand in class that differed from what your classmates said. Perhaps you were the first in your family to try an activity or were the one person who disagreed on a committee when you had to come to a unanimous decision. Talk about how you felt—both the fear of how others might react and the pride in your actions—and why you acted as you did.

Assertive Communication

Assertive communication is a powerful and smart way to convey a message. The first step in assertive communication is just speaking, even when you're not completely confident. Some girls (and boys) are hesitant to say anything in evaluative situations, such as a school or work environment, unless they're completely sure that they're correct or have a better idea than anyone else. But that can prevent others from realizing how much someone brings to the table and can also diminish group performance because the group is not able to use the knowledge and ideas of one of its members. Encourage your daughter to speak up when she might otherwise allow other people to dominate the conversation, and praise her when she does so. Also, let her know that the more she speaks up, the easier it will get, and that the people around her lose out as much as she does when she doesn't share her ideas and knowledge. Because parents have a habit of doing more talking than listening, be aware of your tendency to do that, and try to spend more time listening to your daughter's ideas. That will build her confidence as she learns from your listening to her that what she is sharing is important.

I had a few teachers who validated my identity as a potential young scientist and also some who did the opposite. So it's important for teachers to push female students a bit when they don't speak out in class or don't step up. And teachers needs to make sure that those implicit gender expectations about not being bossy or outspoken don't hold female students back when they really do have a natural talent.

—Hilary Robbins, doctoral student in epidemiology
at Johns Hopkins University

You can also help your daughter express her thoughts in an assertive way. Many girls are accustomed to speaking or acting in a more passive way, and research has found that males use more assertive language than females, although it does vary by context (Leaper & Ayres, 2007; Leaper & Smith, 2004). Here are some exercises you can do with your daughter to give her practice in using an effective communication style. Keep in mind your daughter's age, so your expectations are realistic.

◻ Role model a disagreement with a friend, a teacher, or an employer. Take turns playing each part. Help her understand the difference among responses that are assertive (clearly stating what she feels or knows), aggressive (using language and a voice tone that are hostile and hurtful), and passive (speaking too softly or hinting at what she wants rather than stating it directly). It might be fun and possibly more effective if you play the role of someone who is passive or aggressive and ask her to critique your communication style.

◻ Together with your daughter, find female characters on television or in books who use solid assertive communication. Discuss what they are doing or saying that allows them to come across as strong and worth listening to.

◻ Ask her to write down her thoughts on a topic, such as why tech companies should hire and promote more women. Then ask her to read what she wrote in the most convincing way she can. Give her constructive feedback, and make sure most of your comments are positive and not demeaning. But don't give her false feedback to prevent her from feeling bad. Instead, stick to the facts. For example, did she have an upswing in her voice at the end of a sentence making her sound as if she were asking a question rather than making a statement? Or did she use a lot of modifying words that weakened her thoughts (for instance, saying something like, "I was sort of thinking")? Or does she denigrate her thoughts before expressing them (perhaps saying something like, "I'm probably mistaken, but it could be . . .")? Women are more likely than men to use this sort of tentative language, especially in longer conversations and when speaking in groups rather than in one-on-one conversations (Leaper & Robnett, 2011).

☐ Ask your daughter to pay attention to interruptions in conversations and in classroom discussions. Research has found that men interrupt more than women do, and that this gender difference is larger for interactions in groups as opposed to one-on-one conversations (Anderson & Leaper, 1998). Regardless of your daughter's age, she can begin to practice displaying the kind of confidence that makes it less likely that others will try to talk over her. And if she does get interrupted, she should be prepared to respond in an assertive manner.

> *The earliest memory I have of a mentor was when I was invited to give the alumni speech at the Lockheed Martin Minority Engineering Program graduation. I had tremendous anxiety about speaking in front of the group, and my mentor worked with me to do enough dry runs of the speech that I felt comfortable enough to deliver it live. Anyone who knows me now would never believe that there was a time when public speaking was my greatest fear.*
> —Daria Torres, M.B.A./M.S.E., managing partner and founder of the Walls Torres Group, New Jersey

Showing Strength With Voice Quality and Body Language

Your daughter will find herself in many challenging situations as she grows up. She will need to choose among many possible actions and deal with tough circumstances with a strength that is not only internal, but manifests itself in her demeanor, her facial expressions, and her tone of voice.

> *I first knew I was interested in STEM in fifth grade when I was the only one in my class of 30 constantly raising my hand for every question in science class. My teacher noticed this and would tell me about breaking news in the science world. Before I knew it, I had a giant periodic table on my wall, quotes from famous scientists everywhere, my own tiny microscope, and a subscription to Popular Science.*
> —Marina Tosi, high school student, New York

Many females speak softly, sometimes fading into the background. But that doesn't serve them well as they interact with others whose voices sound more powerful and command more attention than theirs. Give your daughter opportunities to recognize the difference between shouting and speaking in a strong, assertive voice. If she is somewhat reserved in temperament, she will have to take a step out of her comfort zone and practice quite a bit before a stronger voice tone sounds natural to her. Encourage her to practice with you, other family members, and her closest friends. Record her so she can gauge her progress (but only with her permission). And point out role models in the media who use their voice to its best advantage.

Discuss the importance of staying cool under pressure, of managing her emotional responses in challenging situations. Anxiety might show up as a wavering voice, excessive fidgeting, shallow breathing, and a soft-spoken voice. The message to your daughter should be—show confidence while you're still building it, sometimes referred to as "fake it 'til you make it." That doesn't mean that displays of emotion have no place in your daughter's life. But if the people around her at school or at work can easily tell whenever she's feeling stressed, disappointed, or frustrated, they might not pay attention to the important information or viewpoint she is proposing.

If your daughter is one of the many girls who speak softly and prefer to blend into the background in social and school settings, here are some tips for her to use that will allow her to have more of an impact as a speaker:

- ¤ Make eye contact with others you're speaking to. Don't stare at them for long periods, but just long enough to show that you're not afraid. Look away when they look away. Be aware that, in some cultures, making direct eye contact is considered rude.
- ¤ Stand up straight—again, a way to demonstrate power and confidence.
- ¤ Smile when you feel good about something that someone has said, not just because girls are expected to put on a happy face.
- ¤ Raise your hand firmly and straight up when you want to be called on in class. Many girls show their ambivalence about speaking up by the limp and awkward way they raise their hands. They shouldn't have to loudly call out, "I know the answer" to get a teacher's attention (which some students do), but they shouldn't show passivity in their body language either. It's too easy to be ignored if they do so.
- ¤ Practice breathing exercises—filling your abdomen with air and exhaling in a conscious, intentional way. Breathing from your diaphragm helps make your voice louder without yelling, which helps you speak with authority.

Let your daughter know that she shouldn't expect to go from passive to impactful in one day. She's on a journey with stops and starts. But remind her that if she's motivated to make this important change, she will be able to do so and will find school and social situations more enjoyable. Suggest that she take some small steps first—like giving a one-word answer to a question when previously she hadn't responded at all. Everything does not have to be done at the same time. Praise her when she's made progress instead of focusing on her setbacks. She doesn't need to be reminded of what she's doing wrong, but rather of what's she's accomplished.

Giving Powerful Presentations

Public speaking is one of the most common fears. However, almost every job in a STEM field requires good speaking skills. And even if your daughter does not end up in a STEM career, she will still have to speak in groups, starting while she's in school and then afterward in various work and community situations. Whether she's fully comfortable speaking in groups or hates participating in class discussions, the tips below will help her give better presentations.

Reading an Audience

Before your daughter begins to prepare a presentation, she should consider how she will customize it for her audience. Will she be standing by her exhibit at her school's science fair while parents, teachers, and other students walk by and ask questions? Will she be giving a speech in front of the entire junior class at her high school to explain her positions as a candidate for class president? Will she be talking to incoming middle school students about what they should know before starting school?

The same tone, presentation length, vocabulary, and type of humor will not work equally well with all audiences. She should find out whether the presentation includes a question and answer period, whether the audience expects to participate, and whether she can use visual aids, which can enliven a presentation. Will she be taped? Will she have a microphone? Will there be a place for her notes? The more she knows about her audience and their expectations as well as about the setting, the more comfortable she will be.

Part of the skill in accommodating to an audience is about making adjustments on the fly. Are people beginning to look at their phones or tablets? Are they yawning or fidgeting? She may need to vary her tone more, ask a provocative question, or tell a story to get her audience back. Presentations are performances, and the more experience she has, the better she is likely to get.

> *When I have given workshops for middle school students on what I love about being a social scientist, I have told them it allows me to be 'nosy' for legitimate reasons! Any good scientist is a curious person who really wants to figure out why something does or does not happen. For chemists, it might be why this combination of ingredients affects a substance a certain way. For a social scientist, it is wondering how specific experiences cause humans to react, why some people react one way and others another way.*
> —Sylvia Barsion, Ph.D. in educational research, measurement, and evaluation; writer and consultant, New York

If your daughter feels anxious while she's presenting, suggest that she focus her attention on a couple of people in the audience who seem to be encouraging and engaged. Maybe they're nodding or smiling. She could keep going back to them for the additional support she needs to continue her presentation in the most optimal way.

Structuring a Presentation

Solid preparation is key to giving a great presentation. That means that she needs to decide on the presentation's objective—basically, what she wants her audience to walk away with. The most important part of a presentation is typically the beginning—she will either grab her audience's attention or watch it quickly drift away, depending on what she does during that first minute. These are some possible ways to begin:

- a compelling and relevant story;
- a startling, but true, statistic about the topic;
- a cartoon or a joke; or
- an interesting question.

In some way, she should return to that opening anecdote, research finding, or beginning question during her presentation so that everything blends together seamlessly.

> *In Nicaragua, I was asked to do a community health assessment, design a survey, go around to do interviews in the community, compile the data, and try to see patterns and identify priorities for the health program. In doing that I really saw how powerful it was to be able to back up our proposal with those numbers that came from the health survey.*
>
> —Hilary Robbins, doctoral student in epidemiology at Johns Hopkins University

It is always a good idea to create an outline for a presentation (something that works in writing a paper, too). That way she can organize her ideas in a logical way and make sure she's not trying to accomplish too much with one presentation. People can take in only so many concepts at one time. Giving examples and inserting humor are valuable ways to enhance a presentation. Remind her to distinguish between a piece of writing and a presentation. Repetition often works in speeches, but not in writing. Practicing the pace of her presentation will help since it is slower than typical conversations. She can use her hands to emphasize a point and make sure that her facial expressions match the content of her presentation.

The end of her presentation should leave her audience inspired and motivated to take action. Although you are your daughter's role model, she can be a role model for others. Public speaking about STEM is a key way for her to influence those who are younger than her as well as her peers, and maybe even her teachers and other adults. The more skilled she becomes as a speaker, the more impact she will have.

CHAPTER 13

Exploring STEM Through Toys, Games, and Activities

> *As a child, I really enjoyed making things, and using LEGOs was very creative. I could just assemble whatever I wanted to so I would make houses, spaceships, towns with cars, all kinds of things. It was just so free form that I really liked doing that, and along the same lines, I was also into crafts, which also was because I could actually create something with my hands.*
> —Bettina Chen, electrical engineer and cofounder of Roominate Toys California

Women who work in STEM fields told us about the kinds of toys they played with and the games and activities they enjoyed as children. It was evident that the themes of exploration, constructing, and experimenting were commonplace—all important aspects of STEM. This chapter will give you ideas for how you can encourage your daughter to explore STEM through a variety of toys, games, and everyday activities, whether it's putting together snap circuits, experimenting in the kitchen, or creating a budget. Observe your daughter, too, to discover more about her interests and figure out how to use them to foster her excitement about STEM.

Everyday STEM Activities

No matter how old your daughter is, you can find or create STEM activities that are age-appropriate and fun. Below are some suggestions for everyday STEM explorations that range from figuring out which type of beverage is most acidic to calculating which sweater to buy at the mall.

Kitchen Science

When children are young, they actually like doing chores and helping in the kitchen. Capitalize on your daughter's early interest by engaging her in measuring ingredients, dividing up desserts, and discussing the temperature at which water freezes when you're making ice pops. It's helpful to have a variety of measuring spoons and cups around. That way she can easily see that 2 half cups of water equals 1 cup or that 3 teaspoons are equivalent to 1 tablespoon.

In addition to doing kitchen activities in which math concepts come alive, you can easily insert chemistry into food preparation. As a start, you and your daughter can experiment to find out which kinds of pots or pans (aluminum, iron, or ceramic, for instance) heat up food most quickly. And then she can find out what happens to the taste when food heats up quickly or slowly. Getting answers is only a small part of this exercise; it's much more about the process of asking questions, making predictions (hypotheses), and explaining results—all part of STEM.

Red cabbage juice tester. One popular activity uses red cabbage juice to find out which liquids are acidic and which are not. Cabbage juice will turn different shades of red when mixed with acids, and different shades of blue when mixed with bases. You will need the following ingredients and supplies: red cabbage, baking soda (bicarbonate of soda), various liquids (e.g., orange, lime, and lemon juice; milk, soda, and tea), water, grater, strainer, cups, large bowl, and a 1-teaspoon measuring spoon.

1. Grate red cabbage into a bowl.
2. Pour cold water over the cabbage and let it stand for at least 45 minutes.
3. Use a strainer to separate the red juice from the cabbage pieces. (Although you can discard the cabbage at this point, you have an opportunity to talk about conservation by using the cabbage to make coleslaw or composting it.)
4. Measure equal amounts of cabbage juice into plastic cups.
5. Put one cup filled with cabbage juice aside. That will serve as the control in this experiment—as a way to compare what happens to the liquid in the other cups.
6. Add one teaspoon of baking soda to the other cups of cabbage juice. The baking soda (which is a base) will turn the juice blue, allowing your daughter to test different liquids to see which ones will turn the juice red again (and how much is needed to do that). If the juice looks like it is turning back to red, the liquid you added is probably an acid. It will take different amounts of different acids to turn the juice the color of the control. If the juice stays blue, the liquid is probably not an acid.

Depending on your daughter's age, you might suggest that she draw an illustration of her findings or write them up to share with her relatives or friends. Just as you might post her artwork on the refrigerator, do the same with her STEM work. Ask her questions as she does this activity, and encourage her to ask questions, too. She could also teach her friends how to do this activity or perhaps do this as a fun group weekend activity.

Fizzing lemonade. Your daughter might enjoy a STEM activity that results in a beverage that is safe to drink. It relies on the principle of acid-base chemical reaction or carbonation, which occurs when an acid and a base are combined. You will need the following ingredients and supplies: two lemons, baking soda, cold water, sugar, glass, a half-teaspoon measuring spoon, strainer, and a stirrer or spoon. Before you and your daughter take each step below, ask her to predict what will happen and then after each action, to explain the reaction.

1. Squeeze the juice of two lemons into a glass and then strain it to get rid of the seeds.
2. Add one-half teaspoon of baking soda and watch the reaction.
3. Stir the mixture and observe again.
4. Add another half-teaspoon of baking soda. Look at what happens.
5. Add some sugar (not too much) to a glass of cold water, and then add that to the lemon mixture.
6. Taste the fizzing lemonade.

Once you have established the basics, encourage your daughter to try out the same activity with other acidic juices. Baking soda is only safe to ingest in small amounts, so make sure that your daughter doesn't experiment with using large amounts of that chemical. And be sure that you use baking soda and not baking powder.

You can find hundreds of other kitchen science ideas on the Internet at sites like PBSkids.org. Before your daughter does them, make sure you've considered possible safety issues. Remind your daughter that just because an idea is on the Internet doesn't mean it's safe.

> *Anything my parents did with my brothers, they did with me. It wasn't like my brothers learned how to change the oil in a car and I learned to cook. That's what made the most difference for me because my parents did things equally with me and my brothers.*
>
> —Gail Ruby, MS in computer science, senior product manager at Motor Information Systems, Michigan

M and M: Math and Money

Regardless of what girls do in their lives, they need to know about budgeting and banking. And that means being competent and comfortable with math. Give your daughter a head start by using math concepts at a very early age, not for the purpose of pushing her ahead, but to help her feel comfortable with math before she faces the kind of stereotyping and gender bias that might undermine her confidence.

Math concepts in everyday situations. If you're talking to a toddler or preschooler, use comparative terms such as bigger or smaller. Ask questions or make comments about a toy's size, and use hand gestures to emphasize the difference between "just a little" and "a lot." When you're setting the table, ask for one more spoon or two more bowls. Or say something like, "We are only three people, but we have four plates. Let's put one away." Maybe when you're cutting up a favorite dessert, purposely make the portions a bit uneven. Then you can ask, "Who should get the largest piece?" and "Which is the smallest piece?"

Lots of parents express pride when their children at a very young age can count to 10 or 20. But if the counting is just based on rote memorization, it doesn't really mean much. Instead, focus on helping your daughter to understand that three is greater than two and that three is less than four. Use concrete objects to make your point, and show that using math is a part of everyday life. Probability games are fun and only require a single coin. Ask your daughter to predict how often a coin will land heads or tails up if you toss it 100 times. Then discuss your findings.

Math is a vital part of music. Whether you're dancing to a particular tempo or recognizing that one note is held twice as long as the one before, you're using math. Dance steps are timed, and when the music speeds up, those steps have to keep up. Musical instruments have a certain number of strings or keys. Make sure your daughter sees that math is not only all around her, but that it also plays a role in the beauty of the world.

Keeping score in board games, such as Monopoly, requires math skills. Even word games such as Scrabble use math when comparing possible moves—would it be better to take advantage of a triple letter tile or a double word tile? Strategy games such as dominoes, checkers, chess, and Parcheesi boost mathematical thinking, memory, sequencing skills, and spatial skills.

Money matters. Think about whether you are giving your daughter opportunities to learn about bill paying, banking, and investing. If you are including your daughter in these important discussions and actions, that's great. But if you're not, turn over a new leaf, and let your daughter become competent in a skill that will have practical applications every day of her life. Below are some topics and terms she should be aware of, and if you don't feel that you're knowledgeable enough, the two of you can learn together.

Stocks. A great gift for a special occasion might be a share in a company that a girl is interested in. It could be the corporation that makes her tablet or the company that produces blockbuster movies. By owning a very tiny piece of a company, girls will be more motivated to follow the ups and downs of the stock market and read annual reports that discuss a company's performance and its future plans. As a stockholder, your daughter might want to send a letter to the Board of Directors with a compliment or a complaint, and perhaps even suggest that the company work harder to diversify the board so that it is more representative of the population that uses its products.

Online bill payments. Many people pay their bills electronically, and no one sees cash changing hands. But your daughter needs to keep in mind that money can only be transferred electronically to a store or landlord if the bill payer's money is available in a bank.

ATMs. Your daughter should know that the money spitting out of the machine is not the bank's—it's yours.

Credit and debit cards. Discuss the value of having a solid credit rating, one that will allow her to borrow money for a car or a house some time in the future. Explain the difference between a credit card (basically borrowing money that, if paid back quickly, does not cost any fees) and a debit card (subtracting money that's already been placed on a card or is in an account—by you or someone else).

Comparison shopping. Whether you're picking up groceries for tonight's dinner or deciding on a hotel for a vacation, you're likely to do some comparison shopping. Your daughter can assist you in making informed financial decisions. For instance, at the supermarket, compare whether the larger size is really more economical than the smaller one (that's not always the case). Do generic or store brands cost less than big-name brands? If the items differ in size, your daughter will have to do a bit more math, which involves looking at the unit price, but you could make finding the best deals into a fun game, particularly if your daughter brings along a friend for some fun competition. When she's shopping for an item in a department store, ask her to compare discounts. For example, which is a better buy—an item marked 40% off or one that's been discounted at 25% off but with an additional 25% off that?

One of the ways to add to the above list is by listening to your daughter's questions or reading a relevant news story that highlights an issue. Instead of bombarding your daughter with information, allow her to lead the way. The idea is to help her see that math is needed every day in decision making and that the more experience she has with its practical aspects, the less intimidated she will be.

You might also introduce your daughter to careers related to money, including accountant, loan officer, tax attorney, financial planner, chief financial officer in a company or organization, and economist. Go back over your list of role models and see if you can identify those in money-related jobs. They might be willing to answer your daughter's questions and allow her to see what a career in a money field might be like.

> At family gatherings when I was a child, I would sit with the men, listening to them talk about the stock market and their businesses and challenges. As I grew older and became a banker, I became an active member of that conversation. I always loved those conversations, and I knew I belonged when they asked me for my advice on things.
>
> —Karen W. Solorow, president of Coaching for Success and former banker, New York

Giving allowances. The amount of money that children get for their allowance varies from family to family. Although some parents decide that they would rather not give their kids an allowance, it's an appropriate way for you to teach your daughter about the value of money. Here are some important guidelines:

- *Make the amount age-appropriate and fair.* A 7-year old shouldn't be getting the same amount as her sister who's in high school. Decide, possibly with your child, when allowances can be increased. It could be at the beginning of the calendar year or the school year, or it could occur at birthday time. Be prepared for some negotiating, so think ahead about what is reasonable.

- *Decide whether an allowance will be tied to doing chores.* Parents have varying views about the relationship between chores and allowance, with some believing that children should get an allowance only if all of their chores have been completed. That can get pretty complicated as you and your daughter argue about the meaning of "completed." One way to handle the allowance-chore relationship is to give an allowance unrelated to regular chores, but give extra money for certain special chores (perhaps the ones that are only done once a month). If regular chores are not done, you can come up with other consequences unrelated to money.

- *Allow your daughter to choose what to do with her allowance.* You still have an opportunity to influence her by discussing how you divide up household money—some goes for basic necessities, such as food and housing, but part may be put aside for special occasions, such as a vacation. Explain how you make decisions about donating to causes you believe in. Allowing your daughter to make decisions about her money gives her an opportunity to learn about planning ahead and to feel more competent. She can either buy something small at the toy store after saving her allowance for a couple of weeks or save some of her money for 2 months to get something bigger and better.

- *Discuss with your daughter what expenses she will need to pay with her allowance.* And that should be part of the way you decide how much is fair to give her. For example, will movies and

My Budget for the Week (or Month) of _____

Income	
Allowance	
Gifts	
Work	
Other	
Total Income	
Expenses	
Snacks	
Entertainment	
Transportation	
Gifts	
Other	
Total Expenses	
Difference Between Income and Expenses	

Figure 5. Weekly budget worksheet.

snacks with friends come out of her allowance? What about gifts for her friends and family members? If she isn't expected to pay for anything, it will be hard for her to learn about saving and spending.

Making a budget. At some point in your daughter's life, it would be helpful for her to learn how to create and live on a budget. Why not have her gain the experience before she goes off to college? Start a discussion about budgeting by distinguishing between needs and wants—children of elementary school age and older can understand that difference, particularly if you help with some examples from your own life. Then use the chart in Figure 5 or some adaptation of it. The "Other" category under Expenses could include fees for a sports team, dues for an afterschool club, or supplies for a business. The "Work" category might include income from your daughter's entrepreneurial venture (as a dog walker or a greeting card designer) or money she earns as an assistant in a family business. Using a spreadsheet on a computer is a great way to combine technology and math.

Gender Bias at the Toy Store

A walk through the aisles of a large toy store will give you a good idea of the scope of the gender bias issue your daughter faces. Consider doing your own field research with your daughter. Although there are some terrific STEM-related toys, games, and activities available, the packaging is often used to appeal to particular consumers and perhaps discourage others. Below are some observations from one such trip to a toy store:

- ¤ A set that includes the ingredients for making a bouncing ball packaged with a small picture of a boy wearing a white lab coat, eyeglasses, and a bow tie—a stereotypical view of a scientist.
- ¤ Two educational games sitting right next to each other—one about mastering kindergarten level math shows a smiling boy working on an arithmetic problem while the other game is about mastering reading and shows a smiling girl writing in a workbook.
- ¤ Packages of construction toys depicting boys building structures or showing samples of what can be built (with girls not appearing on the packaging).
- ¤ Many toy boxes depicting boys actively working on a project (unless it's art or cooking-related) while girls are either absent or somewhere in the background. One box showed a mom and sister playing background roles while a boy was working. Another showed a mom looking on while two boys worked together building a playground.
- ¤ A construction toy box with a spiral car run that's higher than the little boy who's playing with it. No girl is in sight.
- ¤ A kit for making sand art showing a girl looking at her creation—with a lot of purple and pink.

- Various microscope kits, each one shown with a boy on the package.
- A chemistry set with a picture of a boy holding up a test tube vial.
- A kit for creating a planetarium model pictures boys, while a solar system that simply requires pressing a button to light up a room shows a girl.
- A lab set with a boy wearing safety glasses holding a vial of colored liquid while a girl in the background is holding two pieces of purple plastic.
- A rock dissection kit with two pictures of boys working on the rocks.
- Foam building blocks for toddlers showing a boy examining his construction.
- An activity cube for infants and toddlers with a boy discovering how gears work.
- A building set with large blocks largely in bright pink and lime green and a girl just looking at two of the blocks. Another set from the same company shows blocks in primary colors with a boy putting one block on top of another.
- A crime lab set with three photos on the package—a large picture of a boy using a tool, a small picture of another boy using a microscope, and a girl shown with her mouth open in awe but not doing anything.

On the positive side, the following were found:
- A building toy with tubes in primary colors showing a picture of two preschool girls working together on a project.
- A brainteaser challenge that requires users to undo a knot composed of plastic pieces in colors ranging from red to purple to turquoise, an apparently gender-neutral toy.
- A construction set that encourages users to create rooms with electrical components with a girl pictured on the box cover.
- An elevated tracking system with gender-neutral toy figures.
- A multicolored game emphasizing perception of patterns, endorsed by various organizations.

¤ A toy telescope with a girl pictured peering through it.

What can you do with these observations? Point out to your daughter instances of bias as well as positive examples of nonsexist toy packaging. Ask her to describe what she notices and discuss the significance of what is available on the shelves of toy stores. If you make a purchase of an item, such as a microscope with a boy featured on the box, you can cover that with a photo of your daughter or a picture from a magazine or the Internet featuring a girl using a microscope. And make your voice heard by toy manufacturers. Figure 6 includes an example of a sample Tweet you might want to post.

> *I received a chemistry set for a birthday gift one year. I used to go down into the basement and do a few experiments from the booklet each day (there were a lot of experiments so I was down there quite a bit). My favorite was one where you mixed together two clear liquids and the mixture changed to a bright yellow. I used to do that one over and over again.*
> —Jennifer Tosi, B.A. in engineering, vice-president at Morgan Stanley, New York

Indoor Fun

Whether it's raining or too cold or dark to be outside, your daughter can do lots of things that will allow her to explore STEM indoors. One of the most effective ways for your daughter to learn about electricity (and following directions) is with snap circuits. Kits of all sizes with simple-to-follow directions are available at many stores and online. Once girls see that putting together circuits in a particular way will make a fan whir or a light go on, they will want to continue to experiment with batteries, wires, and switches.

> @XYZtoys @XYZceo My daughter thinks you can do better than having only a boy on your geo set box. Change toy packaging = help girls see their future in STEM!
>
> ___
>
> **Figure 6.** Sample tweet.

Making Dough

If your daughter is between 4 and 10, making play dough with her is an activity that combines various STEM elements and discovery. You will need the following ingredients and equipment: 1 cup of flour, a half-cup of salt, 2 teaspoons of cream of tartar, 2 tablespoons of vegetable oil, 1 cup of cold water, two drops of food coloring, measuring spoons and cup, a mixing bowl, and a small pot.

1. Mix all of the ingredients
2. Cook the mixture in a small pot over medium heat until the dough seems to hold together
3. Allow the dough to cool before shaping it.

Your daughter can experiment with making batches of different sizes (allowing her to calculate changing amounts) and colors and also seeing what happens with different amounts of food coloring and combining different colors to create new ones (the science of color).

It's Called Oobleck

If your daughter is too old to make play dough, she may well be interested in exploring a unique substance called Oobleck, a non-Newtonian fluid that changes from solid to liquid state and back again, depending on the force applied. The strange name comes from an old Dr. Seuss book called *Bartholomew and the Oobleck* in which a king wanted something totally new to fall from the sky and what falls is called Oobleck. Before starting this activity, make sure you are working on a washable surface (e.g., not wood), and that you do not allow the substance to go down the drain as it can easily clog pipes. You will need the following ingredients and equipment to make your own Oobleck: water, 1 cup of cornstarch, 1 or 2 drops of food coloring for each mound of Oobleck, measuring cups, a large bowl, and resealable plastic bags or containers.

1. Start by putting one cup of cornstarch into a large bowl.
2. Mix one or two drops of food coloring into a half cup of water (This step is optional but could make the activity more fun).
3. Combine the cornstarch and water and mix the substance with your hands.
4. Now experiment with the Oobleck to see what happens when you squeeze it hard, roll it up into a ball or other shapes, and let it flow out of your hands.

When you're finished using your Oobleck for the day, put it into an airtight plastic bag or container. If it's stored properly, your daughter can play with it again and again. She might also want to demonstrate its special properties to her friends.

Technology Ideas

Learning to code, build a website, design computer graphics, create an app for a smart phone, or develop a video game are all possibilities, particularly if your daughter has access to afterschool programs that specialize in technology. You can also locate books at the library or online that can point you in the right direction, or find someone to introduce your daughter to computer science. Some websites offer coding lessons, which allow a learner to fix a game before trying to create a new one. The Internet also provides help with making "vines," 6-second videos, which can increase her comfort with technology. And new technologies are constantly being developed. For example, one new product is Jewelbots, which are programmable friendship bracelets that teach girls how to code using an app (http://jewelbots.com).

An important message to give to your daughter with these activities is that making mistakes and learning from them is part of the process. If she expects to be successful right away, she will probably feel frustrated.

So be sure to emphasize that the best way to learn is by experimenting and learning from each experience.

Many of the women we interviewed talked about using chemistry sets and microscopes to explore the world around them. Although experimenting with the unknown is exciting and educational, before your daughter uses a chemistry set or a microscope, make sure she knows the safety rules she should follow, including wearing safety glasses and gloves and not combining chemicals before knowing whether it's safe to mix them.

> *I loved card games and puzzles, Connect 4, and any game that required me to solve something to reach the end result. I loved unique games or challenges like Labyrinth or Jenga because they force you to think methodically. I think seeing the whole picture is what I love the most about business, and games that can give me that view are the ones I love most.*
> —Elizabeth Dodson, cofounder of HomeZada, California

Taking Objects Apart and Building Structures

One of the most interesting ways to learn about how something works is by taking it apart and then seeing whether it can be recreated. Variations include substituting one piece for another and leaving pieces out to see what happens. Of course, if an object is valuable, this is not the best activity for it. But toy cars or trucks that are ready to be discarded as well as old or broken mobile phones or electronic devices would make perfect candidates for a "taking apart" activity.

Designing and building structures are practice for the engineering feats your daughter might accomplish one day. Developing plans is a technique architects use. She can create prototypes out of building blocks of different sizes, shapes, and consistency. She can use craft sticks and glue or a deck of playing cards to create buildings that remain standing even when blown on.

> My favorite toys growing up were focused on building and creating something new. I loved LEGOs, Imaginex, Lincoln Logs, and my brother's track-building set. I also loved drawing and could be kept quiet with a pad of paper and some crayons for as long as my parents needed.
> —Michelle DePinho, civil engineering student at Manhattan College

As your daughter gets older, her projects can get very sophisticated—incorporating simple machines, such as wedges and inclined planes, and a variety of structures that represent different uses—from apartment complexes to playgrounds to office buildings. An incredible number of materials and kits in wood, metal, plastic, foam, and even paper can be purchased or you can use recycled materials. What is most important for your daughter's experience is for her to find delight in experimentation and accomplishment, as her projects integrate various elements of STEM. Although many kits come with directions for creating specific structures, make sure your daughter has the opportunity to be creative, varying how materials are used.

Old Favorites Still Strong

Although the packaging of many of the building sets that have been around for years retain much of their boy-centered messaging with words and images, they can provide hours of fun and experience understanding math (spatial relationships) and engineering concepts (support structures). K'NEX provides material—bricks, rods, and connectors—to create a wide variety of objects, from bugs to robots. Some of the kits are relatively simple with larger pieces and are meant for preschoolers, while other kits offer intricate designs and more complicated instructions. Lincoln Logs, fondly remembered by many women in STEM and now a K'NEX product, provide wood and plastic logs for imaginative construction projects.

Erector sets can provide girls with experience building, using tools, and learning about motors, with some kits appropriate for children as young as 7. The original Erector toys were created more than a century ago and even inspired a med student in the 1940s to create the world's first artificial heart pump.

Another classic brand is LEGO, which has grown into a major industry with contests (Lego Robotics), stores, video games, and even a movie. In recent years, the company recognized that value of attracting more female customers by creating its "Friends" line that is clearly intended for girls (pink and purple and a princess theme are rampant). But it would be better for your daughter to experience a wider variety of LEGO experiences than just those kits designed especially for girls. Fortunately, LEGO has also started adding a few female STEM mini-figures (including those based on real scientists), some designed by fans. You can support more of these fan designs and submit your own through LEGO Ideas (ideas.lego.com). Find kits that allow your daughter to be creative, not just to follow directions (although learning to follow complex directions does have its value).

> *As a child, I liked things with moving parts, sort of like an engineer would. I would drive my parents a little nuts because I would actually destroy my toys trying to figure out how they worked. I would take them apart and then not know how to put them back together again. There was just something in me that was very curious about how things worked.*
> —Carol L. Ensinger, Ph.D., retired pharmaceutical industry chemist and project manager, South Carolina

Designed for Girls

Two companies that have won awards and received significant attention in recent years are GoldieBlox and Roominate, both created by female engineers. Instead of simply changing the color of blocks to appeal to girls, these products provide girls with the opportunity to learn about physics and engineering, fields that few females pursue. And both companies do it in ways that are fun and engaging with ample opportunities for creativity and problem solving.

GoldieBlox kits typically contain a story about Goldie, an inventor, and a construction set with simple machines. Founded by Debbie

Sterling, who saw an unfilled niche in the toy industry, GoldieBlox kits come in a variety of themes, ranging from a spinning machine to movie making. A male character was introduced in 2015, but the colors, stories, and princess references clearly show that these are toys girls will want to play with. Axles, washers, cranks, wheels, and whatever other parts are needed are included in the kits, designed to give girls an early experience with engineering principles and spatial skills.

Roominate Toys, founded by Bettina Chen and Alice Brooks, offers girls the opportunity to build houses with modular pieces for floors and walls and then wire the rooms with lights, fans, and even an elevator. Your daughter can build furniture, stairs, and pools. If she is interested, she can submit photos of her structures to the Roominate website (http://www.roominatetoy.com), on which many girls share their accomplishments. The company has partnered with the University of California at Davis School of Education on a series of activity guides that incorporate the Next Generation Science Standards. The two engineers who created Roominate are a great example of women who saw a need (the dearth of female engineers) and used their training, creativity, and motivation to solve a problem. And they did it as partners, which is something your daughter should appreciate.

> Right now we're developing new apps for Roominate that are going to bring a lot more technology into the product. We're going to have an app that allows you to actually control and program the circuits in your kitchen from your phone. We'll be putting in sensors. You might have a light sensor for one of the rooms or you could have a motion sensor with an alarm system in your house so if something crosses it, the alarm would go off.
> —Bettina Chen, electrical engineer and cofounder of Roominate Toys, California

The possibilities for developing new toys that inspire girls to pursue STEM, particularly in those fields in which women make up a small percentage, are infinite. As a parent, you play an important role as an advocate for your daughter and as a knowledgeable and active consumer.

CHAPTER 14

Stepping Out
Exploring STEM Through Outdoor Activities and Trips

> *When I was in middle school, I was told about the opportunity to go on a marine science trip through the local university. The program put us aboard the schooner Harvey Gamage for 3 days in the Acadia National Park and Penobscot Bay area. We got to do real science and real sailing. We were aboard with other kids who had similar interests, and with real scientists who were excited about their work and eager to share it. That was when I realized I could make a career out of working on and in the ocean.*
> —Kate L. Pickle, deputy director, Science Club for Girls

Outdoor activities and trips, whether they are specifically focused on STEM or not, provide girls with opportunities to experience enrichment, a sense of adventure, and interactions with role models. Extended outdoor activities and trips can mean immersive STEM experiences and exposure to applications of STEM to real-world challenges. Excursions—whether it's for a morning, a day, or a month—offer girls the opportunity to meet professionals engaged in STEM. No matter where you live or your daughter's age, you can find or create engaging STEM experiences. In addition, outdoor family activities and trips enrich everyday routines and offer opportunities for bonding among family members.

Outside Activities

You and your daughter can be creative exploring the outdoors or do activities that may be more fun outside than inside. Even playing ball brings up STEM concepts, ranging from the physics of flight to the principle of gravity. Whether you're playing a casual game of catch in the street or basketball in the community park, you and your daughter can ask questions, make predictions, and discover STEM in action. Collecting data and categorizing objects, such as leaves, birds, rocks, and shells, are STEM processes. If you have collected samples, and not just data (make sure you're allowed to remove those rocks or shells you've found), you can examine them more closely when you get home under a microscope. Getting a very close-up view of dead bugs, dust, and leaves can be fascinating. If you don't think so, make sure you don't show your distaste for the activity, because it's a wonderful way for your daughter to explore STEM.

When you and your daughter are outside, pay particular attention to opportunities to introduce engineering to your daughter, as that's the field she will probably have the least formal education in. Find simple machines (such as levers, inclined planes, screws, pulleys, and axles) in action and talk about how they make work easier, observe solar panels installed on the roofs of houses and discuss their benefits, and figure out why it's so much easier to ride a tricycle than a bicycle.

Scavenger Hunt

One fun activity that can be used in an endless number of variations is the scavenger hunt. This is more exciting with a group, so gather your daughter and her friends for a morning or afternoon of using clues to find hidden objects. Depending on your clues, they might need a magnifying lens, a ruler, a calculator, a smart phone with Internet access, or other tools. Use a nearby park, field, or backyard to set up clues, with each one mentioning something that is STEM-related. You can set up a scavenger hunt so that one clue leads to the next with something big to be discovered at the end or have a list that can be gone through in any order. Some examples of clues are the following:

- Find an area that has a total of 3 + 2 + 6 red flowers in one row (Change the formula to fit the age of the girls in your group).
- Go to an object that is the color of a robin's egg.
- Find an object that is considered a lever and is 6 feet wide.
- Take a photograph of an invasive plant.
- Describe the details of a plant that can be observed with a magnifying glass but not without it.

Magnifying lenses are useful in scavenger hunts, but they can also be used as tools to examine objects that you come across on a nature walk in the woods, at a beach, or on a mountain trail. If you are doing a night scavenger hunt, make use of binoculars and telescopes to search the sky. That would also be an easy way for your daughter to learn about magnification. In fact, whenever you're exploring a new outdoor physical environment, you can introduce STEM concepts and tools, but don't make the experience into an explicit STEM lesson. The activity should feel like an adventure—which it is!

> As a child, I enjoyed walking in the woods with my father to collect leaves for Show and Tell. When I took the shopping bag of leaves to school, I was able to tell the class what type of tree each of the leaves had fallen from. I loved learning. In the summer, I rode my bicycle, and always enjoyed the independence, freedom, and opportunities for discovery and exploration.
> —Michele W., executive consultant, New York

Bubble Play

Most children love to play with bubbles. How about helping your daughter learn how to make her own bubble solution and then experiment with it? That's chemistry in action. You will need the following ingredients and equipment: 1/4 cup of dishwashing liquid, 10–15 drops of glycerin, a quart of water, large bowl, plastic straws, and pipe cleaners bent into various shapes. Look around your house and see what else might work as a tool for this activity.

1. Combine the water, glycerin, and dishwashing liquid in the large bowl
2. Allow the mixture to sit for several hours. (You might want to do that part in the evening, and then do the experimenting the next day.)
3. Dip the various tools into the solution and wave them in the air or blow through them to create bubbles.

The STEM principles involved in this activity are surface tension, evaporation, air pressure, and light reflection. Depending on your daughter's age, the two of you can delve into the explanations on a superficial or deep level. What is important is making predictions and observations, experimenting, and drawing conclusions.

Going Further Afield

Exploring interactive STEM environments can happen in an infinite number of ways if you and your daughter are up for the adventure, challenge, and enjoyment of going on a trip. Even if the main reason for a trip is something other than immersing yourself in STEM, that doesn't mean you can't insert some exploration, learning, and STEM fun into the journey.

How to Make the Most of a Trip

A study of visitor interaction in the Exploratorium Science museum in San Francisco (Tisdale, 2004) resulted in a concept that came to be known by the acronym "APE," which stands for "Active Prolonged

Engagement." The APE framework, which identifies styles of visitor interaction with museum exhibits, suggests that learning is maximized when visitors spend a longer time with a particular display rather than rushing from one to another. Tisdale identified four basic domains of the trip experience, which you can use to maximize the benefit of your own family trips. The physical includes activities that use various senses, such as interacting with exhibits by touch, observation, or listening, while the intellectual domain includes problem solving, data gathering, and analysis of challenges. The social and emotional domains are tapped when interactions among family members or friends who visit a museum together promote a positive emotional experience for everyone.

Plan in advance. Involve your daughter in planning the itinerary. Look at brochures and maps in advance. Think about what you need to bring, both relating to physical comfort and safety (e.g., water, compass, first aid kit, and comfortable shoes) and what you need to make the most of the trip (items such as guidebooks, binoculars for bird watching, and a notebook or tablet). Bring a camera or a cell phone with a camera if picture-taking is permitted by the venue, but pay attention to the rules in order to have a pleasant experience.

When you are on a trip, let your daughter decide how to pace herself, but encourage her to stop to observe, read markers, and use interactive activities (keep in mind the importance of prolonged engagement). If you have children of both genders on a trip, balance discussion equally, making sure that both take turns leading the way through exhibits and playing with hands-on activities. Look for items or displays of interest to your daughter, and help her really notice them by pointing out particular aspects that would appeal to her and asking questions. One finding of the Tisdale (2004) study is that the social interaction between parent and child increased engagement in certain exhibits. Encourage your daughter to make a list of questions for follow up at home. The more that your daughter is able to take ownership of the trip, the more engaged she will be in the experience.

Post-trip reflection. Take advantage of the interest that your daughter has demonstrated on a trip to deepen her knowledge and awareness by following up with questions like:

¤ What did you experience or learn that was new? (This may be especially important if your child has a high level of expertise already in the content area)

¤ What was the highlight of the trip for you?

Other follow-up activities include reviewing brochures or photos from the trip, taking a book out of the library or viewing a video related to some aspect of the trip, visiting a relevant website, or interviewing someone who has spent a lot of time in that place or has particular expertise on an aspect of STEM that you experienced.

Suggestions for Field Trips

Science and natural history museums are wonderful places to visit. In recent years, many have been seeking to enhance the educational value of their exhibits, adding interactive displays and finding ways to keep visitors engaged for a longer time and more deeply with the STEM content. In addition to regular exhibits, many have areas where your daughter can conduct hands-on experiments, construct models, and participate in interactive projects. In addition, these museums often sponsor special events. If you live near a STEM-focused museum, consider a membership, not only for the savings but also because they sponsor member-only events. Zoos and aquariums have interactive and explanatory exhibits as well as opportunities to observe animals in recreated habitats. Botanical gardens engage visitors in the study of botany.

Nature walks are accessible to all. If you live in a rural area or near a park, opportunities are easy to access and free. However, even city dwellers can observe nature by walking around different neighborhoods. You and your daughter can practice observing and noting plants and animal behavior. When visiting hiking trails and parks, look for their visitor centers, which often have interactive and explanatory exhibits as well as trail guides that explain the environmental habitats. Many national, state, and local parks have a center where visitors can see explanations of local environmental conditions, history of the park's founding, pictures of local fauna, and guides with descriptions of the habitats you will walk through. For example, Audubon centers offer opportunities to meet raptors (birds of prey) that have been rescued. Through family walks, you can learn about geology, botany, zoology, and living environments.

> *I enjoyed playing outside—our house backed up to the woods, and my brother, sister and I would walk through them for hours finding small springs, building 'houses' out of rocks and swinging from grapevines. We pretended we were explorers. Also, I would read anything I could get my hands on and just devour books. It helped me to escape to different worlds and travel without ever having to leave my small town.*
> —Elise Sarvas, D.D.S., M.S.D., M.P.H., clinical assistant professor of pediatric dentistry at the University of Minnesota

Trips to amusements parks can provide an opportunity to conduct an analysis of the physics and engineering of roller coasters. Many roller coasters move without engines and provide a fascinating example of how gravity can power movement. Among things to look at are the angles of the roller coasters, the speed at which they travel (often posted by the ride entrance or described in the park's brochure), and the way gravity is used in the design of the ride.

Look into local STEM institutions that permit visitors. For instance, some local water treatment plants offer tours to visitors. San Francisco Public Utilities Commission, Brightwater Clean-Water Treatment Facility in King County, WA, and New York City's Newtown Creek Waste Water Treatment are a few examples. Los Angeles Sewers offers both virtual and in-person tours. See what might be available close to where you live or where you might be visiting. The Hoover Dam located on the border between Arizona and Nevada is toured by about one million visitors annually.

Local bridges can be studied for construction and design elements. Some notable bridges that offer tours covering their design and history include Mackinac Bridge in Michigan, the Golden Gate Bridge in San Francisco, and the Brooklyn Bridge in New York City. City boat cruises, such as the Chicago Architecture Foundation cruise, include an explanation of major architectural building styles.

College campuses and municipalities often have free exhibits open to the public. In 2015, Dayton, OH, offered a Techfest, the University of Washington offered family-friendly Engineering Discovery Days, the University of Wisconsin at Madison offered an Engineering Expo so the public could explore projects by undergraduate and graduate students, and Charleston, SC, hosted a STEMfest with activities and displays at local colleges and venues throughout the city. Check websites for local colleges and universities to find similar events and exhibits, which have the added benefit of introducing your daughter to students and faculty members on a college campus. While visiting a college, you might want to take advantage of a tour for prospective students that includes visits to science laboratories and technology centers.

Visiting the same location multiple times, particularly in different seasons and when there are special events, can be fun. For instance, wildlife viewing at different times of the year offers opportunities to observe migration and nesting patterns of birds and animal behaviors that change with the season. Ecosystems change by season and raise questions, such as how ducks find food in the winter, how turtles stay warm in freezing temperatures, when baby geese hatch, and what deer eat as the weather gets cold.

Your family can also participate in citizen science activities such as bird counts, tree census events, and environmental stewardship activities, such as local beach and park clean-up days. These activities also develop a wider community of children and adults who are involved in and interested in STEM, including professionals. Local newspapers and other publications often include announcements of events. Consider subscribing to e-mail lists for notification from local conservation organizations, such as the Sierra Club and the Audubon Society. Websites such as http://scientificamerican.com and http://nationalgeographic.com describe opportunities throughout the United States.

Trips to workplaces can be illuminating for your daughter, whether they are STEM-focused or not, because technology and other aspects of STEM are found almost everywhere. Most workplaces rely on computers and mathematics as part of payroll and budgeting systems as well as internal and external communication. Building design incorporates engineering, whether in architectural designs or features such as hands-free door opening systems. Scientists may be able to offer laboratory tours and question-and-answer sessions. Ask around among your friends, relatives, and acquaintances to find opportunities for workplace visits by your daughter. Explain that you are trying to expose her to STEM in a variety of environments.

Discussions and activities about STEM can be integrated into any type of trip, even those that are not STEM focused. You can look for unfamiliar plants and animals and applications of technology to everyday problems. You can play math games while in transit and keep track of data (for example, the number of cows spotted or the ratio of red cars to black cars). You could look at the design of buildings and ask questions such as:

- What types of materials were used to design this building? Why?
- How are the separate pieces held together? Is there something else that might have been used that would make the building even stronger?
- What design features are distinctive and what function do they serve?
- What safety features have been incorporated into constructing this building?

While on trips with your daughter, model behaviors that promote scientific and mathematical reasoning, and show your curiosity about the unknown. Use excursions as opportunities to practice assertive communication and a growth mindset by asking questions. Model the joy of learning something new and the humility to ask questions and freedom from needing to be an authority on everything. Modeling an openness to learning and an inquisitive attitude will promote these qualities in your daughter.

CHAPTER 15

Encouraging Persistence, Creative Problem Solving, Leadership, and Teamwork

> *Something that contributed to my success was that growing up I played competitive sports. When you play competitive sports you learn that you don't always win. Girls tend to be very hard on themselves if they don't succeed, more so, I think, than guys. Competitive sports are a microcosm of life. You cannot always win, but you can get better. Girls need to understand that just because they don't necessarily get an A on a particular test doesn't mean that they're failures. If they want it, they have to keep working at it and realize that failure is part of the process. We learn from our mistakes*
> —Carol L. Ensinger, Ph.D., retired pharmaceutical industry chemist and project manager, South Carolina

STEM activities can increase your daughter's interest and skills in STEM fields and can also help her develop persistence, creative problem solving, leadership skills, and teamwork. These skills are critical in STEM and just as useful in other domains. In fact, because these qualities are universally important, you can help your daughter to develop them through activities that aren't directly STEM-relevant, transferring what she learns to STEM fields.

The Importance of Persistence

As mentioned previously, STEM not only has an issue of recruiting girls and women, but also of retaining them, referred to as the leaky pipeline. Those who decide to pursue a career in STEM face numerous obstacles, including stereotypes, bias, and chilly work environments. Moreover, STEM fields may have more than their share of built-in failure and experiences of poor performance. The scientific method, engineering design process, and computer programming all involve learning from mistakes, and having an experiment, design, or code fail is the rule rather than the exception. Furthermore, many introductory STEM courses at the college level are purposefully difficult in order to weed out students from the major who either don't have what it takes to succeed or aren't fully committed. Many STEM courses in college, regardless of level, are also graded on a curve, which forces the average grade for the class to be a C, and only allows the top percentiles of scores to be A's. As a result, if most of the class does very poorly on an exam, a grade of a 60 can be curved up to a B or even an A, and if the reverse happens with everyone doing well, a score of 85 can be curved down to a C. This means that students may end up receiving mixed reviews, including some sort of negative feedback, either in the form of an absolute score or a curved grade.

Gender Differences in Response to Success and Failure

These experiences of failure or poor performance are similarly applicable to boys, but boys don't have to also deal with the stereotypes and other issues that girls do. Additionally, there might be some gender differences in response to success and failure. As previously mentioned, girls have been found to be more likely than boys to believe that their successes in STEM are due to effort and their failures to lack of ability (Meece et al., 2006), which could lead to less persistence following failure. A study conducted by Lawner and Quinn (2016) found that after receiving a very high score on a novel task, college women and men had similar performance state self-esteem (how positive they feel about their intelligence and performance-related abilities at that moment). On the other hand, women had lower performance state self-esteem after receiving a very low score on that task, while men's performance state self-esteem was unaffected by the performance feedback. This finding and those reported by Meece and colleagues (2006) need to be replicated, but they provide some indication that girls and young women are harder on themselves in response to poor performance as compared to boys and young men, which has implications for persistence in STEM.

What Makes Those Who Persist Different?

Children who have a growth mindset tend to persist longer than those who have a fixed mindset when faced with challenges (Dweck & Sorich, 1999). This difference in persistence may be partly a direct effect of beliefs about intelligence, but it is likely also due to the influence of growth mindset on goals and task choice. People with a growth mindset tend to set learning or improvement goals, while those with a fixed mindset set performance goals. As a result, a growth mindset might allow people to see successes while those with a fixed mindset might see failure. For example, if a student's experiment didn't turn out correctly, but she was able to learn something from the results anyway, she would view the experience as successful if she has a growth mindset because it meets a learning goal. And if she didn't do particularly well on a task, but better than she had previously, she would see herself as having succeeded because her performance reflected improvement. In contrast, a student with a fixed mindset might view both of those situations as failures because she had set a performance goal of a particular outcome in an experiment or a high level of performance on a task, and she might then become discouraged and not want to try again.

Children with a growth mindset also tend to choose challenging tasks that allow them to learn, while those with a fixed mindset choose easier tasks that allow them to demonstrate their intelligence and the skills they already have (Dweck & Sorich, 1999). Thus, when children are in situations in which they don't have a choice and must deal with something difficult, those with a growth mindset have past experiences of dealing with challenges that can help them remain calm, not feel overwhelmed, and believe they will eventually improve.

If we focus on longer term persistence, rather than persistence on a discrete task, research with college students has found that professional role confidence predicts persistence in engineering (Cech, Rubineau, Silbey, & Seron, 2011). Professional role confidence comprises two domains: (1) expert confidence—the perception that you have the skills needed to succeed in your field, and (2) career-fit confidence—the belief that the career path for your profession fits with your interests and values. Cech and her colleagues' research measured professional role confidence in engineering courses at the end of engineering students' first year of college, and then used that to predict outcomes during students' senior year in terms of whether they completed an engineering major and how likely they thought it would be that they would be working as an engineer 5 years later. Expert confidence predicted whether students switched to another STEM major, and career-fit confidence predicted their intentions to work as an engineer 5 years after college, even when controlling for demographics, GPA, SAT scores, self-assessed math and writing ability, and family plans. Importantly, professional role confidence also explained gender differences in persistence in engineering.

What Can You Do to Encourage Persistence in Your Daughter?

A key way to encourage persistence in your daughter is to model persistence yourself. Think about the last time you were faced with a challenge, whether in your career or in any other area of your life. Did you:

- ¤ View the situation as a challenge or a threat?
- ¤ Give up easily or keep working at it?
- ¤ Set a performance goal or a goal to improve or learn something from the challenge?

¤ Think your abilities or something else about yourself was the reason you were struggling, or recognize that the situation would be challenging for anyone?

¤ Feel bad about yourself or your abilities?

¤ Respond in the way you hope your daughter would when faced with a challenge?

If the way you dealt with the challenge was not particularly resilient, think about what you could do differently the next time you're faced with a similar situation. Talk to your daughter about how you responded, particularly if she was aware of what happened. It's also important to model positive responses to success in which you take credit for your success but still emphasize a growth mindset rather than a fixed mindset. Think about the last time you did really well on something. Did you:

¤ Say that your success was just due to luck?

¤ Say it was an easy task and anyone could have done well on it?

¤ Emphasize that effort and hard work played an important role in your success?

¤ Say that your success was due to abilities and skills that you developed?

¤ Show that you were proud of your success?

You can also model persistence and a growth mindset by choosing challenging tasks over easy ones. Part of this involves admitting to your daughter when things are difficult for you, but still showing that you're confident you'll be able to deal with the challenge. For example, perhaps you've thought your daughter's school should start an annual science and technology exhibition but feel anxious about talking to the school board about your idea. Instead of trying to find another way to get the exhibition started that doesn't involve public speaking, you could tell your daughter that you're nervous about the presentation and find public speaking difficult, but that you're confident you'll do fine if you practice and get feedback on the presentation.

> *I danced about 30 hours a week growing up. I think balancing dance and school taught me the discipline I needed to succeed in my industry.*
> —Melissa Glifort, process engineer, Maine

Another significant way you can help your daughter is by responding to her successes and challenges in ways that encourage persistence, confidence, and a growth mindset. Tell your daughter that you're proud of her when she succeeds, but emphasize that it shows how much she's learned and improved and how much effort she put into her work. When she's faced with a challenge, encourage her to keep trying and focus on learning from the situation. And when she has the option of doing something that's easy that she's already mastered or something that's new and a bit harder, encourage her to take on the challenge and tell her that even though it will be difficult, she has an opportunity to learn and grow from the experience. Finally, make sure that you don't prevent her from making mistakes that she can learn from or unfairly ensuring that she succeeds. For example, it's fine to help your daughter with her homework if she's having trouble, but make sure you're asking her questions and guiding her to figure things out for herself rather than doing the work for her and giving her the answers. You can practice outside of the academic domain as well. For instance, you can encourage your daughter to focus on trying to improve her soccer skills rather than quitting the team if she feels that she's not very good at it, and you shouldn't violate rules just to make sure your daughter wins when playing board games. She should learn what it feels like when someone else wins and to not give up when she's challenged.

Creative Problem Solving

Traditionally, creativity has been thought of as something that is key to the arts, but not a major part of STEM. However, creativity is just as important in STEM as it is in art endeavors. Scientists and engineers constantly have to use their creativity to come up with ideas for new products or experiments and to figure out alternative ways of looking at problems or using products or techniques. As mentioned at the beginning of this book, the integral role of creativity and innovation in STEM fields is part of the reason diversity of teams is so important (Phillips, 2014). Particularly critical for success in STEM is creative problem solving. This kind of creativity differs somewhat from the kind of creativity emphasized in the arts, but there is substantial overlap. Keep in mind that when your daughter is developing her creative skills in any area, she is developing her ability to solve problems.

> We were always outside and playing these crazy games, being very inventive. I think just building that general creativity got me more interested in science, because in science you have to be very creative to come up with new solutions for these problems.
>
> —Christine Doherty, physiology and neurobiology major at the University of Connecticut

How to Help Your Daughter Develop Her Creativity

A good way to start is by encouraging and providing opportunities for your daughter to explore artistic and creative endeavors. These experiences work even better for developing the kind of creativity used in STEM if they involve looking at an object, situation, or problem in different ways. One example that is appropriate for young children is doing arts and crafts with a mix of typical craft items and everyday household objects, such as cotton balls or egg cartons. To make it more interesting, you can provide your daughter with some specific guidelines—perhaps the final product should include a few specific items or be inspired by or relate to her favorite animal, book, or place to visit. Similarly, if your daughter is young, she can use household objects as musical instruments. Pots and large empty containers make great drums, and if you fill a small container with dried beans or grains, it becomes a maraca.

A more general way to have your daughter practice brainstorming alternate ways of using everyday objects is by making a game out of a common way that researchers measure creativity: the Alternate Uses Test (Guilford, 1967). People are given a set amount of time to come up with as many uses as possible for one specific item, such as a brick or a wire hanger. Responses are then rated in terms of the total number of uses, as well as the originality of each use (do a lot of people come up with the same use for that object?), how many different categories the uses fall into, and the amount of detail. As a game, you can make it a bit simpler by focusing on only one or two of those aspects. For example, each person gets a point for each use that no one else came up with. Alternatively, everyone gets a point for each use they come up with, and then one person in each round gets a bonus point for the most creative use—as voted on by the other players. With variations, this game can be used with children and adolescents of all ages. Even adults will find it fun and informative to test out and improve their creative skills.

Word games can be a great way to demonstrate the perspective-taking side of creativity. You can point out to your daughter that if she shuffles around her letters for Scrabble or Bananagrams or turns the board for Boggle, the difference in perspective will help her come up with many more word possibilities. For older girls, you can add perspective-taking to the Continue the Story game by changing it so that you not only have to continue the story at the point at which the last person left off, but you also have to continue the story from a different character's point of view.

Making Adjustments in Everyday Life

Your daughter can practice the problem-solving aspect of creativity by helping you come up with adjustments to recipes when you're cooking. For example, if a recipe calls for an ingredient that you don't have or that someone in the family is allergic to or doesn't like, ask your daughter to help you brainstorm a suitable substitution. You can even incorporate science as you discuss the role the ingredient plays in the recipe and what other items could do the same thing (e.g., lemon juice and vinegar are both acids, so you might be able to substitute one for the other in a dressing). You can do the same thing if a recipe calls for a piece of equipment you don't have, asking your daughter to help you figure out how to make the recipe without that specific tool.

Finally, all of our examples work even better when you involve more people. It allows your daughter to see wide variety in response to the same task and how people's ideas often relate to their interests and past experiences.

The Importance of Leadership and Teamwork

Many careers in STEM, like careers in other fields, involve working in a team to a certain extent. Although scientists and engineers may have a lot of solitary tasks, they are often part of larger projects that involve collaboration. To be successful in these careers, girls need to be able to work well with others who may be different from them in their skills, background, and even dedication to the project. They also need to know how to lead a team, as well as do their best work and get their ideas heard when they are not the official leader of a team. These are the "soft" skills that are transferrable from one context to another and are often not directly taught in school, but can distinguish those who do okay in their careers from those who truly excel.

> Project based learning takes a problem that is of interest or relevant to the student, and allows her to use all the tools in her toolbox (and learn new ones) to solve it. It promotes teamwork, critical thinking, an iterative process, project planning, asking for help, etc. Most importantly, however, it also provides an avenue by which those students who are not super jazzed about STEM can understand how the role of communicator, photographer, accountant, etc. are equally important in STEM fields.
>
> —Kate Pickle, deputy director of Science Club for Girls, Massachusetts

Tips for Helping Your Daughter Practice Leadership and Teamwork

The best way for your daughter to develop leadership and teamwork skills is by having as many opportunities as possible to work in a team, especially when the experiences vary in the type, size, and structure of the team and her role on the team. Getting feedback about how well she functions as a team leader or member is also important because it allows her to learn about her strengths and recognize areas that need attention.

Team sports are an obvious way for your daughter to develop her teamwork skills, but she can also get involved in other group extracurricular activities, such as a school science Olympiad team. Noncompetitive experiences for leadership and teamwork include participating in student government, committees, and fundraising events (which come with the bonus of involving math and data). If your daughter tends to be less vocal, urge her to take on a leadership role. If she feels comfortable being a leader and often plays that role, encourage her to sometimes find ways to contribute and make herself heard without necessarily being the one in charge. This experience will come in handy at the beginning of her future career when she will likely not have as many opportunities to lead a team. You should also encourage her, whether she's in a leadership role or not, to think about how to best use the skills of everyone in the group.

Beyond team-based extracurricular activities, there are other contexts in which your daughter might try to accomplish something with a group, perhaps within your own family. Family members can provide a supportive environment for your daughter to practice and develop leadership and teamwork skills, whether it's communication, decision making, delegation and division of responsibilities, or conflict resolution. Although adults are the clear leaders of your family, your daughter can take on responsibility and use her skills to help accomplish a family goal—there may even be some areas in which your daughter's skills are above the rest of the family's. For example, if your daughter is adept at using photo-editing software, she can create mock-ups of your family's holiday card. Depending on your daughter's age, you may also be able to put her in charge of a specific aspect of a larger project or even have her act as a coleader, working with you to break a larger project into smaller tasks and delegate those to the family members who would be best at them. You can do this when planning a family vacation or birthday party or helping put together a piece of furniture. With each of these teamwork experiences, give your daughter feedback and encouragement, and point out how she can apply what she learned to working on group school projects or extracurricular team activities.

> *I have always been fascinated with communications as a conduit for building relationships, sustaining careers and leveraging skills to be viewed as a leader. I combined my passion for business with my passion for leadership development into a career as an executive/career coach with an emphasis on communicating with impact and leveraging talent for success.*
> —Karen W. Solorow, president of Coaching for Success and former banker, New York

Beginning to Create a Network

One of the outcomes of a good team experience is the development of solid relationships with others. Help your daughter recognize the value of those relationships, how each person might become part of her personal or professional network. When it is time for her to get help with a project she's working on, she can look to her network to see which individuals have the skills or experience she might need.

A network depends on mutually beneficial relationships. If one person is always asking for assistance, while someone else is typically providing it, the relationship is not likely to last. Emphasize to your daughter that if she meets someone at camp or a science fair or on a family trip, she shouldn't expect the relationship to stay strong if neither person is making an effort to stay in touch or only one person is doing so. With all of the social media available today, it is very easy to stay connected. It could be as simple as sending a quick e-mail, a Facebook message, or a text from time to time. People aren't going to be receptive to requests if that's the only time they hear from a connection. Because networking is very important in career building, you'll find more information about this topic in the last chapter of this book. Regardless of your daughter's age, she can begin to learn how to build strong and genuine relationships.

> *A good IT person not only creates a network, but needs to be a teacher for all those using it. Troubleshooting takes a lot of patience and a degree of creative thinking.*
> —Patty Laughlin, retired Microsoft-certified IT engineer, Missouri End box

Persistence, creative problem solving, and teamwork are invaluable both in STEM and in other domains. To help your daughter make the best use of these skills in STEM, you can use the tips throughout this chapter in a STEM context or add a STEM twist to the activities. However, development of persistence, creativity, and teamwork outside of STEM can also be useful, so encourage the development of these skills in a variety of settings and with a wide range of topics.

CHAPTER 16

Preparing Girls for Engagement in STEM After High School

> *My parents always encouraged learning. When I was young they made sure computer games were educational, enrolled me in community education courses, and reminded me that no matter how frustrating my homework was, math and science would serve me well. They read with me a lot, and it definitely helped in all aspects of my life, especially when it came to my STEM courses.*
>
> —Jessica Kay, B.S. in genomics and molecular genetics and M.P.H., marketing rep at the Detroit Medical Center, Michigan

Beyond the many things you can do as a parent to help your daughter establish an early interest in STEM, there are ways you can help prepare her during high school to continue her engagement in STEM when she enters college.

Choosing the Level of STEM Courses in High School

Preparation for STEM majors and careers can occur in several ways, starting with the courses your daughter takes in school. By high school, students generally have some choice about the courses they take, both in terms of level (for instance, regular, honors, and Advanced Placement courses for the same subject may all be options) and the specific course within a subject area, such as science (for example, the choice might be between physics and environmental science). The choices become greater as students reach their junior and senior years. Although not all schools require 4 years of math and science, strongly encourage your daughter to take math and science every year in high school. Doing so will not only increase her chances of getting into college, but without that background, she would have a more difficult time majoring in a STEM field. Remind her of the importance of keeping her options open.

It's important for your daughter to take on the most challenging courses that she can handle. Not only will taking advanced courses help her get into college, but it will help her be better prepared for the difficulty of college coursework. Some students worry about balancing their GPA against rigorous preparation. However, colleges usually consider the level of the courses taken when looking at a student's record. A somewhat lower grade in a challenging course may well be looked at more favorably than an A in an easy one. If your daughter is not particularly confident in her abilities or is very sensitive to negative feedback, she may want to choose courses that are not as difficult. But remind her that initial difficulties in a class don't necessarily predict how well she will do in the future. Encourage her to seek help from her teachers. She may also be influenced by which courses her friends are planning on taking. Getting opinions from teachers, guidance counselors, or department heads can be helpful, but only if they can accurately assess your daughter's abilities. Because there is some evidence of gender bias among teachers when it comes to assessing students' abilities in STEM (Lavy & Sand, 2015; Riegle-Crumb & Humphries, 2012), it would be wise to take educators' assessment of the appropriate courses for your daughter with a grain of salt, particularly in STEM. Better yet, instead of asking them which course your daughter should take, you can ask what criteria they would use to decide whether a course is a good fit for a student, and then you and your daughter can decide whether you think she would be successful in that class and whether it's the best fit in terms of her abilities and interests.

Deciding on Course Topics

By the time your daughter reaches her junior or senior year of high school, she will likely have options for her science subjects, and possibly in math as well. Your daughter's interest in a particular course might be based on the subject matter, the format of the course (How hands-on is it?), the instructor, and whether her friends are taking the same class. Interest in the subject matter should be the primary criterion, but because a bad instructor or boring course format can turn girls away from a particular area of science or STEM in general, those are important considerations as well. Furthermore, because the different areas of science are related, there may be ways for your daughter to explore her interest in a particular area through a different course, especially when she gets to choose topics for assignments.

> *I had the worst chemistry teacher on the planet. She didn't like girls and did not encourage us, so I went outside the school system. I went to a college to get credit for it because I couldn't tolerate her harassment. Even when I got to college, you had to take at least one chemistry course, and I was so scared of it and had such a bad experience with it that I opted for four physics courses instead. I almost minored in physics just to avoid chemistry, which is sad because I think I would have done well in it.*
> —Karen Panetta, Ph.D., founder of Nerd Girls and associate dean of graduate engineering education at Tufts University

Another thing for your daughter to keep in mind when choosing a course is the possible trade-off between choosing a topic that she finds interesting and the level options for that topic. Schools may not offer multiple levels of science classes for areas that are not as popular, particularly if the school is small. Sometimes interest can outweigh considerations of difficulty, but it's important to consider how taking a course that is too easy or too difficult will affect your daughter's interest in the topic. Getting into classes of one's choice can be a real battle in overcrowded urban schools. As a parent in this situation, you might need to advocate with the department head or the school principal.

In addition to having options for courses in different areas of science, your daughter may also be able to choose which social studies course she takes, and some of the options can be in STEM fields, such as psychology, economics, or sociology. If your daughter has a strong interest in science, encourage her to take a social science course as her social studies course. Depending on the school, your daughter may also have multiple options for math, such as calculus versus statistics, and she may be able to use her elective options to take more than one math, science, or social studies course during a particular year.

Exploring Aspects of STEM Not Covered in School

For a variety of reasons—small size, funding limitations, and overcrowding—some high schools may not offer a full complement of STEM courses. In particular, because it is not a graduation requirement, engineering and technology classes may not be offered at all at your child's school. In addition, advanced coursework in math and science may not be readily available, or the classes may be of poor quality. Outside of regularly offered STEM classes, your daughter can gain familiarity with some of the lesser known areas through reading, web-based activities and courses, and afterschool and weekend activities. Look for experiences that are rigorous and relevant to your daughter's interests.

Applied aspects of STEM can be integrated into core classes. For instance, assignments to read or write a biography provide an opportunity to learn about the life of a woman involved in STEM, including engineers and computer scientists. Some language arts and social studies classes provide the option of creating a three-dimensional project in lieu of a book report, which can provide an engineering opportunity. Use of technology to create reports for all subject areas can enhance the opportunities for your daughter to use her STEM expertise.

Exploring Web Resources

A wide variety of websites offer information and activities about STEM for all educational levels. Khan Academy (http://khanacademy. org) provides user-friendly tutorials on many subjects, ranging from algebra to computer programming. Sodaplay (http://sodaplay.com) offers projects in virtual engineering and allows users to share the models they have created with others. For example, a girl might design an animated animal that is able to walk, which usually takes about 20 hours, and can also play with models that other users have created. Blockly (http://blockly-games.appspot.com), a Google project designed for those without experience in programming, teaches them the basics of programming. Another site that offers online courses in coding is http://code.org, which works to ensure that schools provide access to computer science.

> *Early on, use open-source professional and amateur tools, such as Mozilla's webmaker, popcorn, Scratch, to get girls comfortable with electronic design and coding before they hit adolescence and receive the message that girls aren't good at STEM.*
>
> —Louisa Campbell, principal investigator and project director of gadgITERATION; assistant professor of media design at Parsons School of Design, New York

Access to College-Level Learning

Some colleges permit high school students to enroll in continuing education and college-level coursework, and some high school systems have formal arrangements with local colleges to facilitate enrollment for advanced students. Another option if you cannot access a physical campus is to consider a MOOC—Massive Open Online Course. The largest is Coursera, with more than 100 university partners, including Duke and the University of Pennsylvania. Another is edX with 30 partners, including MIT and Harvard. The challenge of a MOOC is the self-discipline required to complete the coursework; your daughter may need some support in setting up a regular time and place for study. Various levels are permitted, including auditing of the class, and some colleges will award credit for students who fully complete the coursework and assessments (quizzes, exams, and assignments).

At any point in your daughter's education, she can find opportunities to explore new areas. Summer college classes as a visiting student, internships, and international programs are all avenues through which professional women in STEM have discovered careers that they love.

Out-of-School STEM Experiences

Afterschool, summer, and weekend programs can provide significant enrichment opportunities. Many are sponsored by universities and museums. A meta-analysis of 56 studies found that participation in out-of-school programs can significantly increase students' achievement in mathematics as well as reading (Lauer et al., 2003). The best results were found for high school students in mathematics achievement. Quality programs can be difficult to find, as there is no central agency that serves as a clearinghouse. Check local universities and museums and talk to teachers and school administrators. Some localities have a youth services department that may be able to direct you to opportunities.

> *In high school I was chosen as one of the two delegates from Tennessee to attend the National Youth Science Camp—a huge honor. It was great—you'd go to science lectures in the morning and evening, have small seminars on everything from stargazing to C++ programming to yoga, plus all of the outdoor extracurriculars you could want, such as hiking, mountain biking, and spelunking.*
>
> —Elise Sarvas, D.D.S., M.S.D., M.P.H., clinical assistant professor of pediatric dentistry at the University of Minnesota

First Robotics. In 1989, inventor and entrepreneur Dean Kamen started an organization that has inspired thousands of young people to participate in STEM in a fun way. FIRST (For Inspiration and Recognition of Science and Technology) provides programs in STEM that also build confidence and life skills. With hundreds of thousands of volunteers (you could become one—a real inspiration for your daughter), the organization is supported by thousands of companies, schools, and professional associations. Programs provide robotics-based experience and contests for girls and boys from kindergarten through the end of high school. At the youngest age level is the Junior FIRST LEGO League and at the oldest is the FIRST Robotics Competition. Some teams are coed, but many single-sex teams also participate. Girls might start with participation in the Junior FIRST LEGO League in first grade and go to building a 120-pound robot over a 6-week period from a kit of parts provided by the FIRST Robotics Competition as a junior in high school.

> *My high school teachers were very supportive of the FIRST robotics program at our school. I also had a good CISCO networking teacher who got to know and encourage students. It was a small class and he was there because he wanted to be so it was somewhat of an inclusive 'nerd club' environment.*
>
> —Ashley Odom, BS in computer science and public policy, MBA; senior consultant at the Public Consulting Group, Massachusetts

Girls Who Code. Girls Who Code was founded in 2012 by Reshma Saujani to increase the number of girls in computer science. Girls Who Code has clubs in more than 25 states where 6th- through

12th-grade girls learn to code through project-based activities. The clubs also aim to expose girls to role models in tech by bringing in speakers as well as organizing field trips. Girls Who Code also has 7-week summer immersion programs in more than 10 cities across the country that are specifically for rising juniors and seniors in high school. The summer program not only teaches girls about many aspects of computer science, including robotics and mobile development, but also includes mentorship, exposure to role models, and field trips to schools and tech companies.

Junior Membership in Professional Organizations

One excellent way to foster a sense of identity with the STEM field, learn about current developments in the frontiers of professional knowledge, and access scholarships and contests is to join a professional STEM association as a junior member.

The American Association for the Advancement of Science offers a student membership that includes a subscription to *Science*, a prestigious weekly professional journal that contains articles written at a layperson's level, and access to archived articles online. The content is excellent for use in high school papers and projects and covers the full range of STEM advancements. *Science* has recently had female editors in chief, and each issue includes plentiful information about women making advances in the field.

Future Business Leaders of America, a national business organization, offers middle and high school students opportunities to learn about various aspects of the business world and has a section on the tech aspects of business. College and high school students can join the American Mathematical Society with benefits that include student blogs, career advice, travel grants and fellowships, and free subscriptions to Notices and Bulletins. Your daughter also might be interested in the free math help that she can access on the AMS site (http://www.ams.org).

> *In high school, my math teacher invited me to join Math League, which is basically a test top students take and compete against other schools. I also was invited to join Science League. Being a member of these allowed me to realize that I was good at these subjects.*
> —Amanda McKnight, student majoring in chemical engineering and chemistry at the University of New Haven.

The National Academy of Engineering provides access to http://engineergirl.org, which provides information about programs and scholarships as well as the opportunity to ask questions about the field. The "Try on a Career" section gives information about each subfield of engineering, including educational requirements, lifestyle, starting salary, and examples of projects. Your daughter might want to check out the Association for Women in Mathematics, which provides opportunities such as Sonia Kovalevsky Mathematics Days, during which high school and middle school girls take workshops and participate in problem-solving competitions. The organization also holds an annual essay contest on biographies of contemporary women in math for students from grades 6 through college. The Society of Women Engineers offers K–12 memberships and career-building events, scholarships, and other opportunities.

> *During high school, but outside of school, I was very involved with the Junior Academy of Sciences, though admittedly my interest was less about the subject area and more about meeting other kids, and, what's that other species? Right, boys. I also spent the summer after 10th grade at a summer math program at the University of New Hampshire, sponsored by NSF.*
> —Caroline Hecht, computer programmer and web developer, Cornell University

In most high schools and colleges, students can form their own clubs by securing a commitment from a faculty advisor and a certain number of fellow students. Organizing a new club is a wonderful way for your daughter to develop her leadership and teamwork skills.

Choosing Colleges

In considering colleges, your daughter should find out about typical class size (with large lecture classes, she might have limited opportunity to ask questions) and the learning approach emphasized, such as whether there is a focus on project work and whether lab opportunities are abundant. Are research opportunities available? Who teaches the courses—are they mainly graduate students or faculty with doctorate degrees? She should also investigate retention figures, which are sometimes tracked by ethnic group and gender. In her college search, your daughter might want to consider all-female colleges, where she might feel more comfortable competing and speaking up. She should also be thinking about the size of the school. Although larger universities have more options, smaller colleges allow for more interaction with professors. In addition, some colleges have agreements with nearby institutions, in which students can take courses not only at their own school but at other colleges as well.

In addition to these broad considerations, it's important to know how a school stacks up for the particular majors your daughter is considering because schools' overall strengths can differ from the strengths of particular programs. Obviously, the first step is to find out what majors your daughter is interested in. Have your daughter make a list of every major she's considering, in order of interest. Even if she is set on a particular major, have her list at least three possible majors as many college students switch majors. Then you and your daughter can find out which schools have those majors and how strong those departments are. Keep in mind that many schools allow students to create their own major by combining courses in related areas. For each major, your daughter should consider the focus and structure of the program, class size, and opportunities for research and other experiences, such as internships or study abroad programs with courses that count toward the major.

> *When I was in high school I was interested in math and science, so when I got to college I planned to major in biology. I didn't even know what engineering was until I became friendly with some classmates who were majoring in engineering. I switched majors as a sophomore once I realized that engineering was the best of both math and science—it is a good way to apply math skills for a practical purpose.*
>
> —Jennifer Tosi, B.A. in engineering, vice-president at Morgan Stanley, New York

Outside of specific majors, your daughter may also want to consider whether schools have clubs or organizations related to her academic interests, scholarships, interdisciplinary or other special academic programs, and ways of meeting general education requirements that incorporate her interest in a specific area, such as a first-year writing course that focuses on writing in the sciences. In addition, your daughter may be interested in dorms or living groups that focus on a particular interest. For example, the University of Connecticut has a freshman dorm for women in STEM majors called Women in Math, Science, and Engineering (WiMSE).

Because there are a lot of factors to keep in mind, particularly when you add in those not related to the academics of a school (such as tuition, size, and location), it can be helpful to use a spreadsheet to keep track of everything. Your daughter can organize the spreadsheet by the importance of each factor so that she doesn't find herself making decisions about where to apply based on aspects that aren't particularly important to her.

Although this section has provided lots of information about what you, as a parent, can do for and with your daughter, the chapters in the next section focus on another important role you can play—as an advocate in the educational system—not only for your daughter, but for all girls.

Advocating in the Educational System

As a parent, you naturally have a strong interest in making sure that your daughter receives an ideal education. This section describes the many ways you can help your daughter get the best STEM education possible, while also paving the way for an optimal learning experience for all children, including those who have disabilities and those who are gifted. Consider the extra power that comes with partnering with teachers, school administrators, and other parents.

CHAPTER 17

Advocating to Create Gender-Neutral and STEM-Rich Classrooms and Afterschool Experiences

> *I went to an all-girls public school and had really good chemistry teachers who were women. The first chemistry teacher had a career in chemistry before teaching, and I graduated in 1980, so this was a lady who in the 1950s and 60s was doing chemistry and could relate real-life examples. Our second-year chemistry teacher was going back to school to get additional certifications. So both of them were pretty inspiring to me in terms of what you could do. And they definitely had a passion for what they did.*
> —Kathy Callahan, retired chemical and business executive, Pennsylvania

Teacher attitudes and behaviors can make a significant difference in your daughter's interest and confidence in STEM. This chapter focuses on how you can use your observations, knowledge, and experience to advocate for classroom and schoolwide actions to support girls' engagement in STEM from kindergarten through the end of high school.

Being Gender Neutral in Language and Attention

Gender-neutral and gender-inclusive language employs words and phrases that are free of reference to gender where appropriate and that avoid assigning gender to activities and roles that can be conducted by all people. For instance, a member of Congress is not necessarily male, and therefore "Congressional representative" is a more inclusive reference than "Congressman." Using the pronouns "he or she" to refer to mathematicians or alternating "he" and "she" would be another example.

The National Center for Education Research's "Encouraging Girls in Math and Science" (Halpern et al., 2007) guide suggested that using gender-neutral and inclusive language in the classroom and calling equally on girls and boys are two impactful practices. The goal is to create an equitable environment in which girls and boys are similarly comfortable and able to learn about STEM. To do this, teachers need to follow up in comparable ways to the responses of all students, regardless of gender, asking them to explain and explore their initial answers and using specific and concrete feedback.

When Lavy and Sand (2015) studied the long-term impact of teacher bias at the elementary school level on students' course selection and achievement in middle and high school math and science class, they found that, in general, girls' performance in math on classroom tests was lower than their performance on national tests, while boys' performance on classroom tests was higher than their performance on national tests. Teachers know the gender of students for classroom tests while national tests are likely to be machine-scored or identified by a student number, which is gender neutral. In other words, the teachers were biased and their grading in class overestimated boys' math abilities and underestimated girls' abilities. However, teachers varied in how much of a gap there was between their male and female students' classroom test grades and their national test scores, which the researchers used as a measure of the teachers' level of bias. Lavy and Sand found that the more biased a girl's sixth-grade math teacher was, the worse she did on a standardized math assessment in eighth grade and on matriculation exams at the end of 12th grade, and the fewer advanced math courses she took in high school. Clearly teacher bias can have a long-term impact on performance and preparation in STEM. As a parent, you may want to compare your daughter's performance on assessments graded by her teacher and those on standardized exams that are graded without knowledge of gender and address any differences with the teacher.

> *My teachers always saw my love of numbers and probably recognized that I was energized by challenges, so they gave me tougher math questions, which I tackled with relish.*
>
> —Karen W. Solorow, president of Coaching for Success and former banker, New York

Teachers should be conscious of the time that girls have with hands-on lab equipment and technology to ensure that it is the same as what boys receive. Fancsali (2002) noted, in a summary of research on girls and STEM, that when working in groups, boys tend to "hog" the equipment. Even if the children state that it is by preference that boys are taking more time, teachers should stress the importance of everyone having equal experience.

Teachers should make sure that feedback to boys and girls is equivalent—that boys aren't praised more or in different ways than girls are. Promoting a growth mindset is also critical, as described in earlier chapters. When commenting on student work, teachers should praise effort and be specific in their feedback to build competence and confidence. This applies across all areas of study, not just for STEM subjects. When giving negative feedback, it is important to be clear about how students can improve and to also make it clear that they're giving critical feedback because they know the student has a lot of potential and can do better with some guidance. This is especially important for students who must deal with negative stereotypes about their abilities in general or in the specific subject (Steele et al., 2002).

Teachers Setting Norms

Teachers set the norms for student discussions and should be conscious of the amount of time that boys and girls are speaking and that they follow up equally with boys and girls to deepen the thinking and responses of all students. Gender-neutral language should be a classroom norm followed by all students, not just the teacher. Classrooms need to be safe spaces for all students, and respectful language and behavior should be the standard for teachers and children alike. It is important to address inappropriate student comments publicly and immediately so that all students—bystanders as well as those involved in making and receiving comments—are aware of the classroom norms for acceptable behavior. Publicly commenting affirms the safety of the individuals who may feel demeaned, and the immediacy clears the air for the students to focus on work.

At the post-high school level, a study at three community colleges found that "microaggressions," which are brief, everyday comments or behaviors that are insulting, led to poorer academic performance (Suarez-Orozco et al., 2015). Microaggressions are based on status or identity and include staring, ignoring, and making comments that are demeaning. Although the Suarez-Orozco et al. study was done with college students, it is likely that similar results would occur for those who are younger. As a parent, when you hear about microaggressions at your daughter's school, that's a good time to talk to a teacher or administrator about the adverse effects of these kinds of incidents on school performance and about the possible courses of action that can be taken to improve the social atmosphere.

> *I was in a class with 28 males and one other female. The teacher once asked us if we were in the class—and in the engineering program—because we wanted to find a good husband. We were pretty insulted, livid actually. But we won him over when we kicked butt in the class and both got A's.*
> —Jennifer Tosi, B.A. in engineering, vice-president at Morgan Stanley

The Girls Incorporated organization offers a set of guidelines called "Tips for Encouraging Girls in STEM" at http://girlsinc.org/resources/tips-encouraging-girls-stem.html that can be used by teachers. One key guideline refers to helping girls embrace the "ick" factor. Societal messages to girls encourage them to avoid getting messy or touching things that they find "gross." Teachers can address this negative attitude by modeling, avoiding language that reinforces a sense of disgust, and encouraging girls to get their hands on items such as worms for dissection, messy (but safe) chemicals, and goo.

Reinforcing the idea that girls have STEM-related skills is another action teachers can take. A number of the women in STEM whom we interviewed commented on the importance of positive feedback by teachers in developing their confidence and commitment to STEM.

> *High school teachers have a big role in helping girls pursue STEM because high school can be a very unsupportive place for girls who excel in math or science. Real-world applications and examples will increase engagement, but there's a bigger social element to navigate—the number of girls in those classes can start waning. High school teachers should first and foremost treat all their students equally, and then think about reaching out to girls who are excelling in those classes and offer advice and support for choosing a STEM career.*
> —Michelle DePinho, civil engineering student at Manhattan College

Fostering a STEM-Rich Classroom

Classrooms that are rich in STEM benefit all students. For girls who may not see themselves as interested in STEM, having a wide variety of appealing materials and interesting experiences may serve to spark their engagement.

With a bit of creativity, STEM can be integrated into all subject areas. For instance, studying the Industrial Revolution offers an opportunity to discuss engineering advances, such as the phonograph and the steam engine. Biographies of women inventors, mathematicians, and scientists can be offered as part of the English language arts curriculum. Data collection and analysis can be included in any subject area—students might be asked to analyze the results of attitude survey data collected from their peers. Conversely, areas of interest to girls can be integrated into STEM. For instance, using technology, engineering, and math to solve a social problem could appeal to girls' social consciousness. Current events relating to STEM can be incorporated into lessons, and students can write a script for a TV show that demonstrates some of the concepts from their biology curriculum.

> *Teachers have so much on their plates with testing and other requirements, so thinking about incorporating engineering into their curriculum can be very daunting. They should not try to do it themselves. There are huge numbers of repositories and open source materials. Every professional organization, including the Institute of Electrical and Electronics Engineers, has educational outreach toolkits to help do this, and they're usually low-cost or no-cost and require no more than a half-hour preparation on the educator's part.*
> —Karen Panetta, Ph.D., founder of Nerd Girls and associate dean of graduate engineering education at Tufts University

As a parent, note the bulletin board content when you visit the classroom. Classroom bulletin boards can include images of women and girls engaging in STEM as well as visual STEM content such as solutions to mathematics problems and posters showing science project results. Sharing articles that you find about STEM that relate to your daughter's school curriculum can support the teacher's effort to find appealing materials to post. In addition to a physically enriched environment, a climate of excitement and enthusiasm about STEM promotes engagement and can be contagious.

> *What is most effective in our school is our problem based learning approach. By establishing a realistic situation and learning the techniques, vocabulary, and science behind the problem, students not only learn how to solve the problem, but they can also explain why their solution works, and know that it was their solution.*
> —Jeffrey Copperthite, math and engineering teacher at a specialized math and science high school, Connecticut

Encouraging Participation in Afterschool STEM Programs

Parents are in a strong position to advocate for extracurricular activities that will enhance their daughters' range of STEM experiences. Afterschool STEM clubs and research opportunities in local labs or universities can help to fill in the gaps in formal education and offer your daughter a way to engage with STEM on her own terms, following her own interests. Guidance counselors and teachers might also be aware of afterschool and college scholarships as well as contests that girls can apply for.

Your goal of expanding STEM opportunities is aligned with the pressures that school systems are under to meet the growing need for STEM-proficient students. Practically and strategically, you can assume that the absence of programs and opportunities reflect lack of resources rather than resistance to change. Share the resources in this book with teachers and school officials in a helpful and friendly spirit, affirming the challenges that underresourced educational institutions face.

> *My AP biology teacher noticed I liked biology and offered me a job with his friend doing research in the summer—I didn't know at the time that it was research on snakes! Tracking snakes meant long hours in the woods and getting bitten, and being a boy or a girl added nothing to your qualifications.*
> —Elise Sarvas, D.D.S., M.S.D., M.P.H., assistant clinical professor of pediatric dentistry at the University of Minnesota

Many national organizations, such as Girl Scouts and Girls Who Code, establish local groups or clubs in community settings. Sometimes, the most convenient place for their meetings is after school using the school building. Often, schools are happy to offer space when the school day has ended and do not charge for its use. In other instances, a fee is required to pay for cleaning or utility services. When schools recognize that an organization will offer curriculum (such as STEM) that enriches what they provide, they may welcome these organizations. As a parent, you may want to advocate to bring these organizations into your school.

The journal *AfterSchool Matters* is available in print and online through the Wellesley Centers for Women at Wellesley College's National Institute on Out of School Time (NIOST) at http://niost.org. This resource includes many articles on promoting girls' involvement in STEM through informal learning settings. The STEM Funders Network has launched the Building the Field: Designing and Implementing Community-Based STEM Learning Ecosystem Initiative (http://stemecosystems.org) to support the improvement of student performance in STEM fields and to increase participation in STEM careers. Although this initiative is not directed specifically toward females, it creates and connects STEM-rich environments and provides tools to educators, which support formal and informal STEM opportunities for all students.

With your support, schools can integrate STEM experiences into both extracurricular and supplemental activities. At all levels, teachers are looking for educational trips that can enhance and reinforce classroom learning. Some ideas for trips were described in Chapter 14 and can be adapted by schools. Volunteering to chaperone such a trip will help teachers and offer you another opportunity to bond with your daughter.

Students can initiate afterschool clubs in high school by recruiting a certain number of students and securing a faculty sponsor. School-sponsored afterschool and summer programs can supplement course offerings. Schools at all levels play an important role in disseminating information to students and families about summer and afterschool STEM programs, such as camps and weekend programs, as well as recommending individual students to participate in these STEM-focused activities. A parent offering to share information that the entire school can benefit from is a welcome advocate.

Instead of waiting for students to volunteer for extracurricular opportunities, teachers should be encouraged to seek out students who would benefit from them, particularly those who are from underrepresented groups (youth of color and girls). The experience of being recruited for a special challenge or activity is a powerful experience, one that can increase feelings of self-worth and a sense of belonging.

“ *With the Internet, there are so many free online courses and videos clips to pique interest in STEM fields, examples of women who have been remarkably successful in STEM fields, and an established network of mentors (including online mentors, such as iMentor and MentorNet).* ”

—Sylvia Barsion, Ph.D. in educational research, measurement and evaluation; writer and consultant, New York

Participating in a Science Fair—It's Her Project

If your daughter's school holds an annual science fair, encourage your daughter to participate in it. Keep in mind that it's the process of preparing the project, not winning, that is the objective. That means that your daughter should be the one who comes up with the idea and turns the idea into an exhibit, while learning new concepts and practicing persistence in the face of challenges. Although you can certainly help your daughter with brainstorming, answering questions, and suggesting resources, it is her science fair project and not yours. She will benefit much more when she does it herself, resulting in increased confidence and competence. Of course, if she decides to partner with a classmate, that's great, too—as long as she's truly an equal partner. That experience can be a reminder to her that STEM work is often collaborative and that working with someone else can mean learning from and building on each other's ideas and having fun.

If your daughter's school doesn't hold an annual science fair, consider getting together with other parents as well as school administrators, teachers, and students to organize one. As part of the day, think about including special guests—maybe a local female scientist, a STEM university researcher, and an entrepreneur involved in a STEM field. You might enlist the help of local companies that can provide support in the form of supplies. Although science fairs usually take the form of competitions, they do not have to be. Judges might question participants about their exhibit and give feedback. The emphasis should be on learning, exploring, and sharing.

> *In the fourth grade, I did a science fair project about autism. My younger sister has autism and epilepsy. For the fair, instead of doing an experiment you could talk about a scientific topic. At the time, not a lot of people knew about autism. My fourth-grade teacher didn't know what autism was. When the judges came up, I got to educate them. I won first place, so it was very exciting, and that bolstered my confidence in STEM.*
> —Christine Doherty, physiology and neurobiology major at the University of Connecticut

Engineering challenges and exhibitions can also engage students. Some schools now sponsor invention conventions or fairs in which students are challenged to create their own solutions to everyday problems. If one is occurring in your community, encourage your daughter to investigate it—as an observer or a participant, depending on the level.

Promoting Career Exploration

The school setting can be a powerful place for girls to learn about career options and to explore their talents and interests. Teachers have the opportunity to gain familiarity with individual students' strengths and hobbies and to connect these to potential career interests. Guest speakers from STEM fields that relate to curricular themes can enliven classroom experiences, while providing access to role models. Learning about some of the lesser known STEM fields and encountering role models in a group setting can foster a shared awareness among peers. For students who lack computers at home, school may be the best place to access web-based career exploration sites.

If you are a STEM professional or know women in STEM who might be willing to address a classroom or participate in a career day activity, let your daughter's teachers know. They may not have access to speakers through their own networks or are too busy to make the necessary arrangements for a school visit. Authors of children's books related to STEM careers might well be interested in coming to your daughter's school because that is a popular way of publicizing their books. If the author is local, you might not even have to pay a fee.

> *I would definitely encourage my daughters to pursue careers in STEM, and have already taken steps to promote the benefits of STEM in their early academic life. They have been enrolled in supplemental math programs since first grade to ensure they are confident in math. Initially, they didn't like math; now it is one of their favorite subjects. I also ensure that the girls participate in science fairs with items that interest them like erupting volcanoes.*
> —Racquel L. Santana, vice president of eBusiness strategy
> & execution at Travelers Insurance, Connecticut

The National Girls Collaborative Project (NGCP) is a key advocacy organization committed to informing and encouraging girls to pursue careers in STEM (http://ngcproject.org). NGCP organizes statewide networks that you can connect to through its website. It also conducts research and disseminates information on evidence-based practices and provides support for organizations to collaborate. You can search the directory for programs in your area, encourage quality programs to register, and share information about this resource with youth-serving organizations. You can also recommend it to local education officials as a resource to improve their STEM activities.

Teachers can recommend students for internships, special programs, and scholarships. Particularly if your daughter is shy, encourage her to share her interests with her teacher, and make sure that the teacher is aware of topics that are especially meaningful to her. It is important for your daughter to begin to see how her hobbies, interests, and talents can be connected to a wide variety of careers, some of which she has never considered before.

> *I worked in a lab at Ohio State University the summer before my senior year in high school, and in middle school I participated in Science Olympiad. In both cases, it was great to be surrounded by other people who were as obsessed with science as I was and always made me feel as though my love of science as a girl was nothing weird, but totally normal.*
> —Tara Mandalaywala, Ph.D., researcher of social
> cognition in primates at New York University

How to Advocate Effectively With Teachers and Administrators

As a parent, it is your right and responsibility to advocate for your daughter with teachers and administrators—while partnering with your daughter. It can be intimidating to speak to people with expertise in education about how they can do their jobs better, but remember that you are the expert on your child's needs. Parents may also worry about their child being singled out for negative attention if they raise a concern. Be positive and confident in your approach. Educators are usually interested in reaching all of their students and helping them succeed, and most are interested in continually improving their skills. If you approach them in a helpful and cooperative spirit, they are likely to be receptive. Work to build a relationship with your daughter's teachers year-round (not just when you have a complaint), which will increase their willingness to listen to your concerns without being defensive. End-of-year and holiday notes of thanks are very welcome by educators. If you have an area of expertise, volunteer to share it with the class; it doesn't have to be STEM-related. Whether it's speaking at career day in your daughter's class or chaperoning a field trip, connect with your daughter's teacher (and with her classmates). What is important is the positive rapport you're building.

In order to maximize the effectiveness of your communication, use the principles of assertive communication: maintain a respectful attitude toward the person you are advocating with, make "I" statements, and try to include positive feedback with your criticism. Make sure to acknowledge the very real barriers to granting your request and offer any assistance that might be useful. For instance, you might say something like the following: "I know that budgets for science labs are very limited but I would be very happy to speak or write about what this means to my daughter at the county budget meeting" or "I know that it must be difficult to get through the curriculum with 36 students who are all learning in different ways, but my daughter will understand the lesson better if she can hold the welding equipment herself and not only watch the boys do it." Offer to hear the teacher's concerns and goals and how you can support him or her to secure more classroom materials, such as putting out an appeal to fellow parents or assisting the teacher with setting up a donation request through the web-based classroom fund-raising page Donors Choose (http://www.donorschoose.org).

Using research literature to back up your requests can be a good way to approach a teacher or administrator while increasing your confidence. Provide guidelines and materials as informational resources. Feel free to use the articles and materials cited in this book. The articles can also contextualize the issue of equality in the classroom as a widespread social problem rather than as a deficit in this individual teacher.

> *I am so disappointed in my very quiet second daughter's teachers that she is never encouraged in STEM. I find that often when trying to encourage women to pursue STEM, people will portray the subject as being social. Yet women I know in STEM very much enjoy that their work involves less social interaction and more interaction with machinery or formulas. We need to entice the quiet girls who say they want to be librarians and writers and who like spending hours alone knitting and sewing to consider STEM jobs where they can spend hours alone computing or calculating. My outgoing daughter who could do well with humans or machines is the one being encouraged.*
> —Christina Sormani, Ph.D., math professor at City University of New York

Use written communication as well as oral. Particularly if the feedback you are giving is of a sensitive nature, putting it into a note enables you to state exactly what you want (and to edit your words carefully) while giving the teacher or administrator time to reflect and thoughtfully prepare a response. It also gives you an opportunity for someone else to read through what you are sending to see if it is communicating precisely what you wish. Just keep in mind that written communication loses the benefit of tone and inflection. A message that you would deliver in person with a smile or other sign of warmth will not be easily conveyed on the written page.

It's usually a good idea to address your individual concerns to the teacher directly before going up the chain of authority and that your first conversation be private. On the other hand, for systemic issues (such as funding for equipment) or very serious concerns (ongoing inappropriateness of a teacher who has been unresponsive to requests for an individual meeting), talk to other parents and go together as a group to meet with the school's administration. Find out the official channels and use them, but don't be afraid to move forward if you're blocked.

In all cases, be sure to show appreciation not only for changes made but also for listening and maintaining an open dialogue. The more that you are able to show gratitude and offer positive feedback, the more receptive educators will be to future change efforts, and you will reinforce the changes they have made.

CHAPTER 18

Working With Schools to Create Adaptations in STEM for Students With Disabilities

> *Technology has changed the way children with disabilities learn math and science. Forty years ago when I first started teaching children who were blind or had visual impairments, one of the few technologies available was the Kurzweil, a bulky piece of equipment that cost $50,000 and therefore was basically inaccessible to almost everyone. Now, one Kurzweil software version is readily available to translate written material into Braille for those who are visually impaired and another is available for children who have learning disabilities.*
>
> —Judy Strauss-Schwartz, teacher of the blind and visually impaired and certified orientation and mobility specialist, New York

Knowing about people with disabilities who have distinguished themselves in STEM can be inspiring to everyone, not just to those who have a disability. Temple Grandin made important advances in agricultural science, not in spite of her autism but perhaps because of it. Carol Greider didn't allow her reading disability to stand in her way and won a Nobel Prize in medicine for her work identifying an enzyme critical for cancer treatment.

Every student, including those with disabilities, has the right to a rich STEM education. This chapter provides information about adaptations and technologies that can be used in the classroom and innovative strategies that can open the STEM world to children with a wide variety of challenges. Although some schools have wonderful special education departments and access to the latest technology, many teachers need an advocate, like you, to partner with them to obtain the services, resources, and adaptations that students may need.

Adapting STEM Education for Students With Disabilities

If you are the parent of a child with a disability, make sure she is receiving all of the accommodations that are listed in her Individualized Education Plan (IEP) or 504 Plan. An IEP typically provides a broad range of services and equipment to a child with a specific diagnosed disability. A 504 Plan is usually for students who need specific accommodations, such as extended time on standardized tests, but can function well on an everyday basis. These plans outline the services to which a student is legally entitled.

Every child needs an advocate, but your advocacy actions are critical for a student with a disability, particularly if she is mainstreamed in a regular class and does not have a teacher specially trained in working with students with special needs. A wide range of supports are available but not necessarily readily considered. Others are quite expensive, but a school district may need to purchase a particular piece of equipment if mandated by a child's IEP or 504 Plan.

Matching Adaptations to Children's Special Needs

For students who have learning or visual disabilities, a huge number of audiobooks on STEM topics are available. Teachers can usually order classroom textbooks in an audio version at the same cost as those in print. Worksheets used by regular classroom teachers can be adapted—increasing contrast, changing colors, or enlarging print—as needed by individual students. In some instances, simple changes can make a real difference. For example, children who have low vision or are physically weak can use soft-lead art pencils instead of regular ones because they make a darker impression on paper and require less pressure.

> *I make tactile objects for students who are severely visually impaired or blind, using a wide variety of materials, such as duct tape, paper clips, miniature clothes pins, bubble plastic, pipe cleaners, Wikki sticks, and Braille labels and numbers. I even created a tactile board to illustrate DNA concepts for a high school student.*
> —Judy Strauss-Schwartz, teacher of the blind and visually impaired and certified orientation and mobility specialist, New York

Israel, Maynard, and Williamson (2013) noted that children with learning disabilities typically underperform in STEM for a variety of reasons, including the difficulty of focusing on abstract concepts, the complex vocabulary used in textbooks, and the lack of integration of STEM with other subjects. They suggest that teachers individually meet with students to find out about their concerns, use the vast array of digital resources that can make the material more accessible, and integrate exciting hands-on work (such as designing bridges or testing water purity) into the curriculum.

Although individuals diagnosed with autism spectrum disorder (ASD) pursue higher education to a much lower degree than those with most other disabilities, those who do attend are more likely to choose a major and a career in a STEM field. Indeed, 34% of those identified as having ASD in a college sample had declared a STEM major, which is higher than the 23% who did so in the general population (Wei,

Yu, Shattuck, McCracken, & Blackorby, 2013). However, the Wei et al. study also pointed to a very large gender gap among students with ASD—only 3% of females with that diagnosis who were in college declared a major in STEM while the figure for males with ASD was 39%. Although males are significantly more likely to be diagnosed with ASD than females, the extreme gender gap in majors highlights the urgent need for increasing STEM engagement among females with ASD at as early an age as possible.

Baron-Cohen (2009) suggested that high-functioning individuals with autism often have an aptitude for analyzing and constructing systems for explaining things, which may draw them to STEM fields. Although that propensity might be at play for males, which would account for the disproportionately higher percentage of males with ASD opting for a STEM major, research is needed to determine why females with ASD do not show the same preference. It may well be that the same issues described earlier in this book that keep females out of or leaving the STEM pipeline apply to females with ASD, maybe even more so since they're dealing with two stereotypes. When more is known about how and why autism manifests differently in males and females and how other people's reactions to that disability are influenced by gender, parents and teachers will be better able to develop strategies for encouraging STEM engagement tailored to females with ASD.

Research has indicated that when students who are deaf and hard-of-hearing (DHH) are taught by skilled instructors who teach from an understanding that their students are cognitively different from their hearing peers, those with a hearing disability do as well in learning STEM content as their hearing peers (Marschark, Sapere, Convertino, & Pelz, 2008). What those effective teachers are doing is matching their teaching methods to their DHH students' needs.

Parents of deaf children have a critical role to play by communicating in sign language and providing their children with access to STEM content that is age-appropriate and accessible. If a hearing classroom has a deaf student, teachers should make sure the student receives help with word problems, perhaps breaking down the problem into small pieces.

There is a distinct line dividing students who have parents who sign and students with parents who do not sign. Deaf children with signing parents have access to communication at home and are likely to be in the top classes and have reasoning skills way beyond their counterparts. Lip reading does not count as effective communication since it only catches, as a rule, 20% of the conversation and does not help to teach a first language.

—Jordan Katz, certified teacher of math for grades 9–12 and deaf education for K–12, New York

Many children (and their parents) struggle with attention deficit/hyperactivity disorder (ADHD), which often makes learning in school more challenging. Research has shown that when tasks are made more relevant and engaging to students with ADHD, they do better in school (Carlson, Booth, Shin, & Canu, 2002). Although doing that makes learning more effective for all children, it is absolutely critical for those with ADHD. Because of their difficulty attending to relevant information combined with a tendency toward impulsive behavior (Reardon & Naglieri, 1992), it is not surprising that many of those with ADHD have a hard time with STEM subjects, which require sustained attention. Although excessive fidgeting has long been viewed as a symptom of ADHD, research now indicates that increased motor activity might actually be a coping mechanism that allows children to learn more effectively (Hartanto, Krafft, Iosif, & Schweitzer, 2015). The implication for classroom management is clear—instead of trying to get children with ADHD to stop moving, give them objects with which they can fidget. The result may well be enhanced learning. In some cases, children with learning disabilities or ADHD "hyperfocus," making it difficult to get them to move away from a particular activity that has engaged them completely, but that characteristic could actually be an asset for inventors and researchers. Parents and teachers might be able to channel that extreme focus found in some students with ADHD into using technology or working with another appealing aspect of STEM.

Using Special Educational Strategies

Educators have developed a wide variety of strategies to reach students with disabilities. The engineering design process, a type of problem solving that involves gathering information, understanding challenges, evaluating progress, and testing solutions, can be effectively used to create and continually modify the kind of environment children with disabilities need to develop competence in STEM. As a parent, you can support teachers by brainstorming types of resources that can be used to establish the kind of classroom experience that works best with children with different types of special needs. Using the engineering design process means that the learning environment is constantly monitored and revised, with the goal of creating the most suitable classroom experience for each child. If your daughter is in middle or high school, she can learn about the engineering design process while using the strategy along with her teachers to figure out which accommodations would work best for her.

One of the most important considerations for good teaching is the recognition of learner variability present in a classroom. Providing different ways for students to learn takes into account the varying amounts of time different children need to develop competence in a subject, the range and type of stimulation that is optimal, and the level of complexity that can be achieved. Children learn more effectively if they have opportunities for hands-on exploration with subjects that are made relevant to their interests.

Many teachers have found that delivering content through several modes, rather than a single one, is often more effective in general, but specifically for children with disabilities. For instance, instead of just showing a math problem with a simple graph, teachers can represent the concept with charts, tables, and three-dimensional models.

> *I provide multiple ways for students to provide feedback and do their schoolwork, and I consider every single one of them. If a student asks for a reasonable accommodation ('Can I work with Susan? We work very well with each other'), I will provide it. I think other teachers can benefit from listening to their students, accommodating their needs appropriately, and having their students take ownership of their work.*
> —Jeffrey Copperthite, math and engineering teacher in a specialized math and science high school, Connecticut

Teachers are increasingly including inquiry-based instruction into the way they deliver STEM content. This method varies from a totally open learning environment with students determining what and how problems are to be solved to a more structured framework with teachers creating the question and methods of investigation and giving explicit feedback (Watt, Therrien, Kaldenberg, & Taylor, 2013). By attending to the type and degree of disability, teachers can create the most effective type of inquiry learning for individual students. Collaboration among students, between a student and her teacher, and between a regular classroom teacher and a special education specialist are all key pieces of effective inquiry-based STEM learning experiences. Giving children roles in which they can be successful is important for all children, but because those with disabilities often experience a disproportionate number of challenges and failures, teachers may need to give more thought to what they can do that will increase the odds of success. For example, when children are working in teams on an open-ended task, those who have a learning disability might need a bit more support with processing complex information. In general, encouraging a growth mindset will be particularly important because that allows children with disabilities to see the possibility of improving their school performance.

Setting up multiple stations in a classroom is a technique that works well with students with varying abilities. Teachers who use this approach for special days or kinds of work might well welcome you as a volunteer who can supervise one of the stations (with some training), which allows individual students or small groups to get extra attention. For example, if the topic is water pollution, one station gives children the opportunity to investigate ways to purify water using a variety of materials while another station provides opportunities to ask questions of an employee of the local water company. At a third station, children solve problems using charts and graphs about water pollution in their own and neighboring counties. You can imagine many more possible stations for this topic. If these kinds of opportunities are not offered at your daughter's school, consider volunteering (maybe with some other parents) to set up such a day, which would include finding guest speakers, obtaining materials, and developing activities, while making sure that that all children will be able to participate. Many professional STEM organizations have developed curricula they are happy to share and some even provide volunteers who work in a specialized field, such as environmental engineering.

Accommodations for a child with a disability might take the form of setting up a special area of the classroom—definitely not to isolate her but to ensure that she is in the best position to learn in school. For instance, children with chronic physical ailments and/or visual impairments might need a rolling cart right near their desks stocked with their special equipment. Those who are hard of hearing might do better sitting in a front center seat.

Using Technology Effectively

Screen readers and software programs provide magnification for students with low vision. Computers and cell phones provide accessibility to individuals with a wide range of disabilities, including visual, hearing, learning, and motor. Teachers and parents just need to locate the accessibility setting for a particular device and find the enhancement that works for the kind of disability that is present.

CCTV devices are video magnifiers that not only increase the size of print to allow children with vision issues to read, but they can also be used to magnify real objects, making parts of nature, for instance, accessible for the first time to a child.

I have put frogs and stink bugs under the CCTV so that the children I work with who have visual impairments can see them. Their classmates benefit, too, since the magnification allows them to see details they otherwise would miss.
—Judy Strauss-Schwartz, teacher of the blind and visually impaired
and certified orientation and mobility specialist, New York

One piece of equipment that has been found to be particularly useful in teaching STEM to children with disabilities is the iPad. Aronin and Floyd (2013) studied how these devices can be successfully used in teaching STEM in inclusive (mixed ability) preschools. Among the many benefits of the iPad (and other tablets) are the ease of carrying it around to different locations, the number of apps that are available for free or at low cost, and its relative durability. Aronin and Floyd noted that using the Seasons and Weather app can be combined with discussing careers in meteorology and picking the right clothing for different weather conditions in the dress-up corner. They also suggest that students should combine working with actual "manipulatives" with using a related app, such as one related to putting together tangrams.

For students who are deaf, smart boards permit interactive lessons, and graphing calculators allow students to see what each equation looks like graphed out. One challenge that sometimes crops up is when technology includes voice-over videos that explain steps in a problem, as those would not be accessible for deaf students.

Organizational Resources for Girls and Women With Disabilities

Recognizing the importance of including people with disabilities in STEM, many professional organizations and government agencies have developed projects to support this goal, with most focusing on both males and females, but some designed especially for girls and women. You can contribute to equitable STEM education for girls with disabilities by researching and sharing information about services, resources, and professional development opportunities with your local school system or college.

The goal of the Foundation for Science and Disability (http://stemd.org), created in 1975, is to eliminate obstacles that people with disabilities encounter so that they can be fully integrated into the STEM community. In addition to its advocacy work, the foundation sponsors $1,000 scholarships for college students who are pursuing a STEM degree.

As part of the Education to Innovate campaign, a partnership between government and industry that started in 2009, efforts have been made to make STEM education more accessible. In 2012, the White House announced its Champions of Change Initiative. One important part of the initiative is the Disability Employment Champions of Change, which recognizes those who have created educational and employment opportunities for people with disabilities. One person recognized as a Champion of Change is Virginia Stern, who has worked for 40 years to raise expectations of people with disabilities, especially among employers in STEM. Since 1977 she has spearheaded the Project on Science, Technology, and Disability of the American Association for the Advancement of Science (AAAS). In 1996, Stern and her colleagues developed Entry Point to provide paid internships and develop career skills in STEM for students with disabilities.

Project 2061, an initiative of AAAS, offer resources as well as professional development opportunities to teachers. The Women with Disabilities in STEM Education Research Agenda Development Project of the American Psychological Association was designed to promote a research agenda that would identify barriers for women with disabilities in attaining success in STEM education. If you check out http://nsfresources.org/home.cfm, you will find information on projects that were funded by the National Science Foundation (NSF), including guides helpful in teaching various STEM areas. With your daughter's teachers, you can work together to determine which of the projects provides materials and activities accessible for students with disabilities. Girls Communicating Career Connections is a website (http://gc3.edc.org) developed through funding from the NSF that can be particularly inspiring because its video segments targeting girls from underserved groups, including those with disabilities, were produced by young people. The videos were designed to encourage girls to see STEM as relevant to their everyday lives and to consider careers in science and engineering. The site offers supporting materials for teachers. Also funded by NSF is the Concord Consortium (http://concord.org), an educational technology laboratory that provides innovative materials and technology-based activities for topics such as environmental sustainability. The Concord Consortium guides connect their content with Next Generation Science Standards.

Various media outlets offer resources that could be helpful in creating greater accessibility for individuals with a wide range of disabilities. For example, PBS provides an extensive array of information and activities, organized by subject matter and grade level, so that teachers can figure out which ones work with students of varying abilities.

Organizations that focus their efforts on particular kinds of disabilities are another source of information. For example, the American Foundation for the Blind (http://AFB.org) and the American Printing House for the Blind (http://APH.org) offer ideas and resources that are STEM-related specifically for those with visual impairments. For instance, AFB provides product evaluations of various kinds of technology to ensure that they are accessible to individuals with visual impairments. And the APH 2015–2016 catalog carries items that range from three-dimensional RNA and DNA models to Braille-embossed rulers and protractors. You and your daughter's teacher can make use of these important resources.

Parents and teachers of deaf and hard of hearing children can find a vast array of information at The Laurent Clerc National Deaf Education Center at Gallaudet University (http://www.gallaudet.edu/clerc_center). The center publishes an annual magazine called *Odyssey;* its 2015 issue focused on the role of technology. For professionals working in the field of deaf education, an online community is available through the center for sharing practices and getting suggestions from others. A Cochlear Implant Education Center, which is part of Clerc, provides information about the technology.

If your daughter has a learning disability or ADHD, check out Eye to Eye (http://www.eyetoeyenational.org), a national organization that matches middle and high school students with college mentors. Mentors focus on strengthening self-esteem, learning, and advocacy skills in their mentees. The organization runs a summer camp for children with learning disabilities. The founders (who themselves have learning disabilities) also wrote a guide for college students with learning disabilities called *Learning Outside the Lines* (Mooney & Cole, 2000).

When it's time for your daughter to search for the right college for her, be sure to look for the disabilities office at each institution and inquire about the process for obtaining accommodations. In addition, find out about the accessibility of the overall campus. Although the IEP, which is critical through high school, does not carry over into the college level, accommodations and supports at many colleges can be extensive. Some provide adaptive equipment, note-taking partners, readers, and other resources, which can make the difference between success and failure for a student with a disability.

Engagement in STEM can open the world for girls with disabilities and also give them opportunities to contribute in meaningful ways to the knowledge, processes, and equipment of the STEM field. These contributions have the potential to benefit not just those with disabilities but everyone. Think about how different the treatment of livestock would be without Temple Grandin's innovations, and multiply that kind of influence many times for all those with disabilities who are given the opportunity to do STEM work. And then imagine the role you can play in advocating for STEM opportunities for girls with disabilities.

CHAPTER 19

Supporting the Needs of Gifted Students in STEM Fields

> *Going to Duke's Talent Identification Program was decidedly instrumental in who I became. It was important to just have people around who were as intellectually interested and talented as I was. I valued that experience of going there in the summer during junior high and high school and being challenged in a way that my home schools never did.*
> —Stacy Klein-Gardner, Ph.D., director of the Center for STEM Education for Girls at the Harpeth Hall School and faculty member of biomedical engineering and radiology at Vanderbilt University

Although academics may come easier to gifted students, they face the challenge of becoming and staying engaged when material is taught at a pace that is too slow for them and in ways that do not fit their learning styles. Particularly at younger ages, this disengagement can be misidentified, even by trained teachers, as being due to behavior, attention, or learning problems. Although parents of gifted children can advocate for their child's placement in summer or afterschool programs for the gifted or advanced classes, these programs may not exist for every age level or subject, particularly at schools that are smaller or underfunded. Some school administrators also frown upon separating out gifted children from others, arguing that the money spent can be better used in general classrooms, and that keeping talented students in regular classes raises the bar for everyone.

The challenge of encouraging a gifted child's interest in STEM goes beyond placement in gifted programs or advanced classes and includes consideration of the way material is taught, the messages children receive about intelligence, gender bias, issues of belonging, and opportunities outside of the classroom. This chapter focuses on all of these issues.

Keep in mind that a student can be gifted in some areas and not others. Also, having a learning disability or other disability does not preclude a child from being gifted, and a child can have skills and abilities that would foster success in STEM even if she doesn't formally test as gifted and may benefit from the same type of programs that are beneficial for gifted students.

Deciding to Enroll Your Daughter in an Advanced Program

When deciding whether to enroll your daughter in an advanced program or class, you may need to weigh different considerations, including some of the ones mentioned in Chapter 16 regarding choosing high school STEM courses. Issues, such as the topics covered, the way material is taught, and the quality of the teacher are just as important for younger girls. At this age, instead of choosing a program that your daughter can easily handle, it might be wise to go a step beyond that and pick one that will really push your daughter beyond her current skills—something that she will initially struggle with but will allow her the opportunity to learn more complex concepts and new strategies.

Encouraging persistence (as discussed in Chapter 15) will help your daughter face the challenge of such a demanding program without becoming overwhelmed, and will give her the confidence to take on future challenges and even enjoy them, which may influence her later decision to pursue a STEM career. A study of individuals who had been semifinalists or finalists of a prestigious STEM science contest in high school found that those who eventually worked in STEM fields rated intellectual challenge as a more important reason for choosing their career than those who worked in non-STEM fields (Heilbronner, 2011).

> What I liked most about my career in pharmaceuticals was that it was challenging. There's never a guarantee that you're going to succeed. It's extremely tough to find medications that safely treat human illness. I think what I found most fun about it was that we kept learning more about how the human body worked and how human illness works. And yet for every question we answered, another two or three popped up.
>
> —Carol L. Ensinger, Ph.D., retired pharmaceutical industry chemist and project manager, South Carolina

Gifted programs for STEM may be particularly helpful for girls. One study of science enrichment programs found that high school girls reported a greater positive change than boys did in motivation, science knowledge, and belonging to a new social niche (Stake & Mares, 2001). Although this study specifically involved summer science enrichment programs, it makes sense that such programs, whether done in school, after school, or during the summer, would be more beneficial for girls because they are less likely than boys to receive messages that they are good at STEM. Similarly, advanced programs may be especially important for those typically underrepresented in such programs, such as those who are African American or Latina. An evaluation of one program that provides gifted high school students from underrepresented groups with the experience they would need to participate in college-level research in genome sciences found that those who participated in the program were more likely than similar students who did not participate to indicate that they planned to take advantage of research opportunities in high school and pursue a career in science research (Fraleigh-Lohrfink, Schneider, Whittington, & Feinberg, 2013).

What Makes Some Programs Better Than Others?

Within advanced programs that provide the appropriate level of challenge for your daughter, some approaches are more helpful than others in encouraging your daughter's emerging interest in STEM. Hands-on activities tend to be more engaging and are advantageous for developing skills. When the science learning environment offers more opportunities for gifted children to explore and engage in inquiry activities—activities involving prediction, experimentation, observation, interpretation, and communication—the more likely they are to set goals that emphasize trying hard at a task, to feel a sense of self-efficacy or competence, and to plan and monitor activities, such as asking themselves questions about the material to ensure understanding (Neber & Schommer-Aikins, 2002; Yoon, 2009). If the gifted programs available to your daughter don't involve hands-on STEM activities, consider asking the teacher or school officials to try to change that. Project-based learning is another strategy that is both effective and challenging, and can be used with children and adolescents of all ages.

> During an 'astronaut' training session at space camp, I learned about the five degrees of freedom chair (5DF), which was used on Earth by the Gemini, Apollo, and Skylab astronauts to practice moving in a frictionless environment. This trainer allows astronauts to move in five different directions: forward and backward, roll, yaw, side-to-side, and pitch. The 5DF ran on air bearings to simulate the frictionless environment of space. It also demonstrated Sir Isaac Newton's Third Law of Motion: for every action there is an equal and opposite reaction. I had always used hands-on experiences to teach science concepts, but this experience amped up my interactive approach to teaching STEM.
> —Denise Scribner, high school teacher of ecology, biology and forensic crime science, Nebraska

Interdisciplinary programs are not only engaging to gifted students, but they also demonstrate how different fields and skills can be applied in one project. Because girls with strong quantitative skills are more likely than boys with equally strong quantitative skills to also have strong verbal skills (Ceci et al., 2009), programs that cross fields may be particularly important for girls who are gifted at STEM. Interdisciplinary programs allow students to explore multiple areas in which they excel without feeling that they have to choose one, and it can even allow them to see how they could potentially combine seemingly disparate interests in a future career. A longitudinal study of mathematically gifted individuals (Lubinski & Benbow, 2006) found that females preferred fields that meshed with their social and personal values over work that was exclusively in the math domain. The implication is that gifted girls should be exposed to interdisciplinary programs that demonstrate how they can combine their STEM talents with their other skills and interests, something that interdisciplinary programs can do well.

Even programs that focus on one particular area can include interdisciplinary projects that reflect how people with different jobs from different fields work together on STEM projects in the real world. Teachers in gifted programs with different areas of expertise can team-teach and ask their students to collaborate on interdisciplinary projects.

> *I try to teach all my engineers an interdisciplinary approach—being able to understand the problems outside your field and apply what you know to solve those problems. I work with Mass General Hospital on patients who have had their larynx removed because of throat cancer. So we're using our signal processing mechanism, and I'm using my computer architecture knowledge to develop a device that would help them regain actual speech. I feel like my engineering background can and should contribute.*
> —Karen Panetta, Ph.D., founder of Nerd Girls and associate dean of graduate engineering education at Tufts University

Potential Issues to Consider With Gifted and Advanced Programs

Although gifted programs can provide enormous opportunities for children, they can also inadvertently cause children to develop a fixed mindset regarding intelligence. Even the term *gifted* can imply that children have been given certain abilities that others don't have, rather than intellect being something that children must work to develop. A report by the American Association of University Women warned that gifted programs should instead try to promote a growth mindset by reminding children that, while they are already advanced, they must challenge themselves in order to further develop their skills. The report also suggested that changing the name of such programs to "challenge" or "advanced" programs can be part of changing that message (Hill et al., 2010). These programs can also help students develop a growth mindset by encouraging learning and mastery goals, rather than performance goals. Furthermore, because the studies mentioned earlier found that exploration and inquiry activities, especially those in which students have multiple options and some degree of choice, led students to set more effort and mastery goals (Neber & Schommer-Aikins, 2002; Yoon, 2009), such activities can also be used to help develop a growth mindset.

Gifted programs in STEM can help girls become friends with other students who have similar interests (Stake & Mares, 2001) and establish their identity as individuals who are good at STEM. However, gifted programs are not immune to problems with gender bias. Just like in mainstream classrooms, girls can receive negative messages about their place in STEM from their advanced teachers, textbooks, and classroom activities. Furthermore, if gifted programs in STEM have more boys than girls, which can occur when biased eligibility or selection criteria are used, the message that boys are better at STEM than girls might be reinforced. These negative messages may be one of the reasons that gifted girls have lower science self-efficacy than gifted boys (Neber & Schommer-Aikins, 2002). Due to the additional bias gifted girls may be subject to in their classrooms, following the suggestions from Chapter 17 regarding gender-neutral classrooms is especially important. If gifted programs in STEM at your daughter's school have substantially more boys than girls, consider talking to school administrators about the way students are selected for these programs and the possibility of bias.

> *I don't think I had a single friend whose mother was a scientist or a researcher or anything remotely similar growing up. There weren't any examples that women could be leaders of the pack in science. So when my teachers would make me a leader of the pack, it really changed my perspective. It was really my teachers who helped me form an identity as someone who was good at science and math. My teachers played a huge role because my parents weren't in science. They were super supportive, and they gave me everything I needed to excel academically, but they didn't have personal experience or connections.*
>
> —Hilary Robbins, doctoral student in epidemiology
> at Johns Hopkins University

What If Gifted or Advanced Programs Aren't Available?

If you live in an area that does not offer programs for children who are particularly gifted, there are actions you can take—within the formal educational system, in the world of out-of-school programs, and in your home. Some ideas are described below.

Advocating for Changes to or Creation of Programs

If your daughter's school doesn't offer a gifted program that includes STEM subjects or advanced coursework in STEM, you can first consider whether other options might serve the same purpose for your daughter. Gifted programs are helpful because they allow bright students to learn more, at a pace that works for them, and in a manner that engages them. Your daughter's school may have programs or opportunities that are not specifically for gifted students, but involve a learning environment similar to that of gifted programs. Contact the school to find out about any nontraditional options that are offered, with a particular focus on those that allow students to have more control over the pace and way they learn, involve hands-on learning, or use an interdisciplinary approach.

If programs exist that include some of the components that help engage gifted students—whether or not the program is specifically for gifted students—but could use some improvement, particularly regarding STEM subjects, you can talk with administrators about making changes to the program's approach. It might be helpful to first talk to other parents who have children in the program or who would potentially be interested in enrolling their children in the program. Then when you talk with administrators, you can demonstrate that the changes you're requesting would benefit more than just your own daughter.

Similarly, if programs don't exist at your daughter's school that would meet her needs as an advanced student, you can talk to other parents to gauge their interest in the creation of a program and then talk to school officials about the possibility of starting one. Showing that the number of children who would enroll in such a program is similar to the typical class size at the school might help school leadership realize that creating the program would be both beneficial and feasible. When changing existing programs and creating new ones, you may also have to consider whether the program would require additional funding, as that can be another major barrier for schools. If the school would need more money to fund the program, work with other parents and the school leadership to brainstorm ways of getting the necessary money, such as through fundraisers or partnerships with local colleges, organizations, and companies.

> *We're starting to move away from the low-level memorization and a lack of real-world relevance to problem solving that is more in depth. We provide students with authentic problems that have to be solved in class so students immediately see why they're learning something and never really have to ask you about that. It's important for students to see teachers working with each other or at least bringing interdisciplinary problems into the classroom and empowering students to solve real problems. I, of course, think engineering is a great way to do that.*
> —Stacy Klein-Gardner, Ph.D., director of the Center for STEM Education for Girls at the Harpeth Hall School and faculty member in biomedical engineering and radiology at Vanderbilt University

Although it might not be possible to enroll your daughter in any type of special program right now, keep looking for opportunities that might become available as your daughter gets older. In the meantime, you can work individually with your daughter's teacher to find out whether she can incorporate some of the beneficial characteristics of gifted programs into the curriculum. Many of the principles mentioned above, such as hands-on activities, are helpful and appealing for all levels of students, which means your daughter's teacher can use these approaches in ways that benefit all students. Another way you can keep your daughter engaged and learning in the classroom is to ask the teacher to provide additional activities for your daughter to work on if she finishes her regular schoolwork before the other students do. You can even give your daughter or the teacher a notebook with ideas and problems for your daughter to use so her teacher doesn't have to brainstorm additional assignments.

> I always loved English and science classes the most, and I alternated between dreaming of being a writer or a scientist. I still dream about being both of those and am constantly looking for more ways to engage in science writing (apart from writing research papers that is).
> —Tara Mandalaywala, Ph.D., researcher on social cognition in primates at New York University

Outside of the classroom you can find many ways for your daughter to experience enrichment, including afterschool, summer, and online programs for gifted students. A number of universities offer summer and online programs for gifted middle and high school students, such as Johns Hopkins University's Center for Talented Youth and Duke University's Talent Identification Program. You can also look beyond programs that are specifically for gifted students. Just as with school programs, your daughter can get a similar experience to a gifted afterschool or summer program from one that doesn't target gifted children, as long as it is engaging and allows her to work at her own pace.

Creating an Advanced Learning Environment at Home

You can also create an advanced learning environment in your own home. Use the tips from Chapter 13 to provide your daughter with opportunities for STEM exploration at home using toys, books, and activities. Keep in mind that with a gifted child, the age recommendations for a toy or book may not be accurate, and items for an older age range might be more appropriate for your daughter. You might create a sort of "homeschool" program to engage her in STEM learning after school or on weekends, giving your daughter "assignments" that she can complete using books and materials you have at home (or can get from the library) and taking her on STEM field trips following the suggestions in Chapter 14.

> *My love for science stemmed from my maternal grandmother's influence—[she] was the only woman student who majored in chemistry at Jiao Tong University in Shanghai, which is considered one of the best universities in China with a strong reputation in science. She graduated at the top of her class in 1937.*
>
> —Amy Zhang, MBA, CFA, money manager,
> daughter of Zihui Feng (next page)

The advantage a supplementary "homeschool" advanced program has over classroom programs is that it can be individualized to your daughter's exact interests, learning style, and pace. Let your daughter lead the direction of the assignments and trips as much as possible. If your daughter seems to really enjoy one particular assignment, ask her questions about it to determine if it was due to the topic or the type of assignment and give her more opportunities that follow from that. For example, if she was really engaged when you took her to visit a recycling facility, ask her questions about the experience to find out if it was because she finds recycling fascinating or if it was because she enjoyed seeing the process firsthand. If it's the former, you can suggest that she get books from the library on recycling to find out more about why some materials can be recycled and others can't and what items they can be turned into through the recycling process. For example, jewelry designers have created bold, lightweight earrings out of recycled plastic water bottles. If it's the process that intrigues her, you can take her on other trips that allow her to see science in action. You can also find ways to incorporate multiple interests your daughter has by creating interdisciplinary activities. For instance, if she is interested in computer coding and also likes history and writing, she could write a play (and even put it on with like-minded friends) about Rear Admiral Grace Hopper who codeveloped COBOL, the first computer language more than half a century ago.

> *I only had one child, my daughter Amy, because of the one-child policy in China. When I took her to the grocery store, she was the one who calculated the costs of the items. People called her 'a human calculator.' I wanted to be sure she received a good education and would not rely on others. I always had high expectations for her.*
> —Zihui Feng, retired chemical engineer from Shanghai; mother of Amy Zhang (previous page)

Advising Your Daughter in College and Beyond

A parent's work is not done when a child finishes high school. Although your role changes quite a bit as your daughter gets older, you continue to be an important adviser to her through college and beyond. But keep in mind how much she can learn from making her own decisions and mistakes. This section focuses on actions you can take to help your daughter make the most out of STEM opportunities at college and off campus and develop a sense of belonging in STEM. Finally, you can partner with her as she looks ahead to a possible career in a STEM field and learns strategies for integrating her work with family life and out-of-work interests.

CHAPTER 20

Making the Most of STEM Opportunities On and Off Campus

> *I started a neuroscience club in college because students interested in the field didn't know where other students were because there wasn't a real neuroscience major. I brought in professors who were working in the neuroscience graduate program who gave talks. We also did outreach, like Brain Awareness Week, a weeklong set of activities usually aimed toward grade school kids.*
>
> —Nicole Flaig, Ph.D. student in neuroscience
> at the University of Connecticut

Before your daughter goes to college, share this chapter or the information in it with her to help her make the most of STEM opportunities on and off campus. Once she gets to college, allow her the space and freedom to find her own path. As a young adult, it is important for her to apply the lessons you have taught her over the years in the relatively protected space of college, which will build her confidence and skills in navigating adult challenges.

Mentors

Earlier chapters described the benefit of mentoring for women's success in STEM. College and university campuses are rich with mentors. These include professors, graduate students, and juniors and seniors. Professors offer access to rich experiences, including participation in research and connections to real-world experiences. Your daughter should seek out these opportunities because professors will not necessarily know of your daughter's interest (unless she is very outgoing in class). Even if a particular professor doesn't typically take on undergraduates as research assistants or your daughter has not taken a class with that professor, your daughter can still ask for a meeting to find out whether some kind of research work might be open to her. Of course, she has to prepare her case, as professors don't want to feel burdened but certainly should welcome someone who can make a real contribution to their work. Research opportunities are usually available only for students after they have completed their first year in college. Professors and graduate students often need students to help with research in their labs, either as volunteers, for course credit, or with a small monetary compensation. Getting to know professors is an avenue to these opportunities for strong students.

> *I never thought I had any STEM propensity or potential until my senior year of college when one of my professors, Janice Lochner, told me I should consider it. I was taking her Physiology of Nutrition class to satisfy a graduation requirement. I wanted to take the class pass/fail, and she refused. I actually ended up being one of the top students in the class, leading a study group.*
> —Ruthe Farmer, chief strategy & growth officer at the National Center for Women & Information Technology, Colorado

Older students can help your daughter navigate campus life and serve as peer mentors. These supports can be critical especially in the early period of adjustment to campus and selection of majors. Research by Dasgupta (2011) showed that the presence of in-group mentors and peers boosts self-image, a sense of self-efficacy, and career aspirations among students. Peer mentors can foster a sense of confidence and competence in mentees and provide a role model reflective of your daughter's own identity. Some colleges have formal programs that connect students who are underrepresented in STEM to each other. Informally, graduate students and more advanced undergraduates often enjoy connecting with newer students and supporting their progress. Graduate student mentors can also provide helpful advice regarding how to prepare for and find opportunities after graduation, even beyond applying to graduate school.

Encourage your daughter to seek out classes and activities taught by female professors. It can be intimidating to seek out meetings with professors, so before she goes to campus, talk with your daughter about strategies for making herself comfortable approaching professors outside of class and during office hours. Talk to your daughter about how to think critically about the people she encounters, so she can identify who is encouraging her interests and who may be biased against women. Although working with female professors provides important advantages, your daughter shouldn't shy away from working with male professors, as many are very supportive of their female students, and a male teacher may be the one doing just the kind of research that most engages your daughter.

> When I finally ended up in a chemistry curriculum, I was fascinated and eager to learn as much as possible. My professor encouraged me to continue on in chemistry, rather than move into food science, because I was doing very well and would have more opportunities in the work force. What I like best about my job is the diversity in my role, the ability to interact on many levels and within various disciplines.
> —Maureen Iannucci, global market manager in personal care and pharmaceuticals for Sonneborn, New Jersey

Enrichment Activities

Enrichment activities as well as outside opportunities are abundant on college campuses. Student clubs and associations provide opportunities to meet like-minded peers and learn skills outside of class. Your daughter can also organize her own activities with other students, drawing on the leadership skills that she has developed. Students who have not found a club that really fits their interests can form their own by working with the student activities office. The experience of creating a new club is another opportunity for your daughter to strengthen her leadership skills and build her network.

Some colleges have chapters of STEM-related membership organizations, such as Alpha Epsilon Delta (a national honor society for scholarship in health), the Society for Women Engineers, and Engineers Without Borders (which combines service and engineering). Colleges also offer many clubs or organizations that focus on various academic and career interests, such as actuarial clubs or computer programming clubs. Another opportunity your daughter could investigate is providing tech support to theater productions, which can integrate an interest in the arts and technology.

> *I'm involved in the American Society of Civil Engineers' steel bridge design competition. College teams have a year to design a steel bridge that meets certain specifications and build it in under an hour so that it can be tested during a regional competition. Although I haven't taken the required classes to actually design the structure this year, I'm learning the design software with other team members, attending the meetings, and helping coordinate the build team that will put together the bridge for competition. It's been a good experience because it's so hands-on and is helping me see how a real engineering project would come together. We have to worry about budget, design code, build specifications, and ultimately work together as a team.*
> —Michelle DePinho, civil engineering major at Manhattan College

Women's leadership and gender equity awareness organizations are active on some campuses and can provide another outlet for developing leadership skills, meeting peers, and promoting women in STEM on and off campus. Encourage your daughter to become involved in organizations that support women's leadership and allow women's voices to be heard on campus. Student activities can be found through the college website or student activities office. Colleges usually host an annual event for student organizations to recruit new members. Volunteer opportunities, such as campuswide service days, and ongoing commitments, such as tutoring in local afterschool programs, sometimes have a STEM focus, such as food insecurity or alternate energy sources.

> *If girls do choose engineering, I encourage them to join clubs ASAP! It is important to be involved in clubs related to that major so they'll know upperclass students who can help out along the way, if needed. Right away, I joined the Society of Women Engineers, and now, as a sophomore, I am my chapter's Executive Assistant. This allowed me to become known to the advisor. I also got a job as a chemistry teaching assistant this past semester and will work as a TA for Chemistry with Applications to Biosystems next semester, which resulted from doing well and forming relationships with professors.*
> —Amanda McKnight, student majoring in chemical engineering and chemistry at University of New Haven

Most colleges have programs that bring renowned speakers to campus. Your daughter can advocate for women in STEM to be represented among those invited. Encourage your daughter to attend these events, and to ask questions of the speaker either during a formal question-and-answer period or right after the presentation (which is easier if she is somewhat reserved). If the speaker is doing research in a field that interests your daughter, she can follow up with a letter indicating how valuable the talk was and asking whether there are any opportunities for her to get further involved. Taking that kind of initiative is very impressive and can help her be a strong candidate for future educational and job opportunities.

Encourage your daughter to take advantage of her college's career services office, which can help her find and sign up for internships and seek summer jobs in her areas of interest. Participating in career days, even as a first- or second-year student, can assist her in making connections within the STEM field that can lead to off-campus enrichment opportunities. Internships and school-sponsored project-based experiences can provide amazing experiences in the real world of STEM, ranging from designing data systems for banks to maximizing access to clean water. The career office can also help your daughter understand the connections between her course selections and future career opportunities, provide information about lesser known careers, and even provide tips and practice for interviews. Because career offices typically have access to the college's alumni, they can also facilitate valuable connections. Many colleges have programs that introduce students to alumni for informational interviews and job shadowing.

> *I have a B.S. in finance from North Carolina A&T State University, a historically Black college known for its School of Business and School of Engineering. During my senior year, I was at the career center EVERY week researching or interviewing. In October—about 5 weeks in—I interviewed with GE for the Financial Management Program. This prestigious program was based on various rotations through the finance departments at GE, and it really spoke to me. The interviewer said, 'I really like you, but you talk too much for finance, so I'll refer you to the Management Development Program and that was my first role!*
>
> —Angie Pace Kirk, human capital strategist and professional development coach

Many colleges have international study and domestic study (in another city) programs, in which students spend a semester on another campus, with some having a STEM focus. Off-campus service projects may offer opportunities to apply STEM skills to real-world problems. For instance, Worcester Polytechnic Institute offers first-year students a Great Problems Seminar through which students solve real-world problems in interdisciplinary teams and all students complete an Interactive Qualifying Project, most of which are conducted abroad or off campus. Projects have included the creation of a hurricane prediction system for Puerto Rico and a sustainable mentoring program for orphans in Morocco.

Some colleges may have an office for scholarships and grants, which can help students find and apply for funding from external sources, such as foundations, or from within the university. Scholarships will typically fund students' tuition and possibly other educational expenses, and some also connect students with research or internship opportunities. In addition, some scholarship programs, especially those for underrepresented groups, try to promote a community among the students who have the scholarship by hosting activities and events for the scholars or having older students mentor younger students. Grants, on the other hand, fund a student's research and pay for expenses such as equipment or incentives for participants, which may allow students to do research that they otherwise would not be able to do as an undergraduate. Colleges often have small grants for undergraduate research, but there are also external grants available, including from academic honor societies or professional organizations.

> *I was originally pre-med, and midway through school I realized that I didn't want to be a doctor so I was trying to figure out what else to do. I had taken a programming class over the summer at a local college near where I was living in New York. And decided that I enjoyed that programming class, so I decided to try computers, and that's what I ended up enjoying.*
> —Gail Ruby, M.S. in computer science, product manager at Motor Information Systems, Michigan

Programs that bring first-year students to campus just prior to the start of their first year of college can provide a tremendous advantage to your daughter. They enable her to acclimate to campus life and meet other students without the pressure of classes and to begin making friends among a smaller cohort of students. This kind of program can pave the way for a smoother start to academic classes because she will already have a social base of support.

Colleges also tend to have many programs and experiences specifically for first-year students. Many of these programs combine classes or other academic experiences with an extracurricular or social aspect, which helps students meet others with similar interests and allows them to form a community of like-minded peers. Some of these programs will even place all students in the program in the same dorm.

Taking Advantage of Available Support Systems

Sometimes shyness or anxiety will keep a student from seeking out and making the most of campus opportunities. Unlike high school, college requires a high degree of self-organization and motivation. It can be difficult for a girl who suffers from "imposter syndrome" to see herself as qualified to promote her own participation in a research project with a professor or to apply for a prestigious internship. Encourage her to seek counseling as a matter of normative healthy adjustment to campus life; this is offered for free at most colleges. In addition, encourage her to seek tutoring and help from the campus writing center, if she would benefit from that extra support. Colleges often host a women's center and a multicultural center, as well as centers or offices for international students, various religious groups, nonnative English speakers, and the LGBT community. These centers not only provide a safe space for students from a variety of backgrounds and identities, but also have staff who can connect students with various on- and off-campus resources and opportunities for students to become involved in a leadership capacity.

Beyond feeling confident enough to promote oneself or apply for academic opportunities, college women benefit from participating in class discussions and talking to teaching assistants and professors during their office hours. Many smaller college seminars or discussion sections require participation, which counts for a certain percentage of students' grades. But it's important to participate even in classes that don't require it. Taking part in class discussions helps students be more engaged with the material and understand it better. Furthermore, contributing to class discussions allows students to benefit from each other's insights. Remind your daughter that everyone has different experiences and ways of looking at things, so even if she isn't confident that what she has to say is important or it seems obvious to her, it could very well be something that not everyone in the class has thought of and could enhance the discussion.

> *Because of the afterschool program I was in during high school and the people there who took time to listen to us, I learned that it was okay to object to things and not fit the norms. Now, I'm one of those students who sits in the front of the class, participates, even questions what my professor says, as opposed to me sitting in the back and staying quiet.*
>
> —Keisha, college student

Some young women are reluctant to ask questions during class time because they are afraid it will make them seem like they aren't very smart or weren't paying attention. But often other students have the same question and are just as afraid to ask, so it can benefit the entire class to ask the instructor to clarify something or give an example to illustrate the concept. Most professors would much prefer to get questions in class and explain material again than to have students do poorly on tests or assignments. Similarly, professors usually welcome students asking questions after class, over e-mail, or in office hours—as long as it isn't a question that has very clearly been answered in the course syllabus or other class materials. Bright students may especially be reluctant to go to office hours or ask questions because they're used to being able to do everything on their own and feel that they should only ask for help if they're struggling. However, connecting with a professor outside of class shows that a student really cares about the material and doing well in the class, which can be helpful in any ambiguous grading situation and allows an instructor to connect students with opportunities outside of class. In addition, instructors may be better at explaining material in a one-on-one situation, and newer instructors are often grateful to get questions from students because it helps them know what material they haven't explained well.

College is a time of growth and exploration. It is also the beginning of independent adulthood for your daughter and a time for her to transfer her dependence on you to seeking guidance from adults in the college environment. Be ready to listen and support her, but recognize her adult status and need for independence. She will remember the lessons that you have taught her through your earlier years together.

CHAPTER 21

Increasing Your Daughter's Sense of Belonging in STEM

> *I think probably the most challenging thing for me was the combination of gender and age because I took a job at headquarters working with people who were 10, 15, 20 years older than me. So that took building a sense of security and hypervigilance about what I was doing and considering how well I was fitting in.*
> —Kathy Callahan, retired chemical and business executive, Pennsylvania

When people feel that they fit into a group, they are more likely to enjoy their participation and maintain their connection to its members. This chapter discusses the critical importance for girls and young women of developing that sense of belonging in STEM, a factor that may prevent the leaky pipeline that allows so many talented females to leave the field.

The Importance of Belonging

A sense of belonging actually has important consequences for the retention of women in STEM. One study found that college students' sense of belonging in math—how much they felt like a part of the math community when they were in a math setting—predicted their intentions to take more math classes in the future and even led to higher math grades (Good et al., 2012). Similarly, another study found that the extent to which engineering students, both male and female, felt that their career path fit well with their interests and values during their first year of college predicted their intentions during their senior year of college to work as an engineer 5 years after graduation (Cech et al., 2011).

Even minimal ways of increasing belonging, such as having the same birthday as another student or sharing interests, have been found to lead to increased motivation and persistence on a task (Walton, Cohen, Cwir, & Spencer, 2012). Focusing specifically on women in STEM, a qualitative study involved interviewing 31 women who began careers as engineers, with 21 who stayed in engineering and 10 who switched to other careers. All 21 who stayed in engineering mentioned having an identity as an engineer, while none of the ones who dropped out did. Furthermore, some of the women who left engineering noted feeling that their identities didn't match with engineering (Buse, Bilimoria, & Perelli, 2013). Similarly, an experimental study with women in engineering majors found that an intervention that bolstered social belonging in their major led women to increase their grade point average and have more confidence in their ability to succeed as engineers (Walton, Logel, Peach, Spencer, & Zanna, 2015). There is also evidence that it may be more difficult for college women to feel that they belong in STEM. One longitudinal study asked women in STEM majors to complete surveys at the beginning and end of their first year in college, and found that, in general, their sense of belonging in their major decreased over time (London, Rosenthal, Levy, & Lobel, 2015).

Tips for Helping Your Daughter Increase Her Sense of Belonging in STEM

In addition to finding that STEM women's sense of belonging in their major decreased over the course of their first year in college, London and colleagues (2015) also explored the factors that predicted women's sense of belonging. They found that support from people close to them (parents, siblings, other close relatives, and friends) for their choice of major was a significant predictor of women's sense of belonging in their major in the spring semester of their first year, even after controlling for many background factors. This study also asked participants to complete daily surveys for 3 weeks, and similarly found that how generally supported participants felt on a given day predicted their sense of belonging in their major on the same day and the next day.

Supporting Her Choice of Major

Make sure your daughter knows that you support her choice of major, and encourage other family members to do the same. Show your interest and support by asking her questions about the major and her classes—even if you don't have much of a STEM background or your background is in a different area of STEM than what she's studying. Challenging her to break complex concepts down to a level that a layperson can understand is a great exercise and will serve her well in her career. You may have questions for your daughter about the potential for job opportunities related to her major, since you probably want her to follow a career path that will allow her to support herself. When you have those conversations, make sure that you show support for your daughter's choice of major and indicate that you know she'll be able to take advantage of the opportunities available to her to create a successful career path.

Because support from friends for her choice of major and general social support are also predictors of belonging, encourage your daughter to become friends with other students in her major and to join relevant clubs and organizations. Suggest that she take advantage of the supports available to her on campus mentioned in the previous chapter. Make sure your daughter knows that she can always talk to you and encourage her to talk to other family members as well. Older siblings or other relatives who have recently attended college can be great resources.

As your daughter becomes an independent college student, it's important to resist the urge to fix her problems for her or immediately give her advice. Sometimes she may just want to vent about what's going on and hear something along the lines of, "That sounds really annoying. It's too bad that you have to deal with that." If you have advice to offer her that you think will be helpful, ask her first if that's what she's looking for, and try not to get upset if she chooses not to take your advice. Remember that the point is to support her, which sometimes means allowing her to make her own decisions, even when you think she's headed in a direction that doesn't make sense to you (unless of course, her health and safety are at stake). Mistakes are opportunities for learning. It's very normal for young adults to reject advice from parents, so encouraging her to talk to another trusted adult may be more effective.

Perceptions of Compatibility With a STEM Major

London and colleagues' study (2015) examined how young women's perceptions of the compatibility of their gender with their major influenced their sense of belonging in their major. As with support for choice of major from close family and friends, the researchers found that perceived compatibility of gender and major predicted women's sense of belonging during the spring semester of their first year. On the daily surveys, perceived compatibility predicted belonging on the same day, but did not predict belonging on the subsequent day, so it's unclear if this effect carries forward from one day to the next. Still, the perception of compatibility between one's major and one's gender seems to be an important determinant of a sense of belonging for college women in STEM majors. Use the information from this book to show your daughter that women can succeed in STEM, how she can succeed in STEM, and how STEM fields can benefit from having women like her in them.

Another key finding from the London et al. (2015) study was that on days when participants had STEM classes, their perceived performance in class influenced their sense of belonging in their major that day. Obviously anything your daughter can do to improve her performance in class is important, for reasons beyond increasing her sense of belonging. However, it's important to note that *perceived* performance was the important predictor of belonging. So your daughter can increase her sense of belonging in her major by viewing her performance in a more positive light. Encourage your daughter to think of her academic performance in terms of small goals, such as participating in a class discussion, and to focus on whether she's improving and mastering a concept or skill, rather than thinking of her performance solely in terms of grades and test scores. This kind of self-assessment might help ward off any feeling of not being good enough (the imposter syndrome).

> *In college, there was one advisor who encouraged me to continue in math and computer science. He emphasized the fact that there are very few women, let alone African American women, in this field. He also said that the knowledge I will gain will take me anywhere I want to go. He was right.*
> —Yvette L. Campbell, B.A. in applied mathematics and dramatic art-dance, past president & CEO of the Harlem School of the Arts

Finding Similarities

The results of Walton and colleagues' 2012 experimental studies on belonging suggested several small ways to increase feelings of belonging in a task-oriented context, including anticipating positive social interactions and finding similarities with others you're working with, even if the similarities are small or irrelevant to the task. Encourage your daughter to get to know other students in her classes and to try to connect with them, even on topics and concerns that are completely unrelated to class. If she feels more similar to the other students and is able to experience some positive social interactions with them, she'll perceive a greater sense of belonging to her major. Your daughter might feel that she's very different from a lot of the students in her major, but there are likely to be at least a few with whom she has a bit more in common and could potentially develop friendships. Tell her to keep reaching out to other students until she finds someone she's compatible with. Even beyond increasing her sense of belonging, it's always good to have a friend in the same major to talk with about classes, study with, and maybe sometimes get help or advice from.

Although, as a parent, you are probably not able to replicate the social belonging intervention used in Walton and colleagues' 2015 study, you can use some of the same principles to help increase your daughter's sense of belonging. The social belonging intervention used quantitative data and quotes from interviews with older students to convey the message that both male and female students initially worried that they didn't belong in their major, but that these concerns lessened over time. They also specifically indicated that both men and women worried about being respected and taken seriously as an engineer, but that those worries subsided as they continued in the program, and that even when females don't share their male peers' interests, they share their interest in engineering. It might be helpful to warn your daughter before she starts taking college STEM courses that she might feel at first like she doesn't fit in, or she might be intimidated by the professors and other students and worry about them taking her seriously. Reassure her that those worries are completely normal and something most students experience—both men and women—and as she settles into the program, they will go away. Framing those concerns about belonging in such a way will allow your daughter to acknowledge those feelings, but also recognize that those initial negative feelings shouldn't mean she should switch majors. It may also be helpful to tell your daughter that even if she continues to not feel that she fits in with the other students in her major, that doesn't mean those concerns about belonging will continue throughout her career. Because there are many careers and types of workplaces stemming from each major, she'll certainly be able to find one with a culture that works for her, even if it's not a typical path for her major.

> *The most important lesson I've learned is that just because I work with men doesn't mean I have to be one. Instead, I've dealt with the environment by realizing my strengths and using these to earn the respect of my male peers. I also try to go above and beyond and work harder than my colleagues so that I am seen as a true asset to the business, not because of my gender but because of my skills.*
>
> —Sheila Flavell, chief operating officer of FDM Group, London

The American Association of University Women made several research-based recommendations for increasing women's sense of belonging in STEM (Corbett & Hill, 2015), including that students make contact with professionals in the field early on. Many professionals will be happy to talk to college students about their careers. The AAUW report also recommended that young women develop a support network of other STEM women, including their professors, teaching assistants, and other students.

Developing Critical Skills

The AAUW report (Corbett & Hill, 2015) suggested that non-technical skills, such as communication, writing, creativity, teamwork, and leadership, can be important for success in STEM. Remind your daughter of the importance of these skills (review the tips from Chapters 12 and 15) and emphasize that it's never too late to work on these areas if she's truly motivated to improve. Recognizing the significance of nontechnical skills may help her see that she has the potential to succeed in STEM, and may even have skills that others in her major don't have, regardless of whether she feels like she fits in with the other students in her major. Finally, the AAUW recommended promoting a growth mindset, which has been described in detail throughout this book. Doing so will allow your daughter to feel more confident in her ability to succeed, even if she sometimes feels that other students or professors don't take her seriously or have stronger skills.

> " *I got a call from Rhode Island that they had two lighthouses powered from a 6,000 foot cable to the mainland, and they decided they were going to have to forgo their national historic designation because they had no power. So I said we can use solar energy with LED technology, which at the time was relatively new. We did the first all-solar lighthouse with LED technology, and we brought the lighthouse back, and now every lighthouse in the United States run by the Coast Guard uses that technology. We went on the Today Show, and I got attacked that these girls were too pretty, that I cast them. And that was really just perpetuating the stigma that women can't be well rounded, they can't be intelligent, they can't dress nice. It was interesting because every girl I brought on that show was an accomplished engineer. They said 'What could they have possibly accomplished at 21 years old? They haven't done anything serious.' Hey, they saved a national historic landmark, what have you done today?* "
> —Karen Panetta, Ph.D., founder of Nerd Girls and associate dean of graduate engineering education at Tufts University

If you examine those situations in your own life in which you felt you truly belonged—whether it was in a work or a purely social setting—you can get a sense of the power of belonging. If your daughter chooses a career in a STEM field, that perception of fitting in may well make the difference between staying in a career she loves and leaving it. Encourage her to find ways to belong so that she does not have to choose between a rewarding career and her social needs.

CHAPTER 22

Looking Ahead

Exploring Careers and Creating a Satisfying Work and Personal Life

> *I believe that my ability to balance work and personal life starts with not being too hard on myself. No one is perfect, so why should I hold myself to a higher standard than the rest of the world? I also try to have a clear grasp on my priorities at any given time. This clarity allows me to make decisions quickly and with minimum regret. Any decision can be made once you have identified your objectives and constraints, so I am continuously refining my understanding of these factors.*
>
> —Daria Torres, M.B.A./M.S.E., managing partner and founder of the Walls Torres Group, New Jersey

By the time your daughter finishes college, she will have made thousands of decisions, some well-thought-out and others more impulsive or not in her best interests. Hopefully, she has learned from her mistakes as well as from those instances in which her actions served her well. As an adult, she will face many more decisions, including those about her career path, whether she wants to attend graduate school, and how she will balance a fulfilling career with a rewarding personal and family life. This chapter allows you as her parent to peek into the issues that will concern her in years to come. As a young adult, she will have many more people to seek advice from in addition to her parents. But you continue to have an influence and opportunities to act as a sounding board as she figures out the next steps in her career and her life.

Career Paths—Not Necessarily a Straight Line

Although many young women think they have to make a career decision in college or right afterwards, data reported by the Bureau of Labor Statistics (2015) indicated that most people change jobs more than 11 times with nearly half of those changes occurring before age 25. These are not necessarily career changes because the longitudinal research needed to provide that information has not been done. But anecdotal evidence certainly points to career changes, particularly for those who have options due to their skills, experience, or education.

> *My science background gave me a very large advantage in a very competitive journalism workforce. It was also an advantage when I took a job in public relations for a major university. I knew the language of science and engineering, and that's what universities earn money on. I am now a startup entrepreneur in a tech company I founded. I switch careers because once I understand how a system works it's not interesting for me anymore.*
> —Karin Kloosterman, M.S. in computer sciences, Tel Aviv, Israel

If your daughter keeps in mind that a career path is not necessarily a straight line, she might feel more comfortable making decisions about work. Anecdotal evidence abounds of women who started out in one field and then found their true passion years later or those who were confident they had discovered the one true path to career satisfaction only to find that their interests had changed and then went on to a totally different pursuit. These are not examples of mistakes but rather of a change of mind, heart, or both.

> *In all of my job changes, these positions came to me. Someone called me on the phone and asked if I would be interested. Usually this was as a result of the fact that every position I worked in, I did at 150%. I would always learn more than required and become indispensable in that role.*
> —Yvette L. Campbell, B.A. in applied mathematics and dramatic art-dance, past president & CEO of the Harlem School of the Arts

Taking Risks

Deciding on a career means taking a risk. A woman takes one path rather than another, decides to further her education or not, follows her interests or allows salary to be the deciding factor, moves far from home for an exciting opportunity or stays locally to be close to family or friends. These are all scenarios played out by real people with real consequences. Your daughter needs to decide how much she is willing to risk each time she makes a decision and how her values play into those decisions.

Tolerance for risk can change—either increasing or decreasing over her lifetime. If your daughter is the type who fearlessly took off the training wheels on her bicycle and wasn't afraid to fall, she will probably feel confident about going full-throttle into a career that will be challenging and risky. As she gets older, she might well continue living life in the same way as she'd always had, or she might become more conservative—taking fewer risks. On the other hand, a girl who was risk averse might become more open to adventure and the unknown—taking greater risks. And the level of risk she is willing to tolerate can fluctuate as family responsibilities change over time.

Conversations about risk, career paths, and passion can help her make decisions. But keep in mind that she is the one who has to live her life. Although your mistakes or decisions can inform her actions, she should never feel that she has to follow (or not) what you've done. Sometimes, as a parent your most vital role is to be a sounding board—listening and asking questions—as your daughter finds her way.

> *I worked for a short time after graduating college for a computer econometric consulting firm after which I went back to school to get my M.B.A. After earning that degree, I went into banking as a deal maker, relationship manager, and business development professional. I loved finance, and banking was a growing industry that was looking for smart women. Many firms, including banks, came onto campus to recruit. I ended up with eight offers, and while not taking the most lucrative one, I did take the one that I felt had the most opportunity for advancement to leadership, and combined my passion for people with my love of numbers and finance.*
>
> —Karen W. Solorow, president of Coaching for Success and former banker, New York

Making a Name For Herself

Women often underestimate their skills and work contributions (Haynes & Heilman, 2013), particularly when comparing themselves to their male colleagues, but doing so can hurt them when applying for a job or an internship. That doesn't mean that your daughter should brag about her talents, but she definitely shouldn't be hiding them behind a veil of modesty. In business today, people talk about their "brand," which is how they present themselves and how they want others to see them. In STEM fields, particularly those that are dominated by men, a woman's brand needs to include confidence, a willingness to take on challenges, a creative bent, an interest in learning, and the resilience to deal with setbacks. Promoting oneself should never be about becoming less authentic, but rather should be about highlighting one's talents and skills.

Your daughter can learn more about how others see her (and then strategize about how to make changes, if warranted). Although you could comment on her behavior (and you probably do), she may feel that you can't be objective. Instead she could ask trusted (and honest) friends and relatives for feedback about how she comes across—how assertive, confident, and knowledgeable she seems. And if they notice areas that she could work on, such as the fact that she typically follows along passively with other people's ideas instead of giving her own, they can suggest ways she can change.

In addition to the way your daughter presents herself in person, she also shows herself in her resume. Because that is often the first thing a prospective employer sees, encourage your daughter to describe herself in the most positive way. Many books and online resources are available to show how changing the wording can make a difference in how a candidate is perceived. Using terms such as "lead and direct" are more powerful than "manage and implement." If your daughter is going into a male-dominated STEM field, her resume needs to demonstrate that she is not just a collaborator but a leader, not just a participant but an initiator.

Gaining Experience

Finishing college is a great accomplishment, but it's typically not enough to land the ideal job. To get her dream job in a STEM field, she will need to have work experience, spend time networking, and build her technical and social intelligence skills.

Finding a Workplace That's a Good Fit

In looking for a job, your daughter should consider the fit between her personal qualities and the way an organization or company functions. Research on the concept of Person-Organization Fit (Verquer, Beehr, & Wagner, 2003) can inform her job search after college. King and Knight (2011) suggested that women should figure out how well their values coincide with an organization's values. Your daughter could think about situations in which she felt happy and figure out what factors were present. She might ask herself questions such as the following: Was she collaborating with a team? Did she have an opportunity to be creative? Was the work challenging and exciting? A different way of developing an awareness of work values is by thinking about situations in which she was unhappy—again asking herself a series of questions, such as these: What was frustrating about the job? Were there certain kinds of people who were difficult to work with? Was she adequately recognized for her contributions? Was she overlooked when important projects were assigned? Was the job boring?

Once your daughter has a good sense of the values that drive her in terms of work, she needs to collect information about various organizations to learn more about their values and how well they mesh with hers. A lot of the research can be done on the Internet, but it's a good idea to talk to people who have some familiarity with the company. As part of her research on organizations, your daughter should find out about the positions women hold and the support they are given to get promotions, as well as whether the policies and practices encourage a healthy work-life balance.

The type of supervision matters also. What kind of supervision does your daughter prefer? Can she handle a micromanager? Does she like clear guidelines and structure? How much autonomy will she be given to be creative? How much does she need or want?

Although being optimistic about finding a position that provides the ideal person-organization fit is a good approach, your daughter may need to do a bit of compromising, as her ideal position might not be available to her. Remind her that even negative experiences have value, as they will show her what to avoid in the future. She might try out a career with an internship. Some internships offer a small stipend while others do not, so that may be an important consideration for your daughter. But it is a valuable way to get into an organization or an industry in which entry-level jobs are few and far between. Your daughter might also acquire information about STEM organizations by subscribing to relevant list serves or following professionals in an industry through Twitter or LinkedIn.

> *I love the flexibility that my career provides. Although I have a 'boss' (the principal investigator whose lab I work in), I have control over the research I do, the questions I pursue, as well as the hours and pace at which I work. In addition to being fascinated by my research subjects and excited to come into work every day, I also love that my research takes me all over the world and exposes me to people and places that I would otherwise be unlikely to meet.*
> —Tara Mandalaywala, Ph.D., researcher on social cognition in primates at New York University

Some STEM opportunities require relocation, which is also a consideration for young adults. Your daughter may be the type of person who feels comfortable moving far away from familiar people and places, or she might need to have someone close by who can be there for her in emergencies. If she's thinking about relocating, she should consider the cost of living relative to her salary. What may seem like a decent income in a small town might not go very far in a large city. It is important to consider the cost of moving, which can be considerable, and if your daughter doesn't think she'll want to stay in that position for very long, it may not be worth the expense. She probably also needs to take into account the cost of visiting family and friends back home. The bottom line is that the position may be ideal for your daughter, and the expenses and sacrifices may make the move worth it. Or not.

Networking

Business career coaches often suggest that young people put together a "Career Board," a group of people who possess a variety of skills and experience, who can share their expertise in job interviewing, presentation skills, and relevant technical subjects. Your daughter can benefit from putting together such a panel and adding or eliminating people as her needs change. As she deals with work challenges and decision-making dilemmas, she has people she can turn to for assistance. Remind your daughter to always write follow-up thank you letters to those who have provided any kind of help to her or they won't be likely to want to do it again.

One of the ways your daughter can use her Career Board is to help her identify and evaluate her strengths and weaknesses. For areas that need development, members of her board can suggest strategies. For example, if she's not a very good presenter (which is important in all kinds of STEM jobs), an experienced public speaker could give her pointers, such as starting off strong with a compelling story, while a seasoned trainer could suggest how she can use PowerPoints more effectively.

In previous chapters, we discussed the importance of networking and how to find and use role models and mentors strategically. One resource that is key in professional circles is LinkedIn. If you are already on LinkedIn, your daughter can start her networking by signing up and linking to you, which means that she can, without too much trouble, connect to people you are linked to. She can then use those people to contact their connections as well. And if you don't have a profile on LinkedIn, your daughter can certainly sign up on her own. She will probably find that many of her friends and acquaintances have a profile on the site, and she can connect with classmates, professors who know her well, and supervisors from positions she's had during college. Because the site is open to potential employers and colleagues as well as faculty, what she includes in her profile is critical. Encourage her to ask a couple of trusted people to review whatever she writes before she posts her information. And she might ask people who know her well to endorse her or write notes of recommendation on the site.

> *Our lab mostly does theoretical neuroscience with music. We look at all aspects of music—pitch, rhythm, and the perception of those things, and we've created a computer model that models how the brain translates sound. My undergraduate degree was in neuroscience, but being a musician, I wanted to be able to combine the two. So I figured that the way music affected me couldn't be singular to me. How does it do that, and can I use it to help people who have mental or emotional disorders, like depression or bipolar conditions? We're not quite at the point of figuring that out, but we're at a good theoretical starting point for going in that direction. So it was mostly just the combination of putting my talents in music and my interest in science together. I like the fact that most of my collaborators and peers are very creative people, and they are highly passionate about music. So it's not all about the rigors of science, it's about what we're studying.*
>
> —Nicole Flaig, Ph.D. student in neuroscience
> at the University of Connecticut

Networking is usually discussed in a business context, but some networks are purely social. And you never know when a member of your daughter's social network will recommend her for something work-related. Building strong networks will be valuable as she deals with various life challenges. Your daughter will want to seek out different people in her networks, depending on what kind of advice or support she needs.

Considering Graduate School

Many, but certainly not all, positions in STEM require a graduate degree. Engineers typically are eligible for all kinds of jobs with a college degree, although some do go to graduate school to specialize further or make it easier to advance. For some careers, such as doing pharmaceutical research, a master's degree is needed or would be preferred. For other careers, a doctoral degree is required, such as if an individual wants to teach and do research at a university level. Before your daughter starts taking the time and incurring the expense involved in more years of schooling, she should do the research to find out what's needed in the field that interests her. If she discovers that a graduate degree is required and decides to make the commitment to go for it, she then needs to investigate where and when to apply.

Although high school seniors and their parents invest a great deal of time, money, and thought into the college application process, the graduate school process is actually significantly more involved. And if you attended graduate school years ago, you'll soon learn that the process is very different today. Graduate departments, particularly those that offer doctorates in competitive fields and at top-tier universities, expect prospective students to enter having already gained relevant work and/or research experience. Professors want students who will assist them with their research and inspire other students with their critical thinking, creativity, and leadership. Many doctoral programs offer support in the form of research and teaching assistantships and even no-strings-attached scholarships and fellowships, but assistantships are less common in master's programs. The type and degree of support should, of course, figure into the decision of whether, when, and where to attend.

For your daughter to be ready for graduate school, she needs to consider how committed she is to the additional years she will spend as a student and what she will probably need to give up to get that advanced education—whether it's distance from a significant other or a well-paying and challenging job. Many students do not get into graduate school the first or even the second time around. But if your daughter is truly committed to a STEM graduate degree and career, she will need to see rejection as a setback rather than a failure.

> For most of my career, I have worked as a social scientist in the field of education. I think my career picked me rather than the other way around! When I graduated from college, I found a job doing absolutely nothing I had trained for in my studies. However, through that job I met a professor who hired me to be his research assistant. The more we worked together, the more he felt I had the talents to become a researcher. He encouraged me to pursue my Ph.D. and I did so. As a result of that doctorate, I was able to teach college courses in research design and beginning statistics. Although I took and passed four courses in statistics during my graduate degree, I remembered how hard it was, and when I taught my first statistics course, I realized I could come up with a practical way to teach beginning statistics, using topics that students actually cared about. This idea really worked and became part of my teaching, research, analysis, and report writing—putting research findings in a clear and compelling context so readers could see why the study was done and the results were important.
> —Sylvia Barsion, Ph.D. in educational research, measurement, and evaluation; writer and consultant, New York

If your daughter is accepted into graduate school, her journey and the role you will play in it have just started. Your emotional support is needed as she acclimates to the challenges of graduate school life, including the stereotyping and gender bias she faces if she is in a program that has traditionally been male-dominated.

Balancing Work and Personal Life

Having both a rewarding career and a satisfying family life is a goal for many women. This issue is particularly relevant for those who pursue careers in STEM who sometimes feel that they have to choose.

Looking around, they may not see many role models who have figured out how to successfully combine those values that are most important to them—their work and their families. You may be surprised (or not) that an issue that you grappled with when you were younger is still alive well into the 21st century.

Work-Family Interaction

Instead of using the term *work-family balance*, which suggests precarious juggling of burdensome work responsibilities with equally overwhelming family demands, Halpern and Murphy (2005) suggested the term *work-family interactions*. Their research, as well as findings from other studies they cite, suggested benefits from combining satisfying work and family and/or out-of-work interests and activities.

Some organizations have recognized the value of creating the kind of flexible workplace arrangements that parents (as well as others with caregiving and other responsibilities) want and need. Studies have shown that when companies offer these kinds of accommodations, absenteeism decreases and productivity and job satisfaction increase (Weber, 2003). Some women in STEM fields have felt that they had to make a choice between devoting themselves to work or having a family or at least delaying having a family in order to advance their careers. One survey of mid-level scientists and engineers at technology companies found that women were more likely than men to report forgoing a marriage/partnership and forgoing or delaying childbearing in order to advance their careers (Simard, Henderson, Gilmartin, Schiebinger, & Whitney, 2008). A "culture of overwork" may be behind women feeling that they have to choose between work and family (Corbett & Hill, 2015). Excessive work, defined as working more than 50 hours per week, has been found to lead mothers (but not men or women without children) to be more likely to leave their jobs in male-dominated fields and to leave the workforce entirely (Cha, 2013). Focusing on engineers specifically, excessive work has also been found to lead women to have lower job satisfaction, lower commitment to their jobs, and lower commitment to the field of engineering (Fouad, Singh, Fitzpatrick, & Liu,

2012). When women who are well-trained leave a field because they do not think they can create a successful work-family interaction, the result is a personal loss as well as a loss to the organization and the field. This is an example of the leaky pipeline that has been discussed throughout this book. Who knows what these women might have accomplished had they stayed in the world of STEM work?

> *I have my own business helping people master all types of technology. I worked as a high school teacher for 5 years and then as an adjunct professor for 8 more years before going out on my own to work privately with clients. My main motivation was setting my own schedule so I would have time to be home for my children, in addition to my preference for teaching adult students. I love working for myself and making my own hours. In addition, I love helping people feel more comfortable in a digital world.*
> —Carol Friedman, MS in educational computing, customized computer trainer

Kerr and McKay (2014) noted that women who were majoring in a STEM field were aware that many females drop out of a STEM career because of issues related to integrating their work with family, but that they thought those challenges would not apply to them. Unfortunately, many female STEM students also thought that it might be necessary to avoid relationships to succeed in STEM—an interesting dichotomy. You can point out STEM role models who have successfully integrated career and relationship goals to your daughter, but also help her be realistic in terms of developing strategies (such as expecting her partner to share in household chores and childcare) that make a life in STEM possible.

You're Her Role Model

How did you make decisions about balancing work and family life? How satisfied were you with the results of your decision? If you haven't talked to your daughter about your experience, consider doing that, even if you weren't happy with the path you took. What's important is starting conversations about this topic. You don't need to have the answers, but it would be good for your daughter to think about her options and begin to figure out ways to create the kind of professional and personal life she wants.

You're not her only role model, so all the pressure's not on you. In several places in this book, we discussed the importance of role models. They're not only significant for showing the variety of STEM careers that are possible, but they can also show the range of possibilities for combining work and family. Some women in STEM do not want to get married or have children, but that doesn't mean that they don't want a real personal life with hobbies, travel, and friendships. Moreover, caregiving is often a role that women play even when they do not have children. Whether they're making sure an elderly parent or ill sibling is receiving the appropriate care or supporting their friends going through various life crises, women (and men) need nonwork time to fulfill their responsibilities.

A key message to give to your daughter is that regardless of the kind of work-personal life she chooses (or sometimes is foisted on her by situations beyond her control), figuring out how many possibilities exist is something role models can demonstrate to her with their real-life stories.

Because work-family balance or interaction is subjectively defined by each person, your daughter has an opportunity to determine how to create that for herself. As with other life situations, no one solution works for everyone. She might not come up with the best possible way to integrate everything that is important to her at the outset and will probably need to learn from her experience, but the one constant is that your support, ideas, and understanding will continue to play an invaluable role in your daughter's life.

As with all aspects of her engagement in STEM, your daughter will find her way with your help and her own resilience. Gathering information, analyzing results, and constructing solutions are tools that are applicable to both the fields of STEM and the processes of making positive life decisions.

References

Adams, J. D., Gupta, P., & Cotumaccio, A. (2014). Long-term participants: A museum program enhances girls' STEM interest, motivation, and persistence. *Afterschool Matters, 20,* 13–20.

Alberts, B. (2012). Trivializing science education. *Science, 335,* 263.

Ambady, N., Shih, M., Kim, A., & Pittinsky, T. L. (2001). Stereotype susceptibility in children: Effects of identity activation on quantitative performance. *Psychological Science, 12,* 385–390.

Anderson, K. J., & Leaper, C. (1998). Meta-analyses of gender effects on conversational interruption: Who, what, when, where, and how. *Sex Roles, 39,* 225–252.

Aronin, S., & Floyd, K. K. (2013). Using an iPad in inclusive preschool classrooms to introduce STEM concepts. *TEACHING Exceptional Children, 45,* 34–39.

Banilower, E. R., Smith, P. S., Weiss, I. R., Malzahn, K. M., Campbell, K. M., & Weis, A. M. (2013). *Report of the 2012 National Survey of Science and Mathematics Education.* Chapel Hill, NC: Horizon Research, Inc.

Baron-Cohen, S. (2009). Autism: The empathizing-systemizing (E-S) theory. *Annals of the New York Academy of Sciences, 1156,* 68–80.

Bechdel, A. (1985). The rule. *Dykes to watch out for* [Comic].

Beilock, S. L., Gunderson, E. A., Ramirez, G., & Levine, S. C. (2010). Female teachers' math anxiety affects girls' math achievement. *Proceedings of the National Academies of Science, 107,* 1860–1863.

Betz, D. E., & Sekaquaptewa, D. (2012). My fair physicist? Feminine math and science role models demotivate young girls. *Social Psychological and Personality Science, 3,* 738–746.

Bhatt, M. (2012). Evaluations and associations: A neural-network model of advertising and consumer choice. *Journal of Economic Behavior and Organization, 82,* 236–255.

Bhatt, M., Blakley, J., Mohanty, N., & Payne, R. (2012) *How media shapes perceptions of science and technology for girls and women* (White paper). San Francisco, CA: FEM Inc. Retrieved from http://fem-inc.com/FEMIncWomenAndSTEM.pdf

Bureau of Labor Statistics. (2015). *Number of jobs held, labor activity, and earnings growth among the youngest baby boomers: Results from a longitudinal survey.* Washington, DC: Author. Retrieved from http://www.bls.gov/news.release/pdf/nlsoy.pdf

Buse, K., Bilimoria, D., & Perelli, S. (2013). Why they stay: Women persisting in U.S. engineering careers. *Career Development International, 18,* 139–154.

Carlson, C., Booth, J. E., Shin, J., & Canu, W. H. (2002). Parent-, teacher-, and self-rated motivational styles in ADHD subtypes. *Journal of Learning Disabilities, 35,* 104–113.

Cech, E., Rubineau, B., Silbey, S., & Seron, C. (2011). Professional role confidence and gendered persistence in engineering. *American Sociological Review, 76,* 641–666.

Ceci, S. J., Ginther, D. K., Kahn, S., & Williams, W. M. (2014). Women in academic science: A changing landscape. *Psychological Science in the Public Interest, 15,* 75–141.

Ceci, S. J., & Williams, W. M. (2011). Understanding current causes of women's underrepresentation in science. *Proceedings of the National Academies of Science, 108,* 3157–3162.

Ceci, S. J., Williams, W. M., & Barnett, S. M. (2009). Women's underrepresentation in science: Sociocultural and biological considerations. *Psychological Bulletin, 135,* 218–261.

Cha, Y. (2013). Overwork and the persistence of gender segregation in occupations. *Gender and Society, 27,* 158–184.

Cheryan, S., Drury, B. J., & Vichayapai, M. (2013). Enduring influence of stereotypical computer science role models on women's academic aspirations. *Psychology of Women Quarterly, 37,* 72–79.

Cheryan, S., Plaut, V. C., Davies, P. G., & Steele, C. M. (2009). Ambient belonging: How stereotypical cues impact gender participation in computer science. *Journal of Personality and Social Psychology, 97*, 1045–1060.

Cheryan, S., Siy, J. O., Vichayapai, M., Drury, B. J., & Kim, S. (2011). Do female and male role models who embody STEM stereotypes hinder women's anticipated success in STEM? *Social Psychological and Personality Science, 2*, 656–664.

Clance, P. R., & Imes, S. A. (1978). The imposter phenomenon in high achieving women: Dynamics and therapeutic intervention. *Psychotherapy: Theory, Research, and Practice, 15*, 241–247.

Clancy, K. B. H., Nelson, R. G., Rutherford, J. N., & Hinde, K. (2014). Survey of Academic Field Experiences (SAFE): Trainees report harassment and assault. *PLoS ONE, 9*, e102172. doi:10.1371/journal.pone.0102172

Corbett, C., & Hill, C. (2015). *Solving the equation: The variables for women's success in engineering and computing.* Washington, DC: American Association of University Women.

Countryman, J., Kekelis, L., & Wei, J. (2010). *Get involved. Make a difference: A guide for classroom visits and field trips for K–12 students.* Oakland, CA: Techbridge.

Dasgupta, N. (2011). Ingroup experts and peers as social vaccines who inoculate the self-concept: The stereotype inoculation model. *Psychological Inquiry, 22*, 231–246.

Dasgupta, N., & Asgari, S. (2004). Seeing is believing: Exposure to counter-stereotypic women leaders and its effect on the malleability of automatic gender stereotyping. *Journal of Experimental Social Psychology, 40*, 642–658.

Davies, P. G., Spencer, S. J., Quinn, D. M., & Gerhardstein, R. (2002). Consuming images: How television commercials that elicit stereotype threat can restrain women academically and professionally. *Personality and Social Psychology Bulletin, 28*, 1615–1628.

Denner, J., Bean, S., & Martinez, J. (2009). The Girl Game Company: Engaging Latina girls in information technology. *Afterschool Matters, 8*, 26–35.

Dezso, C. L., & Ross, D. G. (2012). Does female representation in top management improve firm performance? A panel data investigation. *Strategic Management Journal, 33*, 1072–1089.

Diekman, A. B., Brown, E. R., Johnston, A. M., & Clark, E. K. (2010). Seeking congruity between goals and roles: A new look at why women opt out of science, technology, engineering, and math careers. *Psychological Science, 21*, 1051–1057.

Diekman, A. B., Clark, E. K., Johnston, A. M., Brown, E. R., & Steinberg, M. (2011). Malleability in communal goals and beliefs influences attraction to STEM careers: Evidence for a role congruity perspective. *Journal of Personality and Social Psychology, 101,* 902–918.

Dockterman, E. (2014, September 15). These girls are fighting sexism with a video game about tampons. *TIME.* Retrieved from http://time.com/3319562/tampon-run-girls-who-code

DuBois, D. L., Portillo, N., Rhodes, J. E., Silverthorn, N., & Valentine, J. C. (2011). How effective are mentoring programs for youth? A systematic assessment of the evidence. *Psychological Science in the Public Interest, 12,* 57–91.

Dweck, C. S., & Sorich, L. A. (1999). Mastery oriented thinking. In C. R. Snyder (Ed.), *Coping: The psychology of what works* (pp. 232–251). New York, NY: Oxford University Press.

Eccles, J. S. (2005). Studying gender and ethnic differences in participation in math, physical science, and information technology. *New Directions for Child and Adolescent Development, 110,* 7–14.

Espinoza, P., Areas da Luz Fontes, A. B., & Arms-Chavez, C. J. (2014). Attributional gender bias: Teachers' ability and effort explanations for students' math performance. *Social Psychology of Education, 17,* 105–126.

Fancsali, C. (2002). *What we know about girls, STEM, and afterschool programs: A summary.* New York, NY: Educational Equity Concepts.

Fouad, N. A., Singh, R., Fitzpatrick, M. E., & Liu, J. P. (2012). *Stemming the tide: Why women leave engineering.* Milwaukee, WI: University of Wisconsin-Milwaukee.

Fraleigh-Lohrfink, K. J., Schneider, M. V., Whittington, D., & Feinberg, A. P. (2013). Increase in science research commitment in a didactic and laboratory-based program targeted to gifted minority high-school students. *Roeper Review, 35,* 18–26.

Fusco, D. (2011). *Advancing youth work: Current trends, critical questions.* New York, NY: Routledge.

Glass, J. L., Sassler, S., Levitte, Y., & Michelmore, K. M. (2013). What's so special about STEM? A comparison of women's retention in STEM and professional occupations. *Social Forces, 92,* 723–756.

Good, C., Aronson, J., & Harder, J. A. (2008). Problems in the pipeline: Stereotype threat and women's achievement in high-level math courses. *Journal of Applied Developmental Psychology, 29,* 17–28.

Good, C., Aronson, J., & Inzlicht, M. (2003). Improving adolescents' standardized test performance: An intervention to reduce the effects of stereotype threat. *Applied Developmental Psychology, 24,* 645–662.

Good, C., Rattan, A., & Dweck, C. S. (2012). Why do women opt out? Sense of belonging and women's representation in mathematics. *Journal of Personality and Social Psychology, 102,* 700–717.

Good, J. J., Woodzicka, J. A., & Wingfield, L. C. (2010). The effects of gender stereotypic and counter-stereotypic textbook images on science performance. *The Journal of Social Psychology, 150,* 132–147.

Guilford, J. P. (1967). *The nature of human intelligence.* New York: McGraw Hill.

Gunderson, E. A., Ramirez, G., Levine, S. C., & Beilock, S. L. (2012). The role of parents and teachers in the development of math related attitudes. *Sex Roles, 66,* 153–166.

Halpern, D. F. (2014). It's complicated—In fact, it's complex: Explaining the gender gap in academic achievement in science and mathematics. *Psychological Science in the Public Interest, 15,* 72–74.

Halpern, D. F., Aronson, J., Reimer, N., Simpkins, S., Star, J. R., & Wentzel, K. (2007). *Encouraging girls in math and science: IES practice guide.* Washington, DC: Institute of Educational Sciences, U.S. Department of Education.

Halpern, D. F., & Murphy, S. E. (2005). *From work-family balance to work-family interaction: Changing the metaphor.* Mahwah, NJ: Lawrence Erlbaum.

Hartanto, T. A., Krafft, C. E., Iosif, A. M., & Schweitzer, J. B. (2015). A trial-by-trial analysis reveals more intense physical activity is associated with better cognitive control performance in attention-deficit/hyperactivity disorder. *Child Neuropsychology: A Journal on Normal and Abnormal Development in Childhood and Adolescence,* doi:10.1080/09297049.2015.1044511.

Haynes, M. C., & Heilman, M. E. (2013). It had to be you (not me)!: Women's attributional rationalization of their contribution to successful joint work outcomes. *Personality and Social Psychology Bulletin, 39,* 956–969.

Heilbronner, N. N. (2011). Stepping onto the STEM pathway: Factors affecting talented students' declaration of STEM majors in college. *Journal for the Education of the Gifted, 34,* 876–899.

Heilman, M. E., Block, C. J., & Lucas, J. A. (1992). Presumed incompetent? Stigmatization and affirmative action efforts. *Journal of Applied Psychology, 77,* 536–544.

Helwig, R., Anderson, L., & Tindal, G. (2001). Influence of elementary student gender on teachers' perceptions of mathematics achievement. *The Journal of Educational Research, 95,* 93–102.

Henn, S. (2014, October 21). When women stopped coding. *National Public Radio.* Retrieved from http://www.npr.org/blogs/money/2014/10/21/357629765/when-women-stopped-coding

Hill, C., Corbett, C., & St. Rose, A. (2010). *Why so few? Women in science, technology, engineering, and mathematics.* Washington, DC: American Association of University Women.

Hurd, N. M., Zimmerman, M. A., & Xue, Y. (2009). Negative adult influences and the protective effects of role models: A study with urban adolescents. *Journal of Youth and Adolescence, 38,* 777–789.

Hyde, J. S., & Mertz, J. E. (2009). Gender, culture, and mathematics performance. *Proceedings of the National Academy of Sciences, 106,* 8801–8807.

Israel, M., Maynard, K., & Williamson, P. (2013). Promoting literacy-embedded authentic STEM instruction for students with disabilities and other struggling learners. *TEACHING Exceptional Children, 45,* 18–25.

Jacobs, J. E., Davis-Kean, P., Bleeker, M., Eccles, J. S., & Malanchuk, O. (2005). "I can but I don't want to": The impact of parents, interests, and activities on gender differences in math. In A. M. Gallagher & J. C. Kaufman (Eds.), *Gender differences in mathematics: An integrative psychological approach* (pp.246–263). New York, NY: Cambridge University Press.

Kekelis, L., Larkin, M., & Gomes, L. (2014). More than just hot air: How hairdryers and role models inspire girls in engineering. *Technology and Engineering Teacher, 73,* 8–15.

Kerr, B. A., & McKay, R. (2014). *Smart girls in the 21st century: Understanding talented girls and women.* Tucson, AZ: Great Potential Press.

King, E., & Knight, J. (2011). *How women can make it work: The science of success.* Santa Barbara, CA: Praeger.

Kitzinger, J., Haran, J., Chimba, M., & Boyce, T. (2008) *Role models in the media: An exploration of the views and experiences of women in science, engineering and technology.* Bradford, England: UK Resource Centre.

Kremar, M. (2014). Can infants and toddlers learn words from repeat exposure to an infant directed DVD? *Journal of Broadcasting & Electronic Media, 58,* 196–214.

LaCroix, J. M., Burrows, C. N., & Blanton, H. (2015, February 26). *Sexualized representations of women in video games: Psychological immersion predicts subsequent hostility toward women.* Poster presented at Society for Personality and Social Psychology Conference, Long Beach, CA.

Landivar, L. C. (2013). *Disparities in STEM employment by sex, race, and Hispanic origin: American Community Survey reports.* Suitland, MD: U.S. Census Bureau.

Lauer, P. A., Akiba, M., Wilkerson, S. B., Apthorp, H. S., Snow, D., & Martin-Glenn, M. (2003). *The effectiveness of out-of-school-time strategies in assisting low-achieving students in reading and mathematics: A research synthesis.* Aurora, CO: Mid-continent Research for Education and Learning.

Lavy, V., & Sand, E. (2015). *On the origins of gender human capital gaps: Short and long term consequences of teachers' stereotypical biases* (Working Paper 20909). Cambridge, MA: National Bureau of Economic Research.

Lawner, E. K., & Quinn, D. M. (2016, January 28). *Responses to success and failure: The role of gender and domain.* Poster presented at the Society of Personality and Social Psychology Conference, San Diego, CA.

Lazowska, E. (2014, October 12). Learning from Satya Nadella's comments. *Crosscut.* Retrieved from http://crosscut.com/2014/10/satya-nadella-problem-microsoft-ed-lazowska/

Leaper, C., & Ayres, M. M. (2007). A meta-analytic review of gender variations in adults' language use: Talkativeness, affiliative speech, and assertive speech. *Personality and Social Psychology Review, 11,* 328–363.

Leaper, C., & Robnett, R. D. (2011). Women are more likely than men to use tentative language, aren't they? A meta-analysis testing for gender differences and moderators. *Psychology of Women Quarterly, 35,* 129–142.

Leaper, C., & Smith, T. E. (2004). A meta-analytic review of gender variations in children's language use: Talkativeness, affiliative speech, and assertive speech. *Developmental Psychology, 40,* 993–1027.

Leslie, S.-J., Cimpian, A., Meyer, M., & Freeland, E. (2015). Expectations of brilliance underlie gender distributions across academic disciplines. *Science, 347,* 262–265.

Levine, L., Bowman, L., Kachinsky, K., Sola, A., & Waite, B. (2015, May 22). *Infants, toddlers, and mobile media use.* Poster presented at the Association for Psychological Science Convention, New York, NY.

Liu, F. (2006). School culture and gender. In C. Skelton, B. Francis, & L. Smulyan (Eds.), *The SAGE Handbook of Gender and Education* (pp. 425–438). Thousand Oaks, CA: Sage.

Lockwood, P., & Kunda, Z. (1997). Superstars and me: Predicting the impact of role models on the self. *Journal of Personality and Social Psychology, 73,* 91–103.

London, B., Rosenthal, L., Levy, S. R., & Lobel, M. (2015). The influences of perceived identity compatibility and social support on women in nontraditional fields during the college transition. *Basic and Applied Social Psychology, 33,* 304–321.

Lubinski, D., & Benbow, C. (2006). Study of mathematically precocious youth after 35 years: Uncovering antecedents for the development of math-science expertise. *Perspectives in Psychological Science, 1,* 316–344.

Lyon, G., & Jafri, J. (2010). Project Exploration's Sisters4Science: Involving urban girls of color in science out of school. *Afterschool Matters, 11,* 15–23.

Manjoo, F. (2014, September 24). Exploring hidden bias at Google. *New York Times*. Retrieved from http://www.nytimes.com/2014/09/25/technology/exposing-hidden-biases-at-google-to-improve-diversity.html?smid=pl-share

Marschark, M., Sapere, P., Convertino, C. M., & Pelz, J. (2008). Learning via direct and mediated instruction by deaf students. *Journal of Deaf Studies and Deaf Education, 13*, 446–461.

Massachusetts Institute of Technology. (2011). *A report on the status of women faculty in the schools of science and engineering at MIT, 2011*. Cambridge, MA: Author.

McCabe, J., Fairchild, E., Grauerholz, L., Pescosolido, B. A., & Tope, D. (2011). Gender in twentieth-century children's books: Patterns of disparity in title and central characters. *Gender & Society, 25*, 197–226.

McCreedy, D., & Dierking, L. D. (2013). *Cascading influences: Long-term impacts of informal STEM experiences for girls*. Philadelphia, PA: The Franklin Institute.

Meece, J. L., Glienke, B. B., & Burg, S. (2006). Gender and motivation. *Journal of School Psychology, 44*, 351–373

Mooney, J., & Cole, D. (2000). *Learning outside the lines: Two Ivy League students with learning disabilities and ADHD give you the tools for academic success and educational revolution*. New York, NY: Simon and Schuster.

Morgan, S. E., Movius, L., & Cody, M. J. (2009). The power of narratives: The effect of entertainment television organ donation storylines on the attitudes, knowledge, and behaviors of donors and nondonors. *Journal of Communication, 59*, 135–151.

Mosatche, H. S., & Lawner, E. K. (2010). *Evaluation of the Queens Community House Access for Young Women program: 2005–2009*. New Rochelle, NY: The Mosatche Group.

Mosatche, H. S., Matloff-Nieves, S., Kekelis, L., & Lawner, E. K. (2013). Effective STEM programs for adolescent girls: Three approaches and many lessons learned. *Afterschool Matters, 17*, 17–25.

Moss-Racusin, C. A., Dovidio, J. F., Brescoll, V. F., Graham, M. J., & Handelsman, J. (2012). Science faculty's subtle gender biases favor male students. *Proceedings of the National Academy of Sciences, 109*, 16474–16479.

Muno, A. (2014). And girl justice for all: Blending girl-specific & youth development practices. *Afterschool Matters, 19*, 28–35.

National Institute on Out-of-School Time. (2007). *A review of the literature and the INSPIRE model: STEM in out-of-school time*. Wellesley, MA: Author. Retrieved from http://www.niost.org/pdf/NASA_Authored%20Paper_Wellesley.pdf

National Science Foundation. (2015). *Women, minorities, and persons with disabilities in science and engineering: 2015.* Arlington, VA: Author. Retrieved from http://www.nsf.gov/statistics/2015/nsf15311

Neber, H., & Schommer-Aikins, M. (2002). Self-regulated science learning with highly gifted students: The role of cognitive, motivational, epistemological, and environmental variables. *High Ability Studies, 13,* 59–74.

Noam, G. G. (2012, July 16). *Monitoring and evaluating program quality: The DOS approach.* Paper presented at the Meeting on Evaluation of STEM Programs Funded by the Noyce Foundation, Oakland, CA.

Phillips, K. W. (2014, September 16). How diversity makes us smarter. *Scientific American.* Retrieved from http://www.scientificamerican.com/article/how-diversity-makes-us-smarter/

Picho, K., Rodriguez, A., & Finnie, L. (2013). Exploring the moderating role of context on the mathematics performance of females under stereotype threat: A meta-analysis. *The Journal of Social Psychology, 153,* 299–333.

President's Council of Advisors on Science and Technology. (2012). *Engage to excel: Producing one million additional college graduates with degrees in science, technology, engineering, and mathematics.* Washington, DC: Author.

Price, J. (2010). The effect of instructor race and gender on student persistence in STEM fields. *Economics of Education Review, 29,* 901–910.

Rahm, J. (2008). Urban youths' hybrid positioning in science practices at the margin: A look inside a school-museum-scientist partnership project and an after-school science program. *Cultural Studies of Science Education, 3,* 97–121.

Reardon, S. M., & Naglieri, J. A. (1992). PASS cognitive processing characteristics of normal and ADHD males. *Journal of School Psychology, 30,* 151–163.

Reuben, E., Sapienza, P., & Zingales, L. (2014). How stereotypes impair women's careers in science. *Proceedings of the National Academy of Sciences, 111,* 4403–4408.

Riegle-Crumb, C., & Humphries, M. (2012). Exploring bias in math teachers' perceptions of students' ability by gender and race/ethnicity. *Gender & Society, 26,* 290–322.

Saliquist, J., Eisenberg, N., Spinrad, T. L., Eggum, N. D., & Gaertner, B. M. (2009). Assessment of preschoolers' positive empathy: Concurrent and longitudinal relations with positive emotion, social competence, and sympathy. *The Journal of Positive Psychology, 4,* 223–233.

Scantlebury, K. (2009, December 23). Gender bias in teaching. Retrieved from http://www.education.com/reference/article/gender-bias-in-teaching/

Schmader, T., Johns, M., & Forbes, C. (2008). An integrated process model of stereotype threat effects on performance. *Psychological Review, 115,* 336–356.

Simard, C., Henderson, A. D., Gilmartin, S. K., Schiebinger, L., & Whitney, T. (2008). *Climbing the technical ladder: Obstacles and solutions for mid-level women in technology.* Stanford, CA: Anita Borg Institute for Women and Technology and the Clayman Institute for Gender Research, Stanford University.

Snyder, K. (2014, August 26). The abrasiveness trap: High-achieving men and women are described differently in reviews. *Fortune.* Retrieved from http://fortune.com/2014/08/26/performance-review-gender-bias/

Spencer, S. J., Steele, C. M., & Quinn, D. M. (1999). Stereotype threat and women's math performance. *Journal of Experimental Social Psychology, 35,* 4–28.

Stake, J. E., & Mares, K. R. (2001). Science enrichment programs for gifted high school girls and boys: Predictors of program impact on science confidence and motivation. *Journal of Research in Science Teaching, 38,* 1065–1088.

Steele, C. M., Spencer, S. J., & Aronson, J. (2002). Contending with group image: The psychology of stereotype and social identity threat. *Advances in Experimental Social Psychology, 34,* 379–440.

Stout, J. G., Dasgupta, N., Hunsinger, M., & McManus, M. A. (2011). STEMing the tide: Using ingroup experts to inoculate women's self-concept in science, technology, engineering, and mathematics (STEM). *Journal of Personality and Social Psychology, 100,* 255–270.

Suarez-Orozco, C., Casanova, S., Martin, M., Cuellar, V., Smith, N. A., & Dias, S. I. (2015). Toxic rain in class: Classroom interpersonal microaggressions. *Educational Researcher, 44,* 151–160.

Tisdale, C. (2004). *Phase 2 summative evaluation of Active Prolonged Engagement at the Exploratorium.* Chicago, IL: Selina Research Associates, Inc.

Tobin, K., & Gallagher, J. J. (1987). The role of target students in the science classroom. *Journal of Research in Science Teaching, 24,* 61–75.

Verquer, M. L., Beehr, T. A., & Wagner, S. H. (2003). A meta-analysis of relations between person-organization fit and work attitudes. *Journal of Vocational Behavior, 63,* 473–489.

Walton, G. M., Cohen, G. L., Cwir, D., & Spencer, S. J. (2012). Mere belonging: The power of social connections. *Journal of Personality and Social Psychology, 102,* 513–532.

Walton, G. M., Logel, C., Peach, J. M., Spencer, S. J., & Zanna, M. P. (2015). Two brief interventions to mitigate a "chilly climate" transform women's experience, relationships, and achievement in engineering. *Journal of Educational Psychology, 107,* 468–485.

Watt, S. J., Therrien, W. J., Kaldenberg, E., & Taylor, J. C. (2013). Promoting inclusive practices in inquiry-based science classrooms. *TEACHING Exceptional Children, 45,* 40–48.

Weber, G. (2003). Flexible jobs mean fewer absences. *Workforce Management, 82,* 26.

Wei, X., Yu, J. W., Shattuck, P., McCracken, M., & Blackorby, J. (2013). Science, technology, engineering, and mathematics (STEM) participation among college students with an autism spectrum disorder. *Journal of Autism and Developmental Disorders, 43,* 1539–1546.

Weisz, B. M., Lawner, E. K., Quinn, D. M., & Johnson, B. J. (2015). *Combatting stereotype threat in lab and field settings: A meta-analysis of self-affirmation and role model interventions.* Unpublished manuscript, Department of Psychological Sciences, University of Connecticut, Storrs, CT.

White House Council on Women and Girls. (2012). *Keeping America's women moving forward: The key to an economy built to last.* Washington, DC: Author.

Yoon, C.-H. (2009). Self-regulated learning and instructional factors in the scientific inquiry of scientifically gifted Korean middle school students. *Gifted Child Quarterly, 53,* 203–216.

About the Authors

Harriet S. Mosatche, Ph.D. (developmental psychology), is an executive and leadership coach, author, researcher, and advice columnist. At AskDrM.org, she and her team answer questions from children, adolescents, and parents. **Elizabeth K. Lawner,** formerly a researcher in youth development at Child Trends, is a social psychology doctoral student at the University of Connecticut where she researches the barriers to recruiting and retaining women in STEM. **Susan Matloff-Nieves,** a social worker for more than 30 years, created a nationally recognized girls' program. She is now the Executive Director of Lincoln Square Neighborhood Center in New York City.